Battle for the City of the Dead

Battle for the City of the Dead

In the Shadow of the Golden Dome,
Najaf, August 2004

Dick Camp

ZENITH PRESS

To the American servicemen and women who make
the ultimate sacrifice for their country:

Till the last landings made
And we stand unafraid
On a shore that no mortal has seen.

Till the last bugle call
Sounds taps for us all
It's Semper Fidelis soldier, sailor, and Marine.

And to my wife, Suzi Pool-Camp . . . great love!

First published in 2011 by Zenith Press, an imprint of MBI Publishing Company, 400 First Avenue North, Suite 300, Minneapolis, MN 55401 USA

Zenith Press titles are also available at discounts in bulk quantity for industrial or sales-promotional use. For details write to Special Sales Manager at MBI Publishing Company, 400 First Avenue North, Suite 300, Minneapolis, MN 55401 USA.

To find out more about our books, join us online at www.zenithpress.com.

Library of Congress Cataloging-in-Publication Data

Camp, Richard D.
Battle for the city of the dead : in the shadow of the Golden Dome, Najaf, August 2004 / Dick Camp.
     p. cm.
Includes bibliographical references and index.
ISBN 978-0-7603-4006-6 (hb w/ jkt)
1. Najaf, Battle of, Najaf, Iraq, 2004. 2. Iraq War, 2003---Campaigns--Iraq--Najaf. 3. United States. Marine Corps--History--Iraq War, 2003- 4. United States. Army--History--Iraq War, 2003- I. Title.
DS79.764.N35C36 2011
956.7044'342--dc22
                          2010045938

Maps by: Patricia Isaacs, based on official 11th MEU operational slides unless otherwise noted.

Design Manager: Brenda Canales
Designed by: Helena Shimizu
Jacket design by: Andrew Brozyna

All photographs are from the author's collection unless noted otherwise.

On the cover:
Main: The Wadi al-Salaam cemetery. *Defenseimagery.mil DF-SD-06-03498*
Background: A Marine firing an M-60 machine gun. *Maj. Michael S. Wilbur, USMC*

On the back cover:
A Cobra gunship fires a missile into the Wadi al-Salaam cemetery.
Lt. Col. Glen G. Butler, USMC

Printed in China

Contents

Wadi al-Salaam Cemetery
August 5, 2004

MARINE 1ST LT. MICHAEL Borneo's Combined Anti-Armor Team Alpha (CAAT-Alpha) was deployed to the north and east side of Revolutionary Circle, the main intersection in the city of An-Najaf, "for all of about three minutes," Borneo recalled, "when there was an airburst right in the middle of the circle, about two feet from my vehicle." Shrapnel from the burst peppered the street, striking Borneo's up-armored Humvee and the light armored vehicle (LAV) alongside. The Marines went to high alert, scanning the buildings and alleyways for danger.

"Suddenly we started receiving machine-gun fire from the cemetery," Borneo said. "When I say a cemetery, it's a maze of tombs and above-ground mausoleums, kind of like New Orleans—but it's huge. It goes on for kilometers, with tunnels, weapons caches, and command and control centers." The *Jaish al-Mahdi*, or Mahdi Militia (also known as the Mahdi Army), felt safe there because it was in an exclusion zone, where the Marines did not go because of the cemetery's religious significance to Shiites.

Borneo moved two of his machine-gun vehicles to a position along the wall of the cemetery. They started firing on the enemy with their .50-caliber machine guns. A section of LAVs pulled up and joined in with their 25mm cannon. "It looked like a hornets' nest," Borneo exclaimed. "You could see guys running all over shooting at us. I don't know whether they were trying to flank us, feel us out, or just had an itchy trigger finger and decided to shoot at us . . . but they shot first, and we responded."

First Lieutenant Michael J. Borneo, an aggressive combat veteran, led the Combined Anti-Armor Team Alpha (CAAT-Alpha) in the first encounter with Muqtada al-Sadr's Mahdi Militia. *USMC History Division*

Borneo quickly realized that Revolutionary Circle was a registered target. "We started taking a lot of mortar rounds—one short, one long, then right on us, with the gunners firing for effect—so I quickly backed my vehicles out of the circle." The mortars stopped, but his team continued to take fire from small arms and rocket-propelled grenades (RPG), which for the most part were ineffective.

Within minutes, Marine AH-1W SuperCobras and UH-1N Huey gunships from Marine Medium Helicopter Squadron 166 (HMM-166) reported on station to support the embattled Marines. Captain Stephen H. Mount was the designated section leader for a flight of two aircraft—a UH-1N Huey and an AH-1W Cobra—that was tasked to provide support for Battalion Landing Team (BLT) 1/4 during an attack on the cemetery:

We were flying in a holding area outside the city when we received word that the 1/4 quick reaction force [QRF] was receiving enemy fire from multiple sources in the cemetery. We were cleared by their forward air controller [FAC], call sign Wombat [Capt. Carl Lowe], to provide support. Our instructions were that anyone west of the road in the cemetery was fair game. We made several attack runs with our crew-served weapons at people that were shooting from the cemetery. In one attack against a car park with an overhang, the whole building exploded with twinkles [automatic weapons fire], including an airburst from an RPG that was set to detonate in the air. We engaged with our crew-served weapons and then Dale Behm [pilot-in-command of the AH-1W] put two rockets into the building in a beautiful display of marksmanship.

The Huey, call sign Rocky 05, was directed by Wombat to attack a suspected mortar position. The aircraft began its attack, but, as Borneo recalled, "It happened about 900 meters away from us. As soon as it flew overhead, the enemy immediately started shooting at it with tracers." Mount remembered that

> we came in on a south-to-northwest attack at about 90 to 100 knots, but we couldn't see [the mortar]. As we came around to the right, we got hit. It felt like I got whacked in the head by a bat. There was a loud ringing in my ears, and I lost vision except for light and dark. I involuntarily jerked back on the stick. The nose of the aircraft climbed until it was nearly straight up. Drew [Capt. Andrew M. Turner, copilot] instantly took control, leveled the aircraft, and got some forward momentum just as we slammed into the ground. We hit on the edge of the street, bounced a couple of times, hit a lamppost, and skidded to a stop in a courtyard. It happened so fast, we didn't have time to shut down the engines.
>
> I was in a lot of pain, but I managed to unbuckle the seat and shoulder harness and step out on what was left of the skid. I yanked out my pistol, but it dawned on me that I didn't have a round in the chamber. In the process of trying to cock it—at the time, I had one hand on my head and eye—the magazine fell out. Before I could do anything else, the crew chief [Staff Sgt. Patrick O. Burgess] grabbed me by my flak vest and dragged me behind a wall. I could hear the crack of small-arms fire as the bad guys fired at us. Staff Sergeant Burgess took my pistol, replaced the magazine, and chambered a round. At the time, I was choking on blood—my head was bleeding badly—and I was worried that I would bleed out. I had a throbbing headache, and I still didn't know what happened. Staff Sergeant Burgess looked me over and made me promise not to lie down. I think he was afraid I'd go into shock and die.

Borneo rushed to the rescue. "I took my vehicle, another nicknamed Habit-3, under Corporal Maksymowski, and a section of LARs [light armored reconnaissance platoons] to secure the crash site and make a tactical recovery of aircraft and personnel (TRAP). No one ordered us to go, but we saw it [Rocky 05] go down and thought it would crash in the cemetery. I'm thinking we would have to fight our way through, in a *Black Hawk Down* scenario. Luckily, it landed about 15 meters off the main road, right before the cemetery." Borneo's reaction force reached the site within minutes. The helicopter's rotors were still spinning. "When we pulled up, we saw Iraqis coming up with RPGs and an RPK machine gun to kill or capture the crew.

Captain Stephen H. Mount receiving the Purple Heart for wounds suffered while flying in support of 1st Battalion, 4th Marines. Mount lost his right eye when a piece of shrapnel pierced his flight helmet. *Lt. Col. Glen G. Butler, USMC*

It wasn't going to happen on our watch! We immediately engaged. I killed at least one guy with my M-16, and Lance Corporal Kidder shot another who was carrying an RPG." Borneo's quick reaction ended the immediate threat. As his unit secured the area around the helicopter, two squads from the 81mm Mortar Platoon arrived.

"My squad went into a building and onto the rooftop overlooking the cemetery," Sgt. Jason McManus recalled. "We stayed there until we started receiving some pretty heavy fire. The Iraqi family wasn't too happy with us setting up on the roof of their house."

Borneo commandeered an Iraqi ambulance, assigned one of his men to drive it, and evacuated the wounded pilot. McManus "ended up helping the crew chief and the gunner into a vehicle, which took them to our medical evacuation ["medevac"] station in the forward operating base [FOB]."

Mount remembered

hearing the rescue force pull up because there was a great roar of small-arms fire as they lit up the area. Their corpsman took my pistol . . . I guess he considered me a danger . . . and stabbed me with morphine . . . it really hurt . . . before checking me over. Next, they loaded me into a vehicle and transported me to one of the FOBs. A medevac helicopter

Iraqi Resistance Report*: "Jaysh al-Mahdi Downs American Helicopter Over al-Kufah"

Al-Jazeera's correspondent in al-Kufah has reported that sources in Muqtada as-Sadr's office say that Jaysh al-Mahdi militiamen have shot down an American military helicopter in the city. Parts of the wrecked aircraft were brought for show to the press. Meanwhile Jaysh al-Mahdi militiamen took up positions in a show of strength along the streets of al-Kufah.

flew me to Baghdad, where a doctor told me that I had lost my right eye. It appeared that shrapnel or part of a rifle round came through the window or the skin of the aircraft, pierced my helmet visor, the bridge of my nose, and through my right eye before exiting my temple. A fraction of an inch, and I wouldn't have made it. My flight helmet was returned to me some months later. It had a neat little hole inward, just in front of my left eye, and a rip and tear over my right eye. The hole was the size of a number-two pencil. The surgeons could not believe how it happened because there was no sign of injury to my eyelid. My medical treatment was fantastic . . . all the way.

The badly damaged Huey was also evacuated to keep it from being used for propaganda purposes. McManus was detailed to provide escort. "The second we started off, we started receiving fire . . . We heard on the radio that there was a pretty heavy firefight going on . . . The amphibious assault vehicles (AAVs) were returning fire into the cemetery."

Borneo said, "Once the helicopter was shot down, it was the turning point in the battle. The Iraqi machine-gun fire from the cemetery kicked off an intense three-day battle."

*All Iraqi Resistance Report quotes are taken as is from various online sources.

CHAPTER 1

Valley of Peace

A New Orleans cemetery on steroids.
—Lt. Col. Eugene N. Apicella, 11th Marine Expeditionary Unit (MEU)

THE WADI AL-SALAAM CEMETERY, in the city of Najaf, is known as the Valley of Peace and is claimed to be the largest Islamic cemetery in the world. It is estimated that over five million Shiites are buried within its sprawling twelve square miles. Shiites from all over the Muslim world are buried there, close to the shrine of Imam Ali (Ali ibn Abi Talib)—the son-in-law and first cousin of the Prophet Mohammed—who was assassinated in AD 661. The faithful believed that by being buried close to Ali, they would enter paradise, avoiding Gehenna, the abode of the fallen. Ali's followers, *Sho at Ali*, consider him to be the Prophet's true successor, a great saint, and martyr. Over the centuries, his tomb has become a shrine and the destination for the faithful, "A million pilgrims come each year . . . although no official record is kept," Gavin Young wrote in *Iraq: Land of Two Rivers.*

Ali's opulent tomb is a towering, gold-domed shrine built upon a rectangular, two-story sanctuary that also houses prayer rooms and clerical spaces. Two minarets stand like sentinels at the corners of the main entranceway. "The gates are covered with tiles bearing complex designs and Arabic script," one observer noted. "In some places the tile has fallen away, and birds are nesting in the holes." The exterior of the mausoleum is inlaid with mosaic tiles of light blue and white marble, "which have darkened handsomely with age," according to Gavin Young. Journalist

Wadi al-Salaam cemetery, known as the Valley of Peace, is reputed to be the largest Muslim burial ground in the world. It is estimated that over five million Shiites are buried in its twelve square miles. In August 2004, its crypts and tombs became one vast battleground. *Capt. Richard Zjawin, USMC*

The Imam Ali mosque is one of the most holy Shiite sites in the Muslim world. Within its opulent interior, the faithful pay homage to Ali ibn Abi Talib, the son-in-law and first cousin of the Prophet Mohammed. Ali's followers considered him to be the Prophet's true successor. *Photographer's Mate 1st Class Arlo K. Abrahamson, USN*

Christopher Allbritton wrote, "As we approached the Shrine, the gold dome gleamed in the mid-day sun. The twin minarets glittered. The whole thing is covered with gold, pure-gold, and the tile work is exquisite. I've never seen anything more ornate and beautiful." Allbritton was referring to the 7,777 pure gold tiles covering the dome and the 40,000 gold tiles on the two thirty-five-meter-high minarets. A brick wall surrounds the outside of the tomb. Four gates, adorned with mosaics portraying birds and flowers, provide entry to a wide, stone-paved courtyard. Inside, neon lights reflect off mirrors, mosaics, and walls of hammered silver. Ali's inlaid teak sepulcher sits in solitary grandeur within the magnificent interior.

Despite its religious importance, the shrine has been the scene of great violence. In 1991, Saddam Hussein's Republican Guard damaged the mosque while putting down a Shiite uprising. Hundreds of Shiites were killed in and around the shrine. General Wafiq al-Samarae, the former director of the Iraqi intelligence service, wrote in *Eastern Gate Ruins* that the regime used chemical weapons in the attack. In 2003, during the surge in sectarian violence, a Sunni extremist exploded a car bomb outside the shrine, killing more than 125 people, including the Shiite Ayatollah Mohammed Bakir al-Hakim. The mastermind of the bombing was Abu Musab al-Zarqawi, the violent Jordanian terrorist. A year later, Muqtada al-Sadr's Mahdi Militia used the mosque as a base of operations in their battle with coalition forces.

The Wadi al-Salaam is located a few short blocks north of Ali's shrine, along the main road that bisects Najaf from north to south. An eight-foot-high wall separates the cemetery from the road for much of its

Burying the Dead

Streams of cars and taxis bearing cheap wooden coffins strapped to their roofs line the road outside the cemetery. Teams of men unload the deathly cargo and quickly carry it to one of five family-owned businesses, where the remains are disinfected and washed; women wash female bodies, while men wash male bodies. After being washed, the body is wrapped in a ten-meter long, white cotton shroud and taken to Imam Ali shrine, where it is paraded three times around the tomb. The remains are then carried to the gravesite and placed in a grave carved in a shallow, sloping trench. They are then covered with the mushroom-colored desert sand, while a cleric recites verses from the Quran.

The business of death is the major commercial enterprise in the city of Najaf. "Tens of thousands of grave-diggers, undertakers, masters of funeral ceremonies, tomb watchers, givers of prayers for the dead, intercessors, Koran citers, mediums for communication with the departed and so on make up the bulk of the workforce," according to Amir Taheri, an Iranian author and commentator.

"I always think of the increasing and decreasing of the dead," said Sameer Shaaban, one of the more than one hundred workers who specialize in washing the corpses. "People want more and more money, and I am one of them, but most of the workers in this field don't talk frankly, because they wish for more coffins to earn more money."

Jawad Abuseba, a gravedigger for twenty-two years, said, "There is nothing beautiful in this career, but I cannot do any other job. Death is something everyone must face. My job demands death, and this is our fate, all of us."

Remains are brought to the Wadi al-Salaam cemetery from all over Iraq, and sometimes there are hundreds of burials a day. "The daily tide of cars bearing coffins has been a barometer of Iraq's violence for years," a cemetery worker explained. Saddam Hussein's wars with his neighbors—Iran from 1980 to 1988, Kuwait in 1991, and the subsequent slaughter of the rebellious Shiites—caused burials to soar at a rate of 6,500 a month. One gravedigger observed, "In his day, people were callously murdered," and dumped in unmarked mass graves. In recent years, sectarian violence has brought forth its own harvest. "It is as if Saddam had never left," the gravedigger said. "I believe the people carrying out these murders learnt from Saddam. He was the master."

distance. Entrances pierce the masonry wall, allowing access to the massive burial ground, where thousands upon thousands of ochre-colored mud and brick headstones, graves, and crypts stretch as far as the eye can see in a confused jumble of monuments. One eyewitness reported, "They [visitors] looked upon graves newly made, graves which had sunk, those which were on the verge of sinking, and graves within graves with mounds over them." It is said that only the cemetery's long-time workers can find their way through the maze. There is no discernable pattern to the layout—no straight lines, no paths, no maps. Mourners depend on a crude numbering system to locate their loved ones. At times, new graves are placed on old ones, making identification even more difficult. Yitzhak Nakash wrote in *The Shi'is of Iraq*, "So massive was the transfer of corpses . . . from the mid-eighteenth century that much of the recently built residential areas of the city were old cemeteries that sank with time." During Saddam Hussein's reprisal of the Shiites after the Gulf War, Republican Guard tanks smashed through the cemetery, grinding many of the mud-brick memorials to dust.

Scattered throughout the jumble of graves are vaults, each with two or three subfloors containing a line of crypts. These underground spaces were sometimes used as weapons-storage areas and hiding places by Shiites opposed to Saddam Hussein and, later, opposed to American forces. Taller mausoleums housing the remains of high-ranking Shiite clerics, government officials, and military officers dot the landscape. Minarets one to two stories high tower over the cemetery, providing places of unhindered observation for snipers and machine gunners. In places, the monuments are so closely packed that it is almost impossible to squeeze between them. Lieutenant Colonel Eugene N. Apicella described the terrain as "a New Orleans cemetery on steroids."

The twelve square miles of the Wadi al-Salaam cemetery are a jumble of above-ground and underground tombs, crypts, and two-story mausoleums. One Marine described the cemetery as "a New Orleans cemetery on steroids." *Defenseimagery.mil DF-SD-06-03498*

NAJAF, THE MOST HOLY (*EL NAJAF EL ASHRAF*)

> *My town's imports are coffins*
> *My town's exports are turbans*
>
> —Ahmid al-Safi, Najafi poet

The ancient city of Najaf (*al-Najaf al-Ashraf*, "the most holy") was founded almost by accident when, according to Shiite belief, a camel bearing the remains of the Shiite cleric Imam Ali (Ali ibn Abi Talib) wandered through the desert and stopped to forage on a hilltop. In accordance with his wishes, Ali was buried on the spot. His grave became a shrine, which over the centuries grew into the city of Najaf. In his book *Muqtada: Muqtada*

Imam Ali

Shiites consider Ali ibn Abi Talib to have been their true spiritual leader since the Prophet Mohammed's death in AD 632. The Prophet's death produced discord among the *umma*, the "community of believers," and it was not until AD 656 that Ali became the fourth caliph, after a bloody coup. Rebellious Egyptian soldiers murdered the third caliph and installed Ali, who ruled the caliphate from the city of Kufa. Ali, in turn, was assassinated by a poisoned sword. It took him two days to succumb to the wound. Before dying, he instructed his followers to strap his body to a white camel and to allow the animal to wander. Where it stopped, they were to dig his grave. On the edge of the desert, six miles south of Kufa, the camel went to ground, and Ali was immediately buried. Over the centuries, the current city of Najaf grew up around his tomb, which has become a shrine and the destination for millions of the faithful.

After Ali's untimely death, a relative of the third caliph seized power and established Islam's first royal dynasty in Damascus, completely alienating Ali's followers, the *Shiat Ali* ("partisans of Ali"; the term *Shiat Ali* was later simplified to *Shiites*). They believed that Islam's sacred leadership was stolen from them by Muslims, who would later be called Sunni. Ali's son Hussein attempted to regain leadership, but was killed in a famous battle near Karbala. Journalist Anthony Shadid notes in his book *Night Draws Near, Iraq's People in the Shadow of America's War*, "His [Hussein] tragic death constitutes the central, most powerful drama of the Shiite faith . . .

[T]o the devout, Ashura, the anniversary of his death . . . is the most tragic and sorrowful day of the year."

Thirteen centuries after Hussein's death, the schism between Shiite and Sunni is still being played out. Sectarian violence may prove to be the downfall of America's Iraq policy.

Al-Sadr, the Shia Revival, and the Struggle for Iraq, Patrick Cockburn wrote, "I always found Najaf an entrancing city, one of the strangest in the world. It is a dusty place on the edge of the desert . . . people sometimes describe it as 'the Vatican of the Shia,' but this is true only in the loosest of senses." Cockburn described traveling along the road to the city—"[a] depressing ribbon development"—and seeing the shrine of Ali suddenly appear: "It springs into view like a burst of sunlight in the sky as it rises above the low buildings of brown brick that surround it."

Captain Dale Beam, who often flew over the city, said.

> Najaf is beautiful. It is dominated by the exquisite mosque, with its golden dome. It's the first thing you can see as you fly out of the desert. At night, lit by lights that highlight the dome, it's really neat! The Old City surrounds the shrine on three sides. North of the mosque, you'd see the gigantic cemetery, with its haphazard brown-monochrome mausoleums and crypts that seem to be stacked on one another. There are very few distinct lines, and those that you can see run east and west. An urban sprawl, with modern buildings, covers the southern area of the city, while huge apartment buildings can be seen to the west. Najaf is a city of both old and new, with no distinct dividing line between the two.

Najaf is located approximately 120 miles south of Baghdad, close to the Euphrates River, on the edge of a sparsely populated track of barren land. The city is perched on a high plateau overlooking the Wadi al-Salaam cemetery on its northern and eastern sides. To the west is the "sea of Najaf," a dried-up lake and floodplain. In Arabic, *Najaf* means a "high land where water cannot be reached" because for much of the city's early history, it struggled to survive despite a lack of water. At one point, there were only thirty families in the entire city. The construction of a series of canals enabled it to flourish as a desert market town. In the nineteenth century, Najaf grew and prospered as an important center of Shiite scholarship and theology. "The city hosts the most eminent of Shia seminaries," Amir Taheri wrote, "which at the height of its theological boom in the 1950s, boasted 124 madrassahs [Islamic schools] with 40,000 trainee mullahs. All the grand ayatollahs of the past 150 years either studied or taught there." Iran's Grand Ayatollah Rudollah Khomeini spent fourteen years in exile in Najaf before returning to lead the Iranian Revolution in 1979.

The city of 560,000 is split into two sections, the old and the new. Much of the old section is still surrounded by a high wall, enclosing a labyrinth of narrow alleyways, markets, shops, and brick homes. Many of the homes have deep, vaulted cellars (*sirdabs*) that connect multiple dwellings and extend up to five stories underground. These cellars were "approached through courtyards of old houses," according to Gavin Young, "in which you find small doors that open onto narrow stairways plunging into the bowels of the earth. Romantically sinister . . . they were used throughout the somewhat alarming history of Najaf, as places of concealment and as means of flight from political opponents, or for violent crimes and the secret disposal of bodies." The new section of the city is a low-level sprawl, its boulevards lined by trees and arched brick buildings. Hotels and shops catering to pilgrims abound, cashing in on the thousands and thousands of the faithful visiting Imam Ali's shrine.

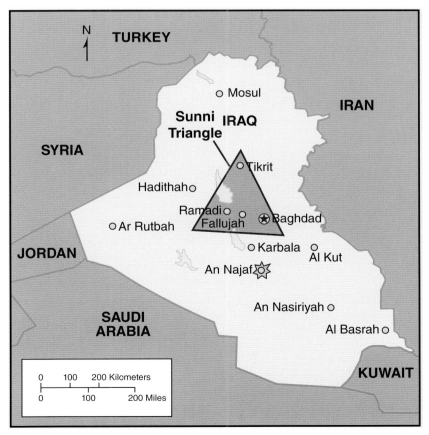

Patricia Isaacs

Najaf is the spiritual center of the Shiite community, and with the overthrow of Saddam Hussein and the ascendancy of the clerics, it became the center of authority for Iraq's Shiite majority. "It is here that major issues of Shiism have been decided for over twelve centuries," exiled Iranian journalist Amir Taheri was told. Taheri postulated, "Whoever controls Najaf and its seminary [Imam Ali's shrine] would enjoy moral legitimacy." The city is also home to the *Hawza Ilmiya*, "circle of religious learning" in Arabic. Control of the shrine also meant access to the mausoleum's treasure, worth an estimated $1 billion. One Coalition Provisional Authority (CPA) official said the shrine was "a cash cow because of the pilgrims' alms." All devout Shiites are obligated to pay a 20 percent flat tax on their income (*sahm-i-Imam*, the Imam's cut) to the foundation that operates the shrine. "The foundation also owns large tracts of farmland and property in Iran and Iraq," Amir Taheri pointed out, as well as "hostels for pilgrims and hundreds of shops in many cities . . . a treasury of gold, jewelry and precious carpets."

During the 2003 coalition invasion of Iraq, Najaf became an important objective for the U.S. Army's V Corps because of its close proximity to Objective Rams, the corps' logistics base. The 3rd Infantry Division, commanded by Maj. Gen. Buford "Buff" Blount, was assigned to isolate the city, clear it, and prevent the movement of enemy reinforcements from the east. Blount, in turn, ordered the 2nd Brigade Combat Team, under Col. David Perkins, to carry out the mission. As the brigade approached Objective Rams, it ran into an Iraqi paramilitary force known as *Fedayeen Saddam*, "those willing to sacrifice themselves for Saddam." Captain Andrew Hilmes, Alpha Company, 1-64 Armor, first made contact about two hours before nightfall. "I was the lead company in the task force," he recalled, "and we were engaged by several hundred militia and Fedayeen fighters who were dug in on either side of Highway 9. They were reinforced with technicals [improvised fighting vehicles, usually open-back civilian trucks] and supplied with prepositioned caches of ammunition."

The battalion deployed on line and swept forward. "It was a one-sided fight, but it was enough to at least cause us to stop and deploy," Hilmes recalled. "Probably over the course of the night we killed over 100 of them. Although they were facing armored vehicles, they were certainly brave, because they kept coming at us. They did not seem to appreciate the fact that we had night-vision equipment and could see them even at night." Captain Todd Wiles, the brigade air officer, reported, "The M-1s [M1A1 Abrams tanks] rolled into the objective and about fifteen white pickups with crew-served weapons mounted on top, . . . and about a hundred troops in black clothing attacked. They were running all over the place . . . low crawling up to the tanks; Bradleys were firing straight through huge dirt berms, thwacking them on the far side."

The heavy weapons of the battalion's tanks and Bradleys quickly eliminated the threat. Major Kevin Dunlop commented wryly, "It is not a fair fight. Trucks with machine guns against tanks and Bradleys can have only one outcome. We were slaughtering them." However, the willingness of the Fedayeen to engage in close combat was a harbinger of things to come.

"What we didn't know at the time was that Najaf was a hornet's nest, just bristling with Baath militia and Fedayeen," Hilmes said. The enemy probed the battalion's lines while it rearmed and rested at Objective Rams. A tremendous sandstorm hit the area as the battalion moved out of the laager. "Visibility was almost nil for a period of three days," Hilmes complained. "It was so poor that we couldn't see the enemy. At certain points, they were actually ramming vehicles into our armored vehicles. I vividly remember watching a civilian bus full of Fedayeen fighters ramming into one of my tanks. The bus must have been going at least forty miles per hour. It literally bounced right off. It probably killed half the guys on the bus, but the rest of them piled out, firing their AK-47s. They were shredded by 25mm high explosives from one of my Bradleys."

On March 27, Capt. Jeff McCoy's Charlie Company, 3rd Squadron, 7th Cavalry, pushed eastward in the sandstorm to secure a bridge across the Euphrates on the northeast corner of Najaf. "We secured the bridge fairly easily," McCoy recounted, "and started deploying when my lead scout element [two Bradleys and a tank] triggered an antitank ambush. The insurgents fired off a pretty organized volley of six RPG rounds." The missiles did little damage—one of the Bradleys lost a radio—but, "it was like stepping on an ant hill!" McCoy exclaimed. "A bunch of dismounted fighters erupted from a complex of buildings." Visibility was down to about twenty meters, allowing the enemy to work in close. Charlie Company opened fire and cut them down without sustaining any casualties, but the attack made McCoy nervous about extending further. He deployed two platoons on the western side of the bridge oriented west and north toward Najaf. The other two platoons, including his headquarters section, were located on the eastern side, where most of the contact was coming from. "I deployed my headquarters element with claymores in an attempt to seal off the area," he said.

The insurgents used vehicles to try and penetrate the perimeter. "Initially it was vehicles loaded with one or two people armed with light machine guns," McCoy explained. "Later on, it graduated to buses and fuel tankers." In one furious exchange of fire, a fuel tanker was set on fire. "It illuminated the area, helping out a bit," McCoy said facetiously, "so that was kind of nice." To reduce the vehicle threat, he brought in air force and navy fixed-wing aircraft to crater the road and the intersection leading to the bridge. Dismounted insurgents continued to press the attack. Most were Fedayeen carrying machine guns. At one point, McCoy received an intelligence report. "We got the 'good news' that perhaps two Iraqi battalions were approaching from the vicinity of Najaf!" He immediately called for help. "Twelve ATACMS [Army Tactical Missile System containing 950 antipersonnel bomblets] were brought in along the road network and a B-1B [Lancer strategic bomber] came in and dropped several two-thousand-pound JDAMs [joint direct attack munitions]." The Iraqi attack was broken up and destroyed by the missile and JDAM combination, although, "My 3rd and 4th Platoons got off a couple of shots," McCoy bragged.

By the evening of the second day, McCoy's company was "approaching black [nearly empty] on ammunition, especially small arms," and the enemy was still attacking. However, the sandstorm had abated, giving the company's night-vision equipment greater range. "We were able to pick up their vehicles pretty far out, engage them with 25mm, and destroy them." At this point, Charlie Company was exhausted and running out of ammunition. Hilmes's Alpha Company, 1-64 Armor, was ordered to help.

"We got a fragmentary order that we needed to move across the river and bail out the cavalry squadron because their situation had become untenable," Hilmes recalled. "That night we did a relief in place." Charlie pulled out, rearmed, and continued the attack. The company lost two tanks and one Bradley in the two-day engagement; the crews were able to escape, however.

"The ammunition was cooking off and raining flames down in front of me," one of the tankers exclaimed. "I yelled, 'Get out! Get out!'" The crew bailed out and ran to a Bradley under heavy fire.

The tank commander was upset. "Blowing up my tank was like blowing up my home. I've lived there for three months. The photos of my wife were in there."

Another expressed anger. "The same people who wave to us when we roll through are the same ones who grab an AK-47 at night and fire them at us. I don't trust anyone anymore."

It wasn't until after the relief that McCoy was able to think about the action. "You're constantly terrified, but you don't realize it until it's over."

Alpha Company, 1-64 Armor, positioned itself at the Kufa bridge to keep the insurgents from getting into Najaf. "The enemy was holed up in the city," Hilmes said. "We really couldn't see them, and for two days we took fire—a very frustrating situation. Every now and then we'd get a shot and would take it, but we were really worried about civilian casualties."

Hilmes's company was supported by Charlie Battery, 1st Battalion, 9th Field Artillery Regiment, under the command of Capt. Matthew Payne. The battery arrived after a forty-hour road march in blackout conditions. "We were shooting within ten minutes of pulling off the road," Payne proudly announced. "We provided our own perimeter security for the two days we were shooting."

At one point, he received word that there were "a thousand fighters in Najaf, and they're going to break out tonight."

"Oh my gosh!" Payne remembered thinking before ordering his men to dig in. "There was always the idea that the artillery would be in a linear battlefield behind tanks and Bradleys . . . but that wasn't the case here." The report turned out to be a rumor.

On the third day, the two companies were relieved by the 2nd Battalion, 327th Infantry Regiment ("No Slack"), 101st Airborne Division, under the command of Lt. Col. Christopher Hughes. His lead element, Bravo Company, moved into position and dug in. "We received some indirect fire from what we called the escarpment in Najaf," Capt. Anthony New recalled. "You could see the golden dome of the mosque off in the distance." Bravo Company responded, bringing on a two-day battle of attrition that saw the battalion using every available weapon. Hughes ticked them off: "Air Force jets, attack helicopters, artillery, tanks, antitank missiles, snipers, psychological operations, infantry . . . I was sure we had broken his [Iraqi resistance] back." As No Slack cautiously entered the city, the paratroopers were met by hundreds of joyful residents "giving the thumbs up sign, waving and smiling," Hughes recalled. "They told us we had destroyed the Fedayeen and Iraqi army positions, and the survivors had fled during the night." *Time* magazine correspondent Jim Lacey wrote, "Najaf had the feel of a liberated city. Smiling citizens crowded every street . . . American soldiers who a day before had been in close combat were now basking in the cheers and applause, their arms tired returning from friendly waves."

Despite the joyous mood of the people, they were still wary. A member of Special Forces told Hughes, "It is amazing the hold Saddam has on these people. They are scared to death of him. Even with hundreds of soldiers in the area, they are afraid he will return." Hughes went out of his way to build trust between his men and the city's residents. In one famous encounter, an angry mob confronted the patrol he was leading on his way to a meeting with Grand Ayatollah Ali al-Sistani. The Iraqis thought the Americans were up to no good.

Hughes, in a totally unexpected, highly unorthodox maneuver, defused the situation. President George W. Bush referred to the incident in an April 12 radio address: "In one city, American soldiers encountered a crowd of Iraqi citizens who thought our troops were about to storm a nearby mosque. Just then, Lt. Col. Chris Hughes ordered his men to get down on one knee and point their weapons to the ground. This gesture of respect helped defuse a dangerous situation and made our peaceful intentions clear." Shortly after the incident, al-Sistani issued a formal *fatwa*, "Do not interfere with the American forces entering Iraq."

Within days, Baghdad fell. The streets of Najaf were filled again with jubilant Shiites. "Freedom brought celebrations and a newfound confidence that was palpable in the streets," Anthony Shadid wrote. "There was a celebratory cacophony . . . with drums and banners, the faithful converged in often spontaneous parades toward the shrine . . . invoking Ali's name." At times, though, the chants and slogans were more political. Posters quickly appeared, showing three stern-faced men in clerical garb, one holding a Kalashnikov (AK-47 Soviet assault rifle) over his head. The caption read, "Crush them under your feet," an obvious reference to the United States and the interim Iraqi government. To Shiites, the three figures were instantly recognizable—Mohammed Baqir al-Sadr, Grand Ayatollah Mohammed Mohammed Sadiq al-Sadr, and Muqtada al-Sadr. The first two were revered clerics who were martyred because of their opposition to Saddam Hussein. The third, Muqtada al-Sadr—black-eyed and glowering, with a black beard and turban—was the son and son-in-law of the other two men in the poster. Muqtada traced his bloodline back to the Prophet Mohammed and was heir to the al-Sadr family legacy.

CHAPTER 2

Muqtada al-Sadr

If we don't deal with this guy [al-Sadr] soon, it might be too late to stop him.

—U.S. Ambassador L. Paul Bremer

IN THE EARLY DAYS of the occupation, Muqtada al-Sadr was something of an enigma. The CPA and the Iraqi Governing Council (IGC) dismissed him as a radical young cleric and demagogue that, if left alone, would quickly fade from the political scene. Hume Horan, a CPA senior counselor on tribal and religious issues, characterized al-Sadr as a "young upstart" and dismissed him as a fringe player. Colonel Joseph DiSalvo, 2nd Brigade Combat Team, thought, "The notion that al-Sadr was the man was absolutely ridiculous. Muqtada himself, as an individual, was nothing. He had a very close circle of influences who were actually riding his coattails; he was just a convenient figurehead."

U.S. Ambassador L. Paul Bremer concurred, describing al-Sadr as, "a rabble-rousing Shi'ite cleric" and excluded him from participating in the twenty-five-member IGC. Al-Sadr denounced the council's formation saying, "The IGC is illegitimate because it was appointed by an illegitimate occupation. We do not recognize it, directly or indirectly, since it exists contrary to the wishes of the Iraqis [read al-Sadr]." He actively fermented rebellion. As the movement gained strength and directly challenged the legitimacy and authority of the American occupation, the CPA demonized al-Sadr as a threat to a democratic Iraq. However, it completely underestimated al-Sadr's political strength among the Shiite masses in the immediate aftermath of the regime's overthrow.

عــاش
عــاش
عاش الصدر
مقتدى للمذهب نصر

Muqtada al-Sadr, the son of a much beloved Shiite cleric, assumed the mantle of leadership when his father was assassinated by Saddam Hussein. Anti-American, he formed the Mahdi Army with the intent to seize power and throw coalition forces out of Iraq. *Maj. R. Bruce Sotire*

Muqtada al-Sadr was thrust into the political arena when his father and two brothers were assassinated by agents of the *Mukhabarat*, Saddam Hussein's secret police. Al-Sadr the elder posed a threat to Saddam because of his opposition to the regime and his wide popularity among the Shiites. He paid for this resistance with his life, taken in a hail of gunfire in Najaf's Revolutionary Circle. "[Al-Sadr's] followers exploded in a paroxysm of rage," Ali A. Allawi wrote in *The Occupation of Iraq, Winning the War, Losing the Peace.* "Thousands took to the streets . . . calling for the regime's overthrow." They were met by Saddam's tanks and security forces, which brutally put down the uprising. Casualties were heavy. According to Allawi, 120 of al-Sadr's key deputies were arrested, as well as over 3,000 supporters, of which 450 were executed. However, Saddam's suppression did not end the movement, members of which came to be known as the Sadrists; it just went deep underground.

Al-Sadr assumed the mantel of leadership after his father's death, albeit with a lower profile so as not to anger Saddam. Continuing his religious studies was essential to maintaining that profile. One of al-Sadr's aides reported that, "senior religious figures advised Muqtada to stick to attending religious classes and to reduce the number of people he met to a minimum so as to preserve his own life. The security forces tracked his movements, even inside his own house . . . but balked at killing him because it feared this would provoke a popular uprising." Al-Sadr's religious studies were also essential to his advance in the clerical hierarchy for, at the time of his father's death, he was only in pre-graduation research.

"Detractors sometimes called Muqtada the video game cleric, Syid Atari," Richard Engel wrote in *War Journal: My Five Years in Iraq*, "because fellow hawza students claimed he spent more time playing Atari than contemplating religious texts." One cleric who studied under the senior al-Sadr said sarcastically, "Muqtada and those people around him, they know nothing. Muqtada, he just sat at his father's computer. He is not an educated man."

Patrick Cockburn disputed this characterization: "Muqtada was keen to burnish his religious credentials and after the overthrow of Saddam studied further under Ayatollah Fayadh, an Afghan ayatollah living in Najaf." In early 2004, al-Sadr elevated him to the rank of *hujjat al-Islam* ("Sign of Islam or Proof of Islam) the third rank from the top in the Shiite clerical hierarchy.

Peter Maass, correspondent for the *New York Times* described al-Sadr's Najaf headquarters: "It is a ramshackle building on an alley across the street from the ornate shrine [Imam Ali Mosque]. Inside, there is a small atrium that most days is crowded with dozens of his aides—clerics in turbans and cloaks who spend much of their time milling around, smoking cheap cigarettes. Al-Sadr's office is nearby, through a set of wood doors. It is a small room with whitewashed walls and thin cushions on the floor." Maass observed people trying to petition the young cleric for a variety of favors: "Muqtada al-Sadr's followers were assembled in a thick line that snaked out of the office door and through the atrium. One after another they stepped forward and knelt before him, whispering their requests into his ear." Al-Sadr granted their requests, cementing his hold on them and earning a reputation for being close to the people.

Correspondent Nir Rosen was "struck by how awkward Muqtada looked and how ill-experienced he was for a man so popular that throughout Shiite neighborhoods he was known only by his first name, a tribute no other Iraqi leader received. I wondered, as I do to this day, if there was some other brain behind his operation. His young, unctuous associates seemed too smug, as if they already knew Iraq was theirs."

Shortly after Saddam's fall, al-Sadr made a four-day "official" visit to Tehran, where he met with senior Iranian officials, including Ali Akbar Hashemi Rafsanjani (former president of Iran) and Ayatollah Khadim al-Haeri, an Iraqi who had lived in the Iranian holy city of Qom for twenty years. Al-Sadr's father had designated al-Haeri to be his official heir and representative and to issue fatwas to his supporters. More ominously, al-Sadr met with Brigadier General Qasim Suleimani, the commander of the Quds (Jerusalem) Force, an arm of the Iranian Islamic Revolutionary Guard Corps

(IRGC), who reported directly to the supreme leader of Iran, Ayatollah Ali Khomeini. The primary mission of the Quds Force is to organize, train, equip, and finance foreign Islamic revolutionary movements. Dan Darling, in the *Weekly Standard*, wrote, "General Suleimani was placed in charge of organizing various Iraqi groups as part of an Iranian plan to dominate the country following Saddam's removal." The London Arabic newspaper *Asharq al-Awsat* reported that at the onset of al-Sadr's uprising, the Quds Force set up training camps in southern Iran, along the Iraqi border, to train al-Sadr's Mahdi Militia and financed his campaign to the tune of $80 million.

The purpose of al-Sadr's Tehran visit, claimed Yossef Bodansky in *The Secret History of the Iraq War*, was to plan a "grassroots campaign aimed at inciting popular resistance—both violent and non-violent—to any form of U.S. or U.K. presence in Iraq."

Bodansky noted that the *Jamaat-i-Sadr Thani*, a group controlled by al-Sadr, was to "organize clandestine networks, tailored after the Hezbollah model, to conduct both anti–U.S. terrorism and other disruptions designated to push Iraq into chaos and civil war." Author Ali A. Allawi confirmed the Iranian strategy: "It [Iran] adopted a policy of 'keeping the pot simmering' . . . and implied that Iran would use its influence, power and money to continue to keep conditions from permanently stabilizing . . . the better to be its [Iraq's] keeper and manager."

Bremer was also aware of Iranian involvement. He noted in an e-mail to Donald Rumsfeld, the U.S. secretary of defense, "Elements of the Tehran government are actively arming, training and directing militia in Iraq . . . they pose a long term threat to law and order in Iraq."

After the Tehran meeting, al-Haeri appointed al-Sadr as his deputy in Iraq. "We hereby inform you that Mr. Muqtada al-Sadr is our deputy and representative in all *fatwa* affairs," his edict noted. It was "a tremendous honor," according to Bodansky. "The appointment gave al-Sadr a legitimacy that offset his lack of formal religious training. Al-Haeri also provided him with a *fatwa* that [gave] Muqtada a license to kill."

One of al-Sadr's first victims was Ayatollah Sayyid Abdul Majid al-Koei, a moderate, expatriate Iraqi cleric who was sympathetic to the United States. On April 10, 2003, al-Koei and Haider al-Rufaii, the *Killidar* ("Keeper of the Keys"), were brutally murdered outside the Imam Ali mosque. Peter Maass asked al-Sadr whether his movement was behind the killings. "Our enemies fight against us," he replied. "They can't fight directly, so they fight by spreading rumors and accusations of being a murder . . . [A]ll of these

Quds Force

The Quds Force (Jerusalem Force) is a special unit of the Iranian Islamic Revolutionary Guard Corps (IRGC). Its name, *Quds* in Arabic means "Jerusalem," a promise that one day the force would liberate Jerusalem from the Jewish colonizers and destroy Israel. It was created during the Iran-Iraq war as a special unit of the IRGC to organize the Kurdish insurgency in Iraq to fight Saddam Hussein's forces. Its primary mission is to organize, train, equip, and finance foreign Islamic fundamentalist terrorist groups. In the past two decades, the force is believed to have helped arm and train Hezbollah guerrillas in Lebanon, Islamic fighters in Bosnia and Afghanistan, and even Sudanese troops in southern Sudan. It is also responsible for gathering information required for targeting and attack planning. Robert Baer wrote in *The Devil We Know: Dealing with the New Iranian Superpower*, "The Jerusalem Force has a long history of backing coups, assassinations, and kidnapping foreigners. It was behind the two U.S. embassy truck bombings in Beirut, the 1983 Marine Barracks bombing, and most of the foreign hostage-taking in Lebanon during the eighties and early nineties."

American intelligence agencies believe the Quds Force is supplying the "explosive formed projectiles" (EPF) that have been so effective in penetrating armored vehicles, including the Abrams main battle tank. One noted terrorist expert says, "It is a remarkably efficient organization, quite possibly one of the best Special Forces units in the world."

According to U.S. intelligence, the Quds Force is organized into eight separate directorates, based on geographic locations:

- Western countries
- Iraq
- Afghanistan, Pakistan, and India
- Israel, Lebanon, and Jordan
- Turkey
- North Africa
- the Arabian peninsula
- republics of the former U.S.S.R.

Experts believe that the force numbers no more than 2,000; however, others say it could number anywhere from 3,000 to 50,000. Whatever its size, "It's a very capable force," according to Mahan Abedin of the Center for the Study of Terrorism. "Their people are extremely talented, [and] they tend to be the best people in the IRGC."

are lies." The death of al-Koei eliminated one of al-Sadr's chief competitors, while al-Rufaii's demise gave him an excuse to take over custody of the shrine's treasury. One year after al-Sadr took over control of the mosque, thieves broke into it and stole much of its contents.

Emboldened by Iranian support, al-Sadr initiated a virulent antigovernment/anti-American campaign. "The government," he declared, "is illegitimate because it was appointed by illegitimate occupation." He urged his followers to "terrorize the enemy," which was a pointed reference to the CPA and the IGC. Bremer was incensed and threatened to issue a "capture or kill" order, but his consistent failure to act made the CPA look inept, because Iraqis were conditioned under Saddam to take government pronouncements seriously. Bremer was severely handicapped because the U.S. military was opposed to action against al-Sadr. Lieutenant General Ricardo S. Sanchez, commander of coalition ground forces, noted in a memo, "My recommendation is to defer the operation . . . [T]he timing is absolutely wrong . . . [I]t would be a strategic blunder for us."

Colonel DiSalvo did not agree. "Al-Sadr should be in jail. He's a murderer . . . The press continually reinforced the theme that al-Sadr was significant, and he's not . . . [H]e's saying the things that attract poor, uneducated, poor people." At the time, the 1st Marine Division, which was responsible for stabilization operations in seven southern governates, was about to rotate home, to be replaced by other coalition forces that did not have authority from their governments for offensive actions. One Polish commander told reporter Richard Engel, "Our forces are peacekeepers. They are not here to fight."

Over the next few months, al-Sadr strengthened his position with a series of moves designed to consolidate his political power. He established parallel government institutions to provide essential services, religious courts that meted out rough and ready justice, and even prisons to take opponents off the streets. A sophisticated communications system was instituted to disseminate his sermons, most of which denounced the United States. Al-Sadr preached, "The smaller devil has gone, but the bigger devil has come. I will fight America." He took to wearing a white robe over his normal dark vestments, signifying a willingness to be a martyr. At the same time, he consolidated his hold on Sadr City, a Shiite stronghold in Baghdad named after his father. Cockburn wrote that Sadr City "was less a district than a twin city to Baghdad, and its two million impoverished people were the core of Muqtada's movement." Al-Sadr also deployed clerics to the major southern cities, Kufa, Kerbala, Kut, Nasiriya, Basra, and Najaf, where they preached the al-Sadr gospel. Their pronouncements struck a responsive cord with much of the Shiite community, who were frustrated by the lack of security, access to basic services, clean drinking water, and electricity, as well as a loss of dignity.

Al-Koei Assassination

Sayyid Abdul Majid al-Koei, the son of a renowned Shiite spiritual leader, was recruited by the CIA to "help in the effort of controlling the city of Najaf and establishing a conduit between the Maraji (Shia religious authority) of Najaf and the Coalition," according to Ali Allawi. He agreed and returned from England, where he had gone into exile after the 1991 attempt on Saddam Hussein's life. Upon his arrival in Iraq, al-Koei was protected by heavily armed guards under contract with an American security firm.

On the morning of April 10, 2004, al-Koei and several others, including Haidar al-Rufaii, made their way to the Imam Ali shrine. Al-Koei's security was left behind because he thought he would be safe in the mosque. The party arrived at the shrine and entered the office of the custodian. Patrick Cockburn described the scene: "Surviving photographs show Sayyid Majid [al-Koei] in a long dark robe sitting on a sofa and smiling gently but confidently at his companions, unaware of any impending danger."

About an hour after their arrival, an angry mob gathered in the courtyard outside the office. Shouting "Long life to al-Sadr," they demanded that the men come out. A gunfight ensued until al-Koei's party ran out of ammunition. The crowd broke in and tied up al-Koei and the others. According to Cockburn, one of the captors said, "You are the hostages of Muqtada and we are taking you to [him] to pass sentence." The men were dragged outside where "swords and knives flashed in the sun." Al-Rufaii was killed, while a badly wounded al-Koei managed to break away and run to al-Sadr's house a few hundred yards away. It was reported that as he lay bleeding, al-Sadr came to the door and refused to help the wounded cleric. He told the crowd to take him away. Al-Koei was immediately killed, and his lifeless body left in the street until his in-laws took it away for burial. Al-Sadr denied any responsibility for the attack.

Yossef Bodansky, however, claimed, "Koei's assassination was organized by a Tehran-controlled hit team operating under the patronage of Jamaat-i-Sadr Thani, a group commanded by Muqtada al-Sadr."

The assassination was investigated by an Iraqi judge, who found sufficient cause to issue an arrest warrant for al-Sadr and several of his senior aides. The warrant was not immediately acted upon until some months later, when one of al-Sadr's top aides was arrested in a predawn raid. The arrest was the cause for a flurry of violent anti-American protests.

MEN IN BLACK

In mid-July 2003, al-Sadr announced the formation of a religious militia, which became known as the Mahdi Army or Militia, Jaish al-Mahdi (JAM) in Arabic, "to fight the American and British occupiers." Lesley Hazleton, in *After the Prophet*, wrote, "The radical cleric Muqtada al-Sadr could not have chosen a more powerfully emotive name for his Mahdi Army. The name itself is a call to action that goes far beyond Muqtada's declared aims of freeing Iraq from American occupation and Sunnis extremism." Lieutenant General Sanchez noted, "When he [al-Sadr] issued a call to arms, busload after busload of Shiites started heading out of Baghdad." Thousands answered the call. It was estimated that by March 2004, the Mahdi Army had grown to between five thousand to ten thousand men armed with rocket-propelled grenades, mortars, machine guns, and Kalashnikov assault rifles. His base of support, estimated to be 3 to 5 million, consisted of young imams, followers of his father, and young, impoverished Shiite city dwellers. One observer noted, "The black-garbed Mahdi Army is drawn from a large and volatile pool: the slums of Baghdad, the poorest of the poor, the Shia who do not see any improvement in their lives since the fall of Saddam. It is the army of the dispossessed."

NBC Middle East correspondent Richard Engel drove to Najaf on the Mahdi Army's first enrollment day. "It was over 100 degrees as our crew walked up a narrow alley behind the Imam Ali mosque," he wrote in his book *War Journal: My Five Years in Iraq*. "The air was thick with sweat. There looked like there were more than three thousand people crammed into the alley, less than eight feet wide. Clerics stood in shaded doorways, fanned by assistants waving pieces of cardboard." Engel went inside the mosque. "The main hall in Sadr's office was packed with a swarm of young men circling and beating their chests under a spinning ceiling fan that did nothing to cool the air. A cleric, who couldn't have been more than twenty-five years old, stood in the center of the crowd, screaming and pointing to the heavens." He climbed a stair to the second floor. "In a room a midget with big bulging eyes, a hunched back, and a wispy beard sat cross-legged on the floor surrounded by Howza students in dirty white robes. Down the hall, young men lined up to sign their names in a logbook, put their hands on the Koran, and swear an oath of allegiance to the Mahdi Army."

Phillip Robertson, a correspondent for the news and culture website Salon.com, was able to arrange a surreptitious meeting in Sadr City with six of al-Sadr's fighters. His contact drove him down narrow, twisting streets flooded with raw sewage into the heart of the Mehdi stronghold, where he met the men in a safe house. He described them as being in their twenties and having similar backgrounds: "They were all laborers, ordinary men who were fighting a guerrilla war against the U.S. blocks from their homes." The fighters talked freely about their hatred of the Americans. "I have attacked the Americans forces every day," one of them said. "When I see a tank or a large number of trucks, we attack from many directions with RPGs, Kalashnikovs and grenades and then disappear back into the city." Their familiarity with the city and their ability to blend in with the crowd made them difficult to stop. After talking with them, Robertson had the impression that al-Sadr had given the men a sense of unity and purpose and a willingness to kill on his orders.

At first, the Mahdi Army was nothing more than a mob of religiously inspired gunmen. One of its early leaders freely admitted, "At the beginning the Mahdi Army was weak and had no real units . . . companies and divisions . . . just groups of armed men. The only condition for somebody who wanted to be a soldier was to be a believer and perform prayers." However, it gradually gained some semblance of organization, thanks in part to the Iranians. The London-based newspaper *Asharq Al-Awsat* reported that the Quds Force of the Iranian Islamic Revolutionary Guard Corps was training between eight hundred and twelve hundred militiamen just across the Iran-Iraq border. The Marines who fought the militia in August were convinced of Iranians involvement. "At one point in the fight," the Marine battalion commander said, "they [Iranians] brought in a sniper who was very good and accounted for many of our casualties." He also believed that the 120mm mortars fired on his men were crewed by Iranians. An Iraqi anti-Iranian militant was quoted as saying, "Iranian intelligence secretly recruited young people to train in Iraq. They gave them $300 to $400 a month and trained them to use weapons to fight the Americans."

In the first few weeks of 2004, al-Sadr directed the militia in well-organized marches and demonstrations against the CPA. The confrontations came to a head on March 28, when Bremer closed down al-Sadr's weekly newspaper, *Al-Hawza*, after it published an inflammatory article praising the 9/11 attacks as "a miracle and blessing from God." Sanchez wrote that Bremer was very upset. "We've got to shut that damned paper down," Bremer exclaimed. "I'm not going to tolerate this." In a fit of pique, he ordered *Al-Hawza* shut for sixty days. "Close the rag down," he commanded. Iraqi police, escorted by heavily armed U.S. soldiers, forced the newspaper staff to leave its building and then padlocked the doors. Al-Sadr used the closing of the paper as an excuse to turn up the heat on the CPA. He called for protests and demonstrations. Thousands of his followers took to the streets. "The rally drew hundreds and then thousands by nightfall in central Baghdad," *New York Times* correspondent Jeffrey Gettleman wrote, "where masses of angry Shiite men squared off against a line of American soldiers who rushed to seal off the area." The newspaper's closing was the spark that ignited widespread opposition to the CPA. "The Mahdi Army was broadly engaged across the south," a CPA report noted, "setting up roadblocks, kidnapping, and torturing Iraqi policemen." General John Abizaid, commander of U.S. Central Command (USCENTCOM), expressed great concern: "We're at risk of losing control of the whole damn region to Muqtada's militia."

On March 31, another major crisis erupted when Sunni gunmen killed and mutilated four Blackwater contractors in the city of Fallujah. President Bush ordered a Marine regiment into the city to arrest the perpetrators and oust Sunni extremists. This new crisis threatened to completely unhinge the American effort in Iraq. "For the first time," Ali Allawi noted, "important constituencies in both the Shia [al-Sadr] and Sunni communities simultaneously rose up in arms in two widely separate locations." Bremer compounded the problem by ordering the arrest of Sheikh Mustafa al-Yaqoubi, one of al-Sadr's top lieutenants, on charges of complicity in the murder of Ayatollah al-Koei. The Mahdi Army was not long in responding. "Muqtada's people are really swarming around our bases," Sanchez reported, "especially in Najaf, where his forces took over a police station and stripped it of all its weapons."

Mahdi Army reinforcements poured into Najaf and its sister city, Kufa, where al-Sadr had taken refuge to preach against the coalition. "All the more canny of Muqtada when he adopted the main mosque of Kufa as his home pulpit," Lesley Hazleton wrote. "In doing so, he took on the spirit not of Ali assassinated, but of the living Imam. Preaching where Ali had preached, Muqtada assumed the role of the new champion of the oppressed." One militiaman said, "[People] heeded the call for the coming battle against the Americans and the defense of the holy sites." Major Barry Wiltcher said that al-Sadr used the cemetery burials to mask his militia's movements "coming in and out of Iran, going into the Shia holy city with weapons, being transported in ambulances."

While large numbers of armed men rushed to the twin cities, they were not even remotely trained fighters. One of those who volunteered admitted that "the Mahdi Army wasn't prepared for the fight. It wasn't even divided into companies and battalions, but was in the form of groups who heeded the call for the coming battle against the Americans." Many of the volunteers heeded al-Sadr's call because they thought the holy sites were in danger of being desecrated.

"We saw hundreds of armed men milling around the tomb of Ali . . . [A]ll the militiamen manning the gates near the shrine were wearing black clothes, black shirts and black ski masks . . . [M]ost of the fighters are young men," correspondent Phillip Robertson reported. "To get into the shrine, one must pass through al-Sadr checkpoints . . . [T]here is no other way in." The militiamen brought their own weapons—chiefly AK-47s and RPGs—or ones they had taken from the old regime. "Some people were selling what they owned in order to buy weapons," a fighter said. "Very few weapons and ammunition were supplied to us."

One night Robertson heard "loud explosions, where the Mahdi Army was attacking the Spanish base." A policeman said, "It was Muqtada al-Sadr fighters who started it." Robertson observed "an absurdly overloaded Volvo sedan sitting low on its springs from the weight of insurgents. Men with weapons were perched delicately on each other's laps. It went racing off into the night, and not long after that, the Spanish base was attacked."

"Blackwater Bridge," in Fallujah, where the remains of four American contractors were hung. The inscription reads, "This is for the Americans of Blackwater that were murdered here in 2004. Semper Fidelis (Darkhorse 3/5, 911)." During the subsequent battle, 3rd Battalion, 5th Marines, captured the bridge. *Bing West*

The policeman complained, "When the Spanish returned fire, they shot randomly, hitting civilian cars."

The Spanish brigade was assigned responsibility for the city, but it operated under a severe political handicap. Its commander told Combined Joint Task Force (CJTF-7) headquarters, "We don't consider al-Sadr a threat. According to our rules of engagement [ROE], we don't have the authority to act against him." In addition, the brigade was being pulled out of Iraq by its government who, according to Sanchez, "decided to pull the plug." Command Sergeant Major Cory McCarty, 1st Infantry Division, agreed: "The big problem I saw was their ROE was very tight, and they were pretty much stuck on defensive type things. The Spaniards and everybody else down in that area were pretty much stuck on the FOB. [They] just kind of watched out the gate and that was all. In talking to the soldiers, they wanted

Iraqi Resistance Report: "The Situation in al-Kufah and an-Najaf"

Qays al-Khaz'ali, spokesman for the Shi'ite Religious leader Muqtada as-Sadr, announced late on Saturday that a military confrontation between Jaysh al-Mahdi, ("The Army of the Mahdi") militia and the American aggressors had become an imminent possibility. In a statement reported by al-Jazeera TV, al-Khaz'ali said that the American side had broken off talks aimed at averting an armed clash between the two sides. "We expect that the American forces will attack the city of an-Najaf at any moment," he said, adding that the attack would amount to "zero hour for the launch of a massive popular revolution." Gunfire could be heard from the north east of the city, an area known as Bahr an-Najaf, where some 2,500 U.S. aggressor forces are encamped. The American invaders seek to disarm the Jaysh al-Mahdi, and the U.S. troops have been ordered to kill or capture Shi'ite Religious leader Muqtada as-Sadr. Tension remains high in al-Kufah, southern Iraq, after clashes between Shi'ite Religious leader Muqtada as-Sadr's Jaysh al-Mahdi (Army of the Mahdi) militia and the U.S. occupation troops in the Umm 'Abbasiyat area north of the city. On Friday Muqtada as-Sadr told supporters he had no intention of dissolving the Jaysh al-Mahdi, and called instead for bringing to trial all those who had beaten Iraqis to death. Muqtada as-Sadr received a measure of support from other Shi'ite religious authorities in Iraq, who described the U.S. demand that Muqtada as-Sadr be handed over to them as a demand that was deliberately aimed at scuttling the negotiations. Shi'ite leaders also warned the U.S. against storming the Shi'ite holy cities of an-Najaf and Karbala', threatening to take up arms in defense of civilians.

to go out there and mix it up like the Americans, but their governments really tied their hands behind their backs."

Major Barry Wiltcher was a liaison officer between the Multi-National Corps–Iraq (MNC-I) and the El Salvadoran, Honduran, Spanish, and Republic of Korea contingents of the Multi-National Corps at the time of the uprising. "The local CPA was screaming that the Spanish weren't providing enough security," he said. "The Spanish leadership did not believe in full-spectrum operations. They believed in peacekeeping or peace enforcement. That's what they signed up for, and they were not about to go out and conduct offensive patrols." During the April uprising, Wiltcher's job was to "send out hourly sitreps [situation reports] after every Mahdi attack." He said, "I assured the CPA that the Spanish could defend the FOB—and they could. They were basically a defensive army, used to conducting security operations. That's what they have been doing for years."

CHAPTER 3

Uprising

The time for killing, torture, and savagery had begun.
—Richard Engel

FIGHTING BROKE OUT IN the southern cities where, "in a coordinated series of attacks," Allawi wrote, "the Mahdi Army had taken over a number of buildings, bridges and police stations." An 11th MEU (Marine Expeditionary Unit) report noted, "In the Najaf-Kufa area the Mahdi was actually better organized than the Iraqi government." The Mahdi quickly took control through a campaign of assassination, kidnapping, and torture of police and government officials. "On one occasion," according to the MEU report, "al-Sadr's thugs kidnapped five Iraqi police and, in one instance, tortured a policeman while allowing the atrocity to be monitored over a government radio frequency." Journalist Nir Rosen remarked that the Najaf chief of police had to pay ransom to get one of his men released. He also noted that "the police had even been infiltrated by al-Sadr's men.

On April 4, a confrontation between al-Sadr's supporters and Spanish coalition forces resulted in over two hundred killed and wounded Iraqis. Marine Corporal Lonnie Young and seven contractors from Blackwater Security Consulting happened to be in the Spanish compound installing radio equipment when Young heard "the unmistakable sound of an AK-47 rifle fire a few rounds out in the street in front of the base." The Marine shrugged into his flak gear and equipment, grabbed his squad automatic weapon (SAW), and charged up the stairs to the roof. "I could see people getting out of a truck and start running toward the compound. One of them dropped down into a prone position and fired several rounds at us." These initial shots were the start of a brutal, four-hour battle pitting the Spanish, Young, and the Blackwater contractors against eight hundred Mahdi militiamen.

Young brought the SAW to bear and "fired off a short burst of 5.56mm rounds at a man carrying an AK-47. I saw him fall onto the pavement and lay motionless." Young continued firing, expending several belts of ammunition. Suddenly one of the men on the roof screamed that he had been hit. Despite the heavy fire, Young ran over to help. "I could hear bullets ricocheting through the air and smacking into a tin air-conditioning duct," he recalled. "I cut off his brown T-shirt and saw a small hole in his left arm that was gushing blood . . . and another hole close to the center of his back." After applying pressure bandages, Young dragged the wounded man to cover and returned to his position. A few minutes later, he heard the unmistakable sound of a bullet hitting flesh. "I looked down and saw a horrific sight . . . blood gushing and squirting out of a guy's face!" For the second time, Young applied first aid and started dragging the man to cover. Suddenly he was hurtled through the air. "I had a burning sensation like I had never felt before on the backside of my left shoulder, and I couldn't see out of my left eye," he recalled. A bullet had pierced his back, and a piece of shrapnel had struck him in the eye.

Despite the wound, Young continued to fire his weapon until an officer ordered him off the roof to shelter. "A small bit of time passed," he recalled, "and the room started spinning. My eyelids felt like they had bricks tied to them, and I was hot all over. I heard the doc say that they had to get me out of there." He was evacuated by a Blackwater helicopter and taken to the U.S. Army hospital in Baghdad for surgery. Young did not have any

Marines of the BLT 1/4 keep their weapons ready and aimed at enemy insurgents in the Old City of Najaf during Operation Iraqi Freedom. *Defenseimagery.mil 040826-M-1726K-005*

major damage, and after a lengthy recuperation period, he retuned to duty. An officer at the compound during the fight praised his performance: "As I look back on all this, I believe that I have Corporal Young to thank that I am still alive." Young received the Bronze Star for his heroic defense of the compound.

Meanwhile, the fighting in Najaf threatened to spiral out of control. Bremer issued a warning: "This morning, a group of people in Najaf have crossed the line, and they have moved to violence. This will not be tolerated . . . ."

Sanchez immediately followed up Bremer's warning by declaring the Mahdi Army a hostile force. The recommendation had been "kicked upstairs," all the way to the White House, where it was approved. "Now, rather than having to wait for the Mahdi Army to attack us," Sanchez wrote, "our military units had the ability to engage as soon as they were identified." The White House also approved a kill-or-capture order for al-Sadr. The approval was incorporated into the final operational plan: (1) capture or kill Muqtada al-Sadr, (2) defeat the Mahdi Army, (3) restore stability in the southern provinces, and (4) assist the CPA in reestablishing civil authority and security.

Bremer heartily endorsed the plan. "Muqtada al-Sadr and his Mahdi Army have declared themselves enemies of the Iraqi people," he said. "This challenge must be addressed swiftly, with no ambiguity, and without leniency. Failure to respond will send a clear signal that violence is effective against the coalition."

The heavy fighting in Najaf and the southern cities stretched U.S. forces to the limit and highlighted the fact that there were not enough boots on the ground. In order to deal with the rapidly deteriorating tactical situation, Sanchez received approval for two operational-level unit movements. First, the 1st Armored Division, which had begun redeploying back to the United States—one third of its force had already been cycled out of Iraq, with some units already in Kuwait and Germany—had its tour extended by four months and was ordered back to the fray. Lieutenant Colonel Thomas Isom was with the advance party in Kuwait when he got the word: "You're not going home, turn around, get back to the area." He had the unenviable task of briefing his men. "It was difficult to tell the soldiers," he recalled. The second operational move involved the highly mobile Stryker brigade stationed in Mosul. "We ordered it to move into Diyala Province, then Baghdad," Sanchez recalled, "and finally, all the way south to operate with the 1st Armored Division."

Left to right: L. Paul Bremer, U.S. Secretary of Defense Donald Rumsfeld, and Lt. Gen. Ricardo Sanchez at a Coalition Provisional Authority briefing in Baghdad. Bremer and Sanchez approved a plan to "kill or capture" al-Sadr. *Department of Defense*

Sanchez designated the area around Najaf as a joint operating area (JOA Striker) and assigned it to the 1st Infantry Division, along with the mission to conduct "offensive operations to defeat anti-coalition forces, capture or kill Muqtada al-Sadr, and establish order in Najaf." The 1st Infantry Division dispatched a composite, brigade-sized force called Task Force Duke, under the command of Col. Dana Pittard. The task force consisted of two infantry battalions and a Stryker battalion, plus support units. According to Pittard, "The movement to An-Najaf was a significant challenge. Not only did the task force have to move over 100 miles to reach FOB Duke (named for the task force), but they also faced constant attacks along their route and had to deal with insurgents destroying key bridges across the Tigris and Euphrates Rivers along their route." The task force's log train, 201st Forward Support Battalion, was confronted by not only blown bridges, but also land mines, improvised explosive devices (IEDs), and two ambushes, which cost one soldier killed in action and two wounded. Despite the enemy resistance and the distance, the road march took only forty hours—a remarkable achievement

Captain Darren Keahtigh, Bravo Company, 5th Cavalry, described how his company, "got the call to pack our stuff and go to Najaf":

> In typical Army fashion, the first two companies departed smoothly. I remember going to bed at 0400 and telling my XO [executive officer]

how I wanted the company lined up and thinking how easy it would be. He gets me up and 0800. "Hey sir," he said, "you have to help me." I asked him how hard it was to line up this sixty-vehicle convoy. I went out, and here's these vehicles, just ash and trash everywhere. I'm pissed. People were told they were going to Najaf and to catch a ride with us. So we pulled them all in and ended up departing at 1200.

Major Peter Zike, fire support officer, 2nd Armored Cavalry, fought his way to Najaf. "They just kept engaging our convoys. I started without any holes in my vehicle and [had] forty-two holes in it towards the end."

Corporal Dan Thompson's six-hour trip to Najaf was less exciting. "We had no enemy contact, except for the lead scout vehicle that took a sniper's bullet through the passenger's side windshield."

Colonel Pittard's composite task force assembled at FOB Duke in the middle of the desert, "a nasty, miserable place, just out of the river basin," according to Lt. Col. Thomas Isom. "There were only a few hard buildings on the site," Thompson remembered, "it was nothing but desert . . . only two plastic port-a-potties for a few hundred men." Pittard's immediate task was to isolate and contain the Mahdi Militia in an economy-of-force mission until CJTF-7 ordered an attack.

"We established presence patrols for probably a week or ten days," Zike recalled. "We would start out mostly on the Kufa side and see how far we could go in, just as a penetration exercise." During one of the penetration raids, militia reinforcements from Najaf tried to cross the river in boats. "We waited until they started crossing and then engaged them with 40mm," Zike said. "The next day, there were bodies floating in the river."

Isom explained that there were two types of "bad guys": "The outer ring around Najaf is what I like to call the 'true believer.' He was the complete fanatic who was willing to do anything—quite literally. These were the types of individuals that would run at a tank with a rifle. The closer you got to Najaf or closer to the mosques, that's when you began finding the trained militiamen." He said dryly, "They were easy to find—they were generally shooting at you!"

The task force established exclusionary zones to protect the mosques, as well as Ali al-Sistani's home. "No indirect fires, fast movers, or rotary-wing within the buffer zone of maybe 500 meters around the Kufa and Najaf mosques," Zike explained. "At times, they [members of the Mahdi Militia] would use the buffer zone as a safe haven. They would fire mortars at us and then go back into the mosque."

Iraqi Resistance Report:
"U.S. Aggressors Advance on al-Kufah"

A U.S. column backed up by helicopters and warplanes stormed the southern Iraqi city of al-Kufah on Friday as a part of the U.S. effort to kill or capture Shi'ite religious leader Muqtada as-Sadr. Battles erupted between members of as-Sadr's Jaysh al-Mahdi (Army of the Mahdi) and the U.S. aggressors. Al-Jazeera's woman reporter in nearby an-Najaf reported early in the day that medical sources there as saying that two Iraqi civilians were killed and seven others wounded in the al-Kufah battles.

Corporal Dan Thompson remembered, "Mortar attacks continued out of Kufa, at exactly fifteen minutes before the hour—every hour—until daybreak. There was nothing we could do about it, and they were almost making a mockery of us, because we can't fire back into the combat exclusionary zone." Occasionally the militiamen would leave the safe haven—a fatal mistake, because they didn't realize they were being watched by an unmanned aerial vehicle (UAV).

"We took fire and saw a white truck driving around," Zike recalled. "We followed them and watched as they set up a mortar tube . . . [W]e engaged them with Hellfire [a AGM-114 high-explosive antitank missile], resulting in two KIAs and several secondary explosions." Zike operated under very restrictive rules of engagement. He had to have positive identification of the target before engaging it. "That day," he explained, "I was 99 percent sure that it was a mortar tube, and I was willing to take the risk because I could see the target on the video feed. That was a good day; it was a good kill."

On April 13, Maj. Chris Budihas, Alpha Company, 1-14 Infantry, was on a leader's reconnaissance on the eastern side of the Euphrates River. "We were trying to locate a place to set up our battalion because the drive from FOB Duke was too long. As we came out of a traffic circle [near Kufa], we were ambushed." The militia had blocked all the roads with fifty-five-gallon drums, forcing the vehicles to cross over the Kufa bridge, which was thought to be mined. "As we drove across the bridge, we found it wasn't mined, so we drove through Kufa, through Najaf, and had a firefight though both of those towns," Budihas recalled. The only casualties Alpha Company suffered were five blown tires —and wounded pride. "We gave the guy hell who was leading for his poor land navigation and the fact that he was getting ready to drive us across a mined bridge . . . [B]ut the enemy has a vote, and they certainly had a vote that day," Budihas said.

Three days later, Charlie Company, 1-14 Infantry, was ambushed by RPGs at one of the traffic circles approximately four kilometers east of the Kufa bridge. "As the company crossed a bridge," Budihas related, "it was ambushed, which initiated a five-hour fire fight." The militia seemed to be well organized; according to the officer, "they were in four- to five-man teams that seemed to know what they were doing. A lot of them were former Iraqi Army guys." As the fight continued, militia reinforcements tried to cross the bridge from Najaf. "I put one of my platoons in an area where they could observe the bridge and actually shoot across and into the river," Budihas said. "One of my machine-gun teams wound up killing a number of them on the bridge." The battalion mortar that was attached to Budihas's company fired over three hundred rounds of high explosive on the enemy, while his own mortar section dropped another sixty. "It was a pretty intense fight," he exclaimed.

On April 22, Task Force Duke was relieved by Task Force 2nd Battalion, 37th Armor, called the "Iron Dukes" under the command of Lt. Col. Pat White. Under cover of darkness, the Iron Dukes deployed without incident into FOB Duke, Hotel, Golf, and Baker and immediately came in contact with the Mahdi Militia. The Dukes had experience with fighting al-Sadr's

Iraqi Resistance Report:
"U.S. Aggressors, Shi'ite Militia Clash on Outskirts of al-Kufah Monday Evening"

Battles broke out on Monday evening between the Jaysh al-Mahdi militia, loyal to Shi'ite religious leader Muqtada as-Sadr, and U.S. aggressor troops at the northern entrance to the city of al-Kufah, according to Agence France Presse (AFP). Jaysh al-Mahdi militiamen posted on a bridge at the entrance to the city battled the U.S. aggressors who sought to cross the strategic objective and advance into the city, according to AFP. The Jaysh al-Mahdi reported that U.S. forces opened fire on the observation point on the bridge killing and wounding an unspecified number of militiamen. In response the Jaysh al-Mahdi destroyed two American military vehicles. AFP reported that dozens of Jaysh al-Mahdi militiamen were deployed in the fields adjacent to the main road and members of the militia were also seen leaving an-Najaf on their way forward to al-Kufah, 10km away, to bolster the front lines there.

An M1064 self-propelled 120mm mortar crewman preparing to fire. The powerful 120mm mortar round can reach out and touch someone over seven thousand meters away. It has a seventy-meter killing radius. *Department of Defense*

militia, having confronted them in Sadr City, Baghdad, between April 4 and 10 and in Kut a week later.

Lieutenant Colonel White organized the task force into four tank and cavalry teams: Headquarters and Headquarters Company operated from FOB Duke; one tank team and the Paladin battery were located at FOB Hotel, on the northern outskirts of Najaf; another team collocated with the El Salvadorian battalion in the heart of the city at FOB Baker; and the fourth team replaced the Spanish brigade at FOB Golf. "We arrived just in time to see them [the Spanish] off, as they were ordered to leave the next day," Cpl. Dan Thompson recalled. "The shaggy, bearded Spaniards busied themselves dismantling their command post and packing away furniture that was purchased with U.S. government money." Thompson was not enamored with the Spanish soldiers. "Look at them, they were getting hit every night, and they knew the general points of origin, but did nothing, nothing for Iraq—only let [al-]Sadr take control of An-Najaf!"

Major Zike shared Thompson's sentiments. "The Spaniards were there, but they didn't want to play."

On the other hand, Zike had a great deal of respect for the El Salvadoran battalion. "[FOB] Baker got attacked one time," he related, "and there was an El Salvadoran lieutenant out there with his pistol, killing insurgents. I thought that was great!"

Associated Press correspondent Dennis D. Gray wrote that an El Salvadoran corporal engaged Iraqi gunmen in hand-to-hand combat. "One of his friends was dead," Gray noted, "twelve others were wounded, and the four soldiers left standing were surrounded and out of ammunition. So Salvadoran Cpl. Samuel Toloz said a prayer, whipped out his switchblade knife and charged the Iraqi gunmen." Gray wrote that Toloz stabbed several attackers, which forced them to back off, just as a relief convoy arrived.

"We never consider surrender," Toloz remarked humbly. "My immediate reaction was that I had to defend my friend, and the only thing I had was a knife. I was trained to fight until the end."

FOBs Baker and Duke were subject to regular militia mortar fire. Corporal Thompson recalled, "Around 0400, loud explosions woke me from my sleep. I sat up in my cot and noticed our second-story room was filled with dust—the shock of the explosions disturbing sandbags and pushing dust through the fabric of the bags stacked in our room along the window." A Hunter UAV spotted the mortar tube in a field that was still hot from being fired.

Major Zike recalled, "We tried artillery, but that did not have the effects we wanted. I had an F-16 on station . . . and using the Hunter as the eyes, we brought it in and dropped a 500-pounder on the mortar."

Thompson said, "Everyone went on top of the roof to get a view of the bomb drop. After a few minutes, you could hear an F-16 coming

Iraq Resistance Report:
"Jaysh al-Mahdi Shells an-Najaf Base Periodically"

U.S. military sources say that the Jaysh al-Mahdi is periodically shelling the U.S. base in an-Najaf. A U.S. commander, Colonel Pat White, reported that American helicopter gunships patrolled the skies after the latest mortar barrage in an attempt to forestall further attacks. He said that the American aggressor forces were practicing "self discipline" so as not to reply extensively to the mortar barrages, as they are awaiting the "right" time to launch maneuvers inside an-Najaf.

A dead insurgent lies in the street after an unsuccessful attack on an American position. The insurgents quickly learned that a frontal attack against U.S. firepower had only one outcome. *Defenseimagery.mil 041109-A-1067B-041*

in fast and low from the west. Seconds later, we heard the boom from the explosion."

Thompson saw evidence of shell damage in the compound and was told that it was mortared every night. "As night fell," he explained, "we waited for the explosions, but all we heard were loud booms in the distance. An AC-130 (call sign Basher) gunship was firing at targets in Kufa . . . [I]t was a comforting sound." As the fire support officer, Zike was directly involved with controlling and approving the gunship's targets. "In my cell, I had the fires [air controllers], two teams of enlisted tactical air controllers, an air liaison officer, and I had the Hunter UAVs."

Zike had priority-of-theater aviation assets while in Najaf, including fixed-wing close-air support, Apache attack helicopters, and Basher. One night, Zike's team identified a suspicious, large, covered object in the back yard of a private residence. "It ended up being a 57mm antiaircraft gun," he pointed out, "so we brought in an AC-130. It expended 38 rounds of 105mm [and] 100 rounds of 40mm on the target. We ended up with a body count of fifty-seven or fifty-eight militiamen."

Zike was extremely cautious in following the rules of engagement. "I asked the judge advocate general to be with us during the operation," he explained, "since we were dealing with civilians in the city." In one instance, Zike was directed to fire on a wounded militiaman, and he refused. "I saved my commander's ass, and even more important, it was the right thing to do." The wounded Iraqi was the result of an AC-130 attack. "We engaged a large force inside a building," Zike said. "The first round was a little bit off, the second round was more accurate, and the fourth round was dead on." A battle-damage assessment team found fifty-eight bodies the next morning. "As in Islamic tradition, the local people would come out and take the bodies so they could be buried within twenty-four hours," Zike explained. "Most of these people were out-of-towners though, because no one claimed the remains. They were out there for about a week, just festering. The heat, the smell of blood, feces, urine—the things the human body excretes after it's dead—is just something that will always stay with me."

Major Todd E. Walsh, Task Force S-3, explained, "Initially it was tough going, with every patrol or logistics convoy subject to ambush whenever they left a FOB. Quick reaction forces, composed of a tank section or platoon, were released when contact was made, to further develop the situation." When an ambush was initiated, the task force standard operating procedure was to get out of the kill zone, establish a base of fire, and maintain contact with the enemy until the reaction force arrived to exploit the situation. The tactic worked, according to Major Walsh. "This finally brought the task force freedom of movement along the main supply routes into and out of the city, as the enemy's outlying forces were attrited."

It became readily apparent that the enemy favored certain areas in the city for initiating attacks, and after identifying enemy-oriented areas of interest, the task force took steps to target enemy cells. Lieutenant Colonel White identified the enemy as "trained and untrained militia," saying, "The trained militia members were organized into four companies. Two companies were employed as defensive companies and controlled key terrain around the Imam Ali shrine and Kufa mosque, while two companies were employed as attack companies throughout Kufa and Najaf." White believed that the untrained militiamen roamed the streets and executed "opportunity attacks" on his patrols and the police using RPGs and small arms. These attacks were often hit and run—a couple of RPGs, automatic-weapons fire, and a mad dash to get out of the area before the soldiers could organize a pursuit.

White believed that almost every mosque and school was being used as a cache for weapons and ammunition and as mortar firing points. "Mosques were also the hiding place of choice for terrorists," Corporal Thompson said. "They would camp out in the mosques, turning them into extremist youth hostels. The problem for us was entering or attacking mosques. We had to respect the religion of the people or risk losing their support."

Colonel White estimated that more than five hundred al-Sadr militiamen were in and around the Imam Ali shrine and another six hundred were near the Kufa mosque. He believed that the Wadi-al-Salaam cemetery was "infested with insurgents . . . and was being used as a weapons and ammunition cache."

Corporal Thompson was frustrated by the militia use of the mosques as firing positions because the militiamen used the mosques in their propaganda. "When these sites are even slightly damaged," he said, "it is our fault."

White cautioned his troops to avoid civilian casualties or infrastructure damage. "Limiting collateral damage was paramount in all our planning and execution," he said. "Soldiers were well aware of the cascading effects a hole in the golden dome or a city block razed during counter-fire would have on the Shia population."

White's strategy was to "concentrate first on the militia—keep up the pressure, stay flexible, and remain unpredictable—[and] focus secondly on Mahdi leaders, target[ing] them and [choosing] the right time to attack." He directed the task force to conduct limited-objective attacks on prayer day to disrupt communication and enemy movement in the city, particularly al-Sadr's movement between Najaf and Kufa.

"He [al-Sadr] would go to the mosque on Thursday, and then a series of three or four vehicles would pull up outside, and he would get in one of them," Zike reported, "sort of like a *French Connection* type of thing." Al-Sadr was considered a high-value target. Zike said, "The first priority was to capture him to exploit his intelligence value . . . but, if we had to kill him, we would." On one occasion, the task force thought they had him. A Hunter UAV followed a car that was thought to contain al-Sadr. A reaction team forced the car to stop, and both the driver and passenger were shot in the process. Al-Sadr was not in the car.

One of the first large-scale operations into the city included elements of a tank company (Crusader) with its M1A2 Abrams tank and two light cavalry troops (Iron and Apache) in M113 Bradley fighting vehicles. The operation was scheduled to kick off at 1645 on May 6. "Elements of Crusader tank company, along with Apache Troop scouts rolled into Najaf," Corporal Thompson recalled, "while Iron Troop approached Kufa from the east, across the Euphrates, in a fake attack that success-fully lured al-Sadr into believing we were attacking from the east." The feint was successful. Swarms of militiamen attacked the army mecha-nized force near the Kufa bridge and were decisively engaged. After the firefight, "Iron [Troop] reported forty enemy dead," said Thompson, who monitored the firefight. He had listened as the tank commander described the battle.

"We're taking heavy RPG fire to the west. I'm going to attack and neutralize the threat," the officer had reported. The sound of small-arms fire could be heard over the radio net every time it was keyed. At one point, an enemy machine gunner opened fire on the tank. "The rounds were flying right past my head," the commander had told Thompson. "My gunner fired his coax [tank machine gun] and just tore him up."

Task Force 2-37 continued to keep up the pressure. On May 30, it launched Operation Smackdown, the first in a series of limited attacks to probe militia defenses around the Kufa mosque. During the attack, two soldiers, 1st Lt. Kenneth M. Ballard and Spc. Nicholaus E. Zimmer, were killed in action, as were twenty-two enemy fighters. A second attack was launched on June 1, resulting in another forty confirmed enemy dead. On June 3, the task force initiated its final attack. Heavy fighting occurred near the mosque, around a school building and courtyard that contained militia mortar positions. The fighting involved room-to-room clearing and the capture of a large amount of ammunition and weapons. The attack force counted another fifty-two militia killed.

Colonel White's strategy had an effect. Al-Sadr's forces had been hammered by superior U.S. firepower. One estimate placed militia casualties as high as 1,000. The survivors were split up and isolated in the old town of Najaf and around the Kufa mosque. One Mahdi fighter reported, "The street fighting was very intense . . . [T]hey destroyed the shops and buildings so Najaf became like a city of ghosts."

Al-Sadr secretly moved about the city. "No one knew where he was going in the dark alleyways of the city," Ali Ahmed, a militia fighter, recalled. Within twenty-four hours after the third attack, the task force received

The business end of a M1A2 Abrams main battle tank. The Abrams is the backbone of the U.S. armored forces. Its 120mm smoothbore cannon fires an armor-piercing, fin-stabilized, discarding-sabot round featuring a depleted uranium penetrator. *Defenseimagery.mil DM-SD-06-00540*

Ayad Allawi, the leader of the interim government. Allawi wanted al-Sadr eliminated, but lacked the political strength to launch an all-out attack against the anti-coalition cleric. *Department of Defense*

rumors that Grand Ayatollah al-Sistani was attempting to broker a truce with al-Sadr and bring about a peaceful solution.

Thompson recalled that the public's reaction was unexpected. "Our translator said, 'It's really a surprise. All the people say they've been waiting for a big U.S. attack and that they want Sadr gone!'"

The fighting in Najaf created a crisis for the newly elected interim government of Ayad Allawi, who had taken the reins of power on June 28 from ambassador L. Paul Bremer of the Coalition Provisional Authority. The crisis generated a complex struggle for control of the city, pitting a number of factions against one another. Muqtada al-Sadr, at the center of the crisis, sought to demonstrate his strength as a political force to be reckoned with. By taking advantage of the political and military turmoil in the country, al-Sadr was able to "steal a march" on the opposition. His anti-coalition stand struck a responsive chord among the Shiite masses, enabling him to mobilize thousands to defend the Imam Ali shrine. Under the guise of establishing an alternative government, he seized the state-owned Samir Hotel, renaming it his ministry of defense. He also set up his own Sharia courts, which handed down sentences that included executions and mutilations. But it was his fiercely anti-coalition diatribes that earned him the enmity of the United States: "No, no to imperialism, no, no to occupation, no, no to falsehood, no, no to the devil [the United States]!"

Both al-Sadr and the Iraqi government were under increasingly heavy pressure to end the fighting. The government was desperate to avoid a confrontation that might damage the Imam Ali shrine, while al-Sadr knew he could not win against U.S. firepower and looked for a face-saving solution. Finally, a political agreement was reached. The United States would pull back to its bases, while the Mahdi Army was allowed to withdraw from the city and keep its weapons—a bitter pill for the American forces. Ali Ahmed said, "Muqtada gave an order saying everybody had to go back to his family. But many of our men stayed inside Najaf saying that the truce was just a lie, and they also moved into nearby regions such as Mashkab, Haidaria, and Abbasia."

Robert Fisk, a foreign correspondent for the *Independent* (U.K.) visited Najaf to see al-Sadr. He stated, "On the drive to Najaf I found that in the first 70 miles, the police have abandoned all the checkpoints. The road is littered with smashed police vehicles and burned-out American trucks." Upon reaching Najaf, he found that all the police had fled to Kufa. He made his way to al-Sadr's air-conditioned office in the Imam Ali shrine. "When I went to see his right-hand man, I asked him, 'What are the terms of the agreement?' He said, 'We have a map, and the Americans are only allowed

Iraqi Resistance Report: "Ceasefire Arrangement Progresses in an-Najaf"

Under a deal worked out between Shi'i religious authorities leaders and the Jaysh al-Mahdi militia loyal to Muqtada as-Sadr militia, the Jaysh al-Mahdi is supposed to pull back from the Islamic shrines in the twin cities of an-Najaf and al-Kufah and hand over security to Iraqi puppet police, according to the puppet governor of an-Najaf 'Adnan az-Zurufi. At the puppet governor's request, the U.S. invader troops agreed to stay away from the Imam 'Ali Shrine in an-Najaf and the mosque in al-Kufah where Muqtada as-Sadr preaches to give Iraqi puppet security forces a chance to end the standoff. By midday Saturday, as-Sadr's fighters remained at the most sensitive religious sites but were no longer brandishing weapons, an aide to the Shi'i religious leader said. The chief of the puppet police in an-Najaf, Sayyid Ghalib al-Jaza'iri, told the U.S. Associated Press (AP) that he would send puppet police in civilian clothes to the site to "assess the situation." He complained that his men were too poorly armed and equipped to take over right away. "We are responsible for all the holy sites now," al-Jaza'iri said. "We went through the city of an-Najaf, we are in control and we have capabilities. And I have a reserve force."

to use two roads.' The man actually produced a U.S. military map with two crayon marks on it, saying, 'They are the roads I allow them to go on. I drew them with crayon, and they accepted it.'"

Phillip Robertson wrote in "The Fake Peace" that "Hours after a deal was struck, armed Mahdi Army forces are back in Najaf—abetted by fresh volunteers." Eyewitnesses claimed to have seen pickup trucks filled with armed men streaming into the city, responding to al-Sadr's call for help. Armed militia occupied checkpoints throughout the city, requiring everyone to show identification. One of them declared, "We have no orders to leave our posts. We will not leave Najaf until there is a direct order."

Another said, "Maybe the fighters who are not from here will leave the city. They will go home and wait for instructions." It was apparent to the observers that despite the cease-fire agreement, Najaf had not been turned over to the civilian authorities. Al-Sadr's Mahdi Militia still controlled the city by intimidating the population. His Sharia courts were still in existence, handing out sentences that ranged from mild reprimands to savage beatings and even execution.

Robertson attended a Friday service, where thousands of al-Sadr's faithful jammed the streets to hear the sermon. "A young man was handed the microphone," he wrote, "and delivered the call to prayer in an anguished shriek, 'Allahu Akhbar!'" Robertson related how the multitude suddenly kneeled in unison toward Mecca and pressed their heads to the ground, making the street ripple and appear to change color. The effect was hypnotic, giving the impression of an irresistible force, a disciplined army of followers. Al-Sadr's power grab went unchallenged in the immediate aftermath of the war because the coalition was focused on finding weapons of mass destruction, capturing Saddam Hussein, and wrapping up the war.

By early 2004, however, the United States wanted to eliminate al-Sadr and his army once and for all. "The Mahdi Army is a hostile force," President George Bush emphasized. "We can't allow one man [al-Sadr] to change the course of the country. It is absolutely vital that we have robust offensive operations . . . At the end of this campaign, al-Sadr must be gone." However, the time never seemed to be right. At one point, a special-operations detachment maintained observation of al-Sadr's comings and goings and devised a kill-or-capture plan, which was never acted upon. Despite the United States' desire to eliminate al-Sadr as a political force, it was very concerned that the fighting might damage the shrine.

"It [the United States] was anxious about the public relations disaster that might ensue if the city of Najaf, in particular the shrine area, was extensively damaged," Allawi wrote. But the United States was also very concerned that al-Sadr's control of the city might fatally weaken the interim government. Allawi noted that the government needed to demonstrate "the efficacy of its new policy of the 'strong state' that would not brook any serious dissent."

The highly mobile Stryker brigade received orders to move into Baghdad and farther south. Stateside, unit-deployment schedules were also expedited, including that of a Marine expeditionary unit.

CHAPTER 4

Back to the Brawl

The MEUs are the most highly trained air-ground-logistics combined-arms unit in the world.

—Col. Jeff Bearor, USMC

11TH MARINE EXPEDITIONARY UNIT
(SPECIAL OPERATIONS CAPABLE)

THE HOME OF 11TH MEU (SOC), Camp Pendleton, is located between San Diego and Los Angeles. Its 125,000-acre training area offered the MEU excellent opportunities for amphibious training along its seventeen miles of coastline and to test its weapons and fire-support procedures on its many live fire ranges. In December 2003, the 1st Battalion, 4th Marine Regiment (Battalion Landing Team [BLT] 1/4), was assigned to the 11th MEU as its ground combat element. In September, the battalion had returned from Iraq, where it had spent eight months conducting stability and support operations after participating in the "march up" to Baghdad with the 1st Marine Division during Operation Iraqi Freedom.

"Following combat operations, 1/4 was assigned to the Military Protectorate of the Province of Hillah, which lasted from May until we redeployed back to CONU.S. [the continental United States] in September 2003," Maj. Coby M. Moran explained.

Lieutenant Colonel Gary S. Johnston, the MEU operations officer, described 1/4 as a "great battalion, very combat ready. Over 50 percent of its men had combat experience." The battalion commander, his staff, company

Insignia of the 1st Battalion, 4th Marines. The Chinese dragon represents the battalion's early history as part of the international force in Shanghai China in the 1930s and 1940s. *USMC*

officers, and staff noncommissioned officers remained from their previous deployment, as well as many of the squad and fire team leaders—they were the cutting edge of the command.

Lieutenant Colonel John L. Mayer, 1/4's battalion commander, was an experienced infantry officer with over twenty years service, and he was no stranger to 1/4. He had served in it for four years as a company commander, the operations officer, and its second-in-command. "From there I went to school . . . Command and Staff, School of Advanced Warfare, and the War Fighting Lab . . . and then to the 1st Marine Division staff," Mayer pointed out, "where I helped plan the liberation of Iraq." He knew he was slated for command of 1/4, so he "made sure the battalion was included in the deployment order." In August 2002, he was given command of the battalion and led it during the "100-mile gunfight," as the slugfest on Highway 7 to Baghdad has come to be known.

Upon his return from Iraq, he had been "lucky enough to keep almost all my officers and senior SNCOs [staff noncommissioned officers]." His operations officer, Maj. Coby Moran, and two of his company commanders had "fleeted up" from billets in the battalion after the invasion. "I was very lucky that my leadership had combat experience," Mayer said. "That's one of the most important attributes for a leader to have. It inspires confidence from their men."

After thirty days leave, Mayer said, "We chopped [joined] to the 11th MEU and began the typical workup that prepared the battalion for a variety of missions. At the time, we believed we were going to do a typical MEU deployment."

Lieutenant Colonel John L. Mayer, commanding officer, 1st Battalion, 4th Marines. Mayer was an experienced officer with over twenty years service, and the deployment to Najaf was his second deployment to Iraq. *Lt. Col. John Mayer*

Colonel Anthony M. Haslam, commanding officer, 11th MEU. *USMC History Division*

The MEU had just completed its first at-sea predeployment training and was on liberty, enjoying a much-deserved Easter weekend before commencing the arduous special-operations qualification exercises. Colonel Anthony M. Haslam, its commanding officer, was home when, as he described, "I received a call saying they [1st Marine Division] were looking for two MEUs to go ashore in Iraq, possibly in the next three to four weeks."

Colonel Haslam asked to expedite the certification process. "We went to the MEF [Marine Expeditionary Force] and requested to push the special-operations certification to the second at-sea period, so if we left early we would be certified." The request was approved.

MEU (SOC)

An MEU (SOC)—Marine expeditionary unit, special operations capable—is the standard, forward-deployed Marine expeditionary organization. It is a self-contained operating force capable of carrying out a wide variety of conventional and special operations of limited scope and duration. An MEU (SOC) is embarked aboard a U.S. Navy amphibious ready group (ARG), which provides it with a quick, sea-based reaction force.

"We made some quick plans with the MEF and went through the special operations exercise," Johnston noted.

"We did an amazing job in literally ninety-six hours," Lt. Col. Eugene N. Apicella, Haslam's second-in-command, boasted, "from the time we sailed and started our second at-sea." The MEU passed with flying colors.

"I tell you what," Haslam exclaimed, "they did great! We got our SOC certification."

Immediately after certification, Haslam authorized a short period of leave and then turned to getting the MEU ready to embark on the ships of Amphibious Squadron 5 (Phibron 5) for the lengthy sea-voyage to Kuwait.

"We left Camp Pendleton on May 27," Moran said, "and embarked on the ships from the San Diego 32nd Street naval base. We sailed to Hawaii, off-loaded, and spent three days live firing at Schofield Barracks. Once that training was complete, we had two days of well-earned liberty before reembarking."

The battalion continued to train during the long transit. "I made all my Marines and sailors wear their complete combat load and carry weapons loaded with blanks while moving about the ship," Mayer said. The loaded-weapons policy was designed to get the men used to carrying them—and used to avoiding accidental discharges, the bane of inexperienced men in combat for the first time. "The men hated wearing their full kit in the crowded ship's passageways," he admitted. "We also did a lot of day and night firing from the flight deck, and we scheduled physical training during the hottest time of day. I knew we would off-load in Kuwait at the hottest time of year, and I didn't want them coming off thirty-eight days at sea out of shape."

While at sea, the MEU received word from Apicella, who was already in Kuwait, that its mission was going to change. Initially it was going to be the Multi-National Force–Iraq (MNF-I) operational reserve near Baghdad, subject to employment anywhere in Iraq. "About a week or two

11ᵗʰ MEU (SOC) T/O

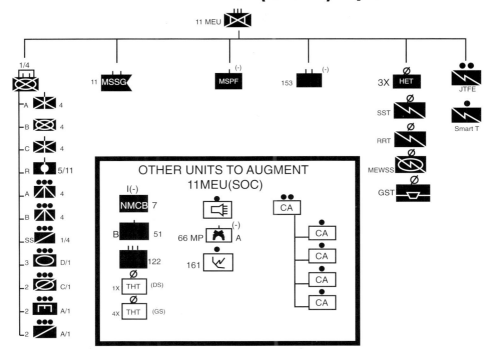

The 11th MEU Table of Organization. The MEU's primary units included a ground-combat element (1st Battalion, 4th Marines), an aviation-combat element (HMM-167), and a combat-service support element (MSSG-11). The MEU had over 2,200 Marines assigned to it. *USMC History Division*

Amphibious assault vehicles (AAVs) in a training exercise off the coast of Camp Pendleton. The AAVs are designed to carry twenty-five combat-loaded troops in a single lift from assault shipping during amphibious operations and to conduct subsequent mechanized operation ashore. *USMC photo*

before we pulled into Kuwait," Johnston recalled, "we were notified of a change in plans. We were going to take over the provinces of Najaf and Qadisiyah. And I'm like, 'Where are those?'" The new assignment caused some consternation because the MEU had completed all the planning for the Baghdad assignment. However, as Johnston said, "We immediately turned to trying to figure out what we needed for the new mission." He soon learned that the MEU was going to be assigned to the Multinational Division–Central South (MND-CS) under Polish control. "It was a huge issue," he emphasized, "because we'd be very thin on the ground, almost an economy-of-force mission. We would have a tough time covering it with our limited mobility assets." In the time remaining before arriving in Kuwait, Johnston worked out an operational plan. "[W]e never received anything from Center South," he said. "As a matter of fact, we gave them the plan, which they kind of tweaked and sent it right back to us."

The MEU plan was "wargamed" by the commanders aboard the flagship over a three-day period. They came up with "a six-month plan that called for the occupation of the Najaf and Qadisiyah provinces," Mayer recalled. "During that time, we would train the ING [Iraqi National Guard], police, and any available regular Iraqi Army troops." Once the Iraqis were sufficiently trained—a task estimated to take four months—the combined Iraqi and Marine force would attack and eliminate al-Sadr's militia. That left two months to conduct follow-up stability operations and restore normalcy. Mayer said the plan "provided the basis for the operation order that served us throughout our time in Iraq. We stuck to it even though the timeline was disrupted by the Mahdi Militia, who attacked us immediately upon our arrival in sector." The Iraqi training was put on the back burner until the Mahdi Militia was forced from Najaf.

The MEU reached Kuwait and off-loaded at the naval base on July 6. It immediately commenced ten days of training, "Knocking the rust off," Haslam declared, referring to the relative inactivity of the thirty-eight-day at-sea transit. After completing the training, the battalion broke into five separate convoys for the road march to its objective area.

"Motorized convoys are always a challenge," Moran explained, "because of breakdowns and problems with communication among the different drivers." In each convoy, there might be rolling stock from battalion, the MEU, the MEU's service-support group, and even the aviation component.

Each convoy consisted of dozens of vehicles under the control of a single commander: one of the three rifle-company commanders, the weapons-company commander, or the artillery-battery commander. The convoy commander was responsible for providing security, maintaining convoy integrity, establishing the speed of march, and routing. "The route took us up Highway 1, the main north-south highway through central Iraq from Kuwait through Nasiriyah," said Moran. (Nasiriya was the site of a 2003 Marine battle.) Their first stop was at Diwaniyah, the capital of Qadisiyah Province. "Alpha Company, several weapons company attachments . . . CAAT-Bravo, 81mm Mortar Platoon, and the battalion snipers . . . stayed there," Moran said, "while the rest of the convoys continued to Najaf, arriving at FOBs Hotel and Duke on the twenty-third." The battalion immediately prepared to assume responsibility in accordance with the theater's standard operating procedure (SOP). The SOP prescribed a ten-day turnover process between relieving units.

RELIEF IN PLACE

The 11th MEU (SOC) officially assumed responsibility for Najaf and Qadisiyah provinces from the U.S. 1st Infantry Division's Task Force Dragon (1-14 Infantry) on July 31, at a formal change of command at FOB Duke. The two provinces covered over 16,000 square miles but were considered "very quiet, very peaceful," according to Lieutenant Colonel Johnston. FOB Duke was located about twenty kilometers northwest of Najaf, in an

A convoy of Humvees (high-mobility, multipurpose wheeled vehicles) near Habbaniyah, Iraq. The four-wheel drive vehicle has at least seventeen variants, including a cargo/troop version, weapons platform, ambulance, carrier for TOW (tube-launched, optically tracked, wire-guided) missiles, and prime mover. *Defenseimagery.mil 071023-M-2819S-002*

isolated desert wasteland that had been an Iraqi ammunition dump. The base was still under construction, but had some amenities—showers, mess hall, air conditioning—that were a step above the tents in the desert that had been used during Task Force Dragon's occupation. Its large size and isolation made it the perfect choice for maintaining security. The MEU soon established its administrative headquarters and logistics storage areas. A detachment of helicopters was also based there.

BLT 1/4 was headquartered at FOB Hotel, four kilometers north of the Imam Ali shrine's exclusion zone, just outside the city's center. Mayer wanted his headquarters there to be close to the shrine and to where the enemy was thought to be positioned. "The FOB's location provided several advantages," Mayer said. "It put our artillery battery within easy range of the entire city; our armored reaction force could easily traverse the main road or through the desert; it was strategically located along the main north-south supply routed; and finally, it was within VHF radio range of the MEU headquarters at FOB Duke." Bravo Company, minus one platoon, provided security for the governor's compound.

The change of command ceremony was conducted with as much military pomp and ceremony as conditions allowed. Against a backdrop of

Major Coby M. Moran, operations officer, 1st Battalion, 4th Marines. Commissioned in 1995, Moran served in a variety of infantry positions, including Operation Iraqi Freedom as Weapons Company commander in 1/4. *USMC History Division*

the national ensign and the organizational colors, Colonel Haslam spoke to an assembly of servicemen and -women and a delegation of Iraqi civilians. "The local leaders of the town came out," Maj. Glen G. Butler recalled, "as well as the mayors of An-Najaf and Diwaniyah. It was pretty cordial." Haslam emphasized that the 11th MEU mission was to help the Iraqis maintain security and provide assistance with rebuilding. He also praised the professionalism of his army counterpart and thanked him for his assistance in the turnover process.

Major Moran recalled, "The army did a very methodical, detailed approach to the relief in place. It was very well done." The battalion staff had an opportunity to "get in the hip pocket" of its counterpart. "A lot of exchanging notes," Moran explained, "a lot of turnover files, intelligence—their whole intelligence package, which identified areas of interest, identified personnel targets [many of al-Sadr's lieutenants] and in this case, the enemy in the AO [area of operations] at the time."

The two units embarked on a ten-day "left seat, right seat" turnover process. During the first segment of the turnover, the more experienced soldier sat in the left seat with the less experienced Marine in the right.

11th MEU (SOC) Press Release, July 31, 2004

FOB DUKE—The 11th Marine Expeditionary Unit (Special Operations Capable) assumed operational control of the An Najaf and Al Qadisiyah provinces from the U.S. Army during a ceremony here today.

Upon arrival in country, the MEU began a 10-day turnover with Task Force Dragon, comprised of elements of the 1st Infantry Division. This task force assumed control of the area of operations in June, relieving the 2nd Armored Cavalry Regiment who had been extended twice in Iraq.

Working for the Polish-led Multi-National Division Central South (MND-C-S), 11th MEU Marines will focus on full spectrum operations that include combat operations; training, equipping and building leadership in the Iraqi security forces; and conducting civil military operations in their area of responsibility south of Baghdad.

Operating from three bases outside the major cities of An Najaf and Ad Diwaniyah, and one air station west of Baghdad, the MEU's aim will be to support Iraq's sovereignty, enable Iraqis to take the lead in their own defense, and set the stage for national elections.

The MEU's area of operations holds great historical and current significance. An Najaf, population 550,000, is home to Iraq's top Shiite cleric Grand Ayatollah Ali ali-Sistani and the radical Shiite cleric Muqtada Sadr and his Mahdi army. The 10th-century Imam Ali Shrine and its neighboring cemetery make Najaf one of the holiest cities for Shiite Muslims. Ad Diwaniyah, population 450,000, is located on a branch of the Euphrates River and on the Baghdad-Basra railroad.

Currently there are seven standing MEU (SOC) command elements, three on each coast: 11th, 13th and 15th on the west coast, while the 22nd, 24th and 26th are on the east coast. The 31st is located on Okinawa.

A Typical MEU (SOC) is augmented with selected personnel and equipment, bringing its strength to approximately 2,200 Marines and Sailors. It is organized into four basic elements:

Halfway through the process, the two switched places. The Marine took over in the left seat, while the soldier was available in the right seat for last-minute mentoring. "The process was very valuable to us," Moran said. "It gave our NCOs and junior officers a chance to go out in the city, physically view the terrain and the environment, and get a good look at what the unit we're relieving currently uses."

Sergeant Jason McManus recalled, "We were definitely proactive in taking over from the army. We practiced quick-reaction drills because we started getting reports that there was a buildup of the Mahdi Army . . ."

Army Staff Sgt. Earl C. Dean said, "It was pretty seamless. We have the same battle drill. Marines are just like my infantry soldiers."

1. A command element, commanded by a Colonel
2. A Ground Combat Element (GCE) commanded by a Lieutenant Colonel, comprising an infantry battalion, reinforced with artillery, reconnaissance, engineer, armor, assault amphibian units and other detachments as required.
3. An Aviation Combat Element (ACE) commanded by a Lieutenant Colonel, comprising a reinforced helicopter squadron with transport, utility, and attack helicopters, a detachment of vertical/ short takeoff and landing (V/STOL) fixed-wing attack aircraft, and other detachments as required.
4. A Combat Service Support Element (CSSE) commanded by a Lieutenant Colonel, task organized to provide logistic support.

MEUs routinely receive special training to qualify them as "special operations capable." To receive this certification, the MEU undergoes an intensive 26-week, standardized predeployment training program. The MEU (SOC) must demonstrate competence across twenty-one conventional and limited special operations missions including:

- Amphibious raids: specialized boat raid and long range helicopter raids.
- Clandestine reconnaissance and surveillance missions.
- Humanitarian and disaster relief
- Noncombatant evacuation operations (NEO)
- Military operations urban terrain (MOUT)
- Limited objective attacks
- Tactical recovery of aircraft and personnel (TARP)
- Gas and oil platform operations (GOPLAT)
- Seizure/recovery of selected personnel or material
- Maritime interdiction operations (MIO)
- In-extremis hostage recovery (IHR)

Marine Staff Sgt. Richard M. Saxton acknowledged, "Everything's gone pretty well overall. The army's definitely been very helpful. They are well versed with the area and know their job well. We've learned a lot from them through map studies—where the hot spots are, where to go, where not to go, key points around the city and other things to look for."

Dean cautioned his counterpart, however, "Complacency is the number one enemy out here. You can go out on a hundred patrols and nothing will happen, but the enemy could be waiting for that one time that you let your guard down and take advantage of it." He admitted, "If something happens, we want to act on it right now. We're not able to do that right now. If we do, it makes the Iraqi National Guard and the Iraqi police that much less effective in the eyes of the people."

Saxton gave Dean a straightforward reply. "We're ready to get started."

The army told the Marines that the city was quiet. First Lieutenant Michael J. Borneo had reason to be skeptical. "The army is telling us that An Najaf was peaceful but, as we're driving through the streets, we see Mahdi Militia on every corner holding RPGs and machine guns. We're staring at them, they're glaring back at us—the whole Mexican standoff thing; and I'm thinking this is weird."

Mayer recalled his initial impression. "The people were not friendly. They stared with open animosity as our vehicles drove by or as we tried to start conversations with them. The Shiite hostility was new to me. It was 180 degrees different from my experiences in al-Hillah less than a year previously." He was of the opinion that "Najaf was a city dominated by terror and oppression. Businesses were closed, schools were not operating, children were not playing—there were little signs of normalcy."

First Lieutenant Jeremy T. Sellars thought the city was friendly at first. His opinion quickly changed. "We were going to go see the ING checkpoints," he recalled. "We turn down a street that Purdy [an army counterpart] said he's never been down before. I remember looking out the window, and Purdy exclaimed, 'Huh, I've never seen these roadblocks here before . . . What's going on?" Their vehicle drove around the barrier. "There's an Iraqi guy standing on the sidewalk with an AK-47," Sellars continued, "and he seemed to be just flabbergasted, like he couldn't believe what he was seeing . . . and then he became the most angry man that I'd ever seen in my life."

As the vehicle continued down the street, "I see a guy with an Iranian rocket," Sellars exclaimed. "I realized then that this is not a police force." Fortunately, no one fired, and Sellars and his crew made it back to their base safely, where they were debriefed on what they had observed. "We looked on the map," Sellars explained, "and discovered that we had inadvertently driven by al-Sadr's house." He indicated the house was not a specific no-go zone, but the army had worked out an unofficial, "We won't drive by your house and harass you, if you don't mess with us" agreement.

Lieutenant Colonel Johnston realized early on that "there were some areas these guys [the army] weren't going." A deal had been struck between the army and the governor to make the cemetery and the Old City exclusion areas. Johnston said these were huge areas that "no one was going into at all."

Mayer was not happy. "We didn't like the exclusion zones, but we figured we couldn't do much about them for the time being."

Iraqi civilians staring at a Marine patrol. Mayer was surprised by the hostility of Najaf's citizens and felt that "the city was dominated by terror and oppression." *Bing West*

First Lieutenant Jeremy T. Sellars, platoon commander, 1st Platoon, Charlie Company. A graduate of Princeton, Sellars entered the Corps through officer candidate school and was commissioned an infantry officer in time to participate in Operation Iraqi Freedom. Najaf was his second deployment. *USMC History Division*

Sellars thought that the inadvertent drive-by had "started the tension between al-Sadr's militia and the Marines." However, Lieutenant Colonel Mayer explained that he had Iraqi friends from his previous tour who told him, "Al-Sadr was positive the coalition sent the Marines back into Najaf to destroy the Mahdi Militia and to kill him." Mayer postulated that "when a Marine patrol went by Sadr's house for the second time, I'm sure he figured it was a direct assault."

All the variables were coming to a head. Mayer said, "When we took over Najaf, it was literally about to explode."

BORNEO PATROL

On August 2, with the city now in Marine hands, the MEU sent out its first patrol. "We made the determination the night before," Lieutenant Colonel Johnston said, "to send the patrol into areas that were adjacent to—not into, but very close to—the exclusion zone. I told everybody that I had a bad feeling about the patrol . . . [M]y spine hairs were tingling."

The BLT assigned the mission to Weapons Company's CAAT-Alpha, codenamed Havoc, commanded by 1st Lt. Michael J. Borneo, a combat-experienced officer from the 2003 invasion of Iraq. Colonel Mayer described him as "someone who stuck his nose into almost every fight. While Marines are known for moving to the sound of the guns, in my battalion, it was usually Borneo's guns that the rest of us were moving to. He was always right in the middle of it." Borneo's orders were to "look at key infrastructure: hospitals, clinics, IP [Iraqi police] stations, civic buildings . . . areas of interest . . . just to get a feel of the AO [area of operations]." The patrol consisted of forty-one men, along with a small contingent of Iraqi National Guard riding in two trucks.

"All the Marines were combat veterans of OIF I [Operation Iraqi Freedom I, the 2003 invasion] and, in fact, had led the battalion's march to Baghdad," Major Moran pointed out. "They had seen months and months of combat." The patrol was mounted in eight heavily gunned, up-armored HMMWVs (high-mobility, multiwheeled vehicles, known as Humvees) carrying an array of automatic weapons: M-3 (.50-caliber machine gun) and M-240G (7.62mm machine gun), Mark 19 (40mm) automatic grenade launchers, and four wire-guided TOW antitank missiles.

As the patrol drove cautiously north along one of the the city's principal four-lane highways, it came to its last checkpoint, a maternity hospital, which happened to be adjacent to Grand Ayatollah al-Sistani's home. Unknown to Borneo at the time, al-Sadr's nondescript home was a few houses away, on the same side of the street. The patrol stopped to allow the Iraqi translator to talk with the inhabitants of the hospital. Suddenly, one of the Iraqi guardsmen yelled out, "RPG, RPG!" and frantically pointed to the walled compound across the street.

Borneo looked to where he pointed and saw "guys running back and forth with AKs, an RPG, and three 82mm mortar tubes." He quickly dismounted and, with half a dozen men, started across the street to investigate. "As we crossed the street," Borneo explained, "they opened fire at us with small arms." As bullets caromed off the roadway and cracked over their heads, the squad fell back under covering fire from the men in the vehicles.

The enemy quickly targeted the vehicles. Several RPGs exploded close by, convincing the drivers to move to covered locations. As his platoon maneuvered, Borneo made a quick estimate of the situation. He decided to split the platoon in two sections—one to the north and the other to the south—to isolate the compound and prevent the enemy from reinforcing or escaping. Author Francis X. Kozlowski, in *U.S. Marines in Battle, An-Najaf*, wrote, "The al-Sadr compound stood in an open area a few hundred meters square, but its perimeter wall and other obstacles provided cover and concealment for the enemy. Storage containers, a junkyard, long berms, and vehicles separated the Marines from the militia fighters, making the battle terrain difficult."

A Humvee mounted with a Mark 19 40mm grenade launcher provides overwatch protection of a dismounted patrol. Note the additional ballistic armor hanging over the doors. *Defenseimagery.mil 040812-M-2306K-070*

The platoon dismounted and took up firing positions from behind their armored vehicles, metal containers, and dirt berms. "At first, we were just exchanging small-arms fire," Borneo recalled, "but then they started shooting 82mm mortars and RPGs at us." As the situation deteriorated, and the platoon began taking heavy automatic-weapons fire, incoming mortar rounds, and RPG volleys, Borneo quickly realized he needed help and requested the assistance of the QRF, located in FOB Hotel, about thirty minutes away. "I'm in contact with approximately twenty to thirty guys," he told Major Moran.

Lieutenant Thomas was monitoring the radio. "You could hear the bullets and the RPGs, which was pretty frustrating," he said, "because I had four tanks and couldn't get into the fight."

Moran approved Borneo's request and released "a platoon from Bravo Company mounted in seven-ton trucks, and called for a Cobra attack-helicopter section to provide close air support."

Several mortar rounds—Borneo counted fifteen—exploded in quick succession. The patrol determined the mortars were being fired from inside the compound, but they could not see the actual firing positions because of the compound's high walls. Borneo explained that his gunner improvised by "using indirect fire from the MK-19 [40mm grenade launcher] to shoot over the top of buildings." He added, "My section leader adjusted fire to get them where they needed to be."

Gunnery Sergeant Jeffrey M. Godfredson, the platoon sergeant, edged his vehicle into a firing position so his gunner, Lance Cpl. Daniel W. Barker, could hose down another mortar position with his 240G machine gun. When Barker ran out of ammunition, another vehicle moved in to take Godfredson's place. Lance Corporal Richard L. Sweetman spotted an RPG team that was firing from the protection of an earthen berm. He fired an AT-4 antitank missile at the enemy team and took it out. At this point, small-arms fire erupted from several buildings surrounding the embattled platoon.

"This whole neighborhood was a Mahdi Militia stronghold," Borneo explained. "They were seriously Sadr friendly . . . and were taking potshots at us . . . [A]ll of a sudden you hear, ping, and bullets just whiz by." Lance Corporal Brad A. Kidder put them under fire with his M-16 rifle and M-203 grenade launcher. "He started doing really direct, really accurate fire on the rooftops and killed two individuals that were sniping at us," Borneo said.

A militiaman tried to sneak out of the compound, but was spotted by Lance Cpl. Eric Johnson, who "sprinted across fifty meters of open ground," according to Borneo, "with machine guns and RPGs shooting at him and climbed on top of a boxcar where he could see down into the compound." Johnson opened fire with his M-16 rifle, killing two militiamen, who were manning a mortar tube. The enemy saw the exposed Marine and turned their weapons on him. An RPG exploded close by, slightly wounding Johnson in the arm, but did not discourage him from continuing the fight. "This kid, this lance corporal, was just doing amazing things," Borneo related. "He's under fire, bleeding from the wound in his arm . . . and he's calling out directions and distance to the enemy and engaging them with his weapon."

Borneo's gunner, Lance Cpl. Brandon W. Shaw, spotted two militiamen firing RPGs from beneath a fuel tanker two hundred meters away. It was a bad decision on the enemy's part. Shaw hit the vehicle with several 40mm grenades and blew it up, ending the threat conclusively. Sergeant Eric W. Clayton's fire team killed another four militiamen with rifle fire, while Pfc. Edward Roacho engaged enemy snipers with his vehicle-mounted .50-caliber machine gun. Lance Corporal Christopher B. Abner dropped a sniper with his M-16, at a range of 150 meters. Despite the heavy enemy fire, only one Marine was slightly wounded, which attested to the disciplined

Gunnery Sergeant Jeffrey M. Godfredson, platoon sergeant, Combined Anti-Armor Team Alpha (CAAT-Alpha). When his team came under fire, Godfredson moved his vehicle into a firing position to suppress enemy fire. *USMC History Division*

suppressive fire of Borneo's men. The militia could not deliver aimed fire before being targeted. It could only "spray and pray," the militia's preferred shooting technique. Militiamen held their weapons out in the open and pulled the trigger without aiming. Borneo was thankful. "It's lucky for us Iraqis don't have the marksmanship of United States Marines."

Major Moran was closely monitoring the progress of the fight. "It was my job to think ahead," he explained, "and I wondered 'Where is this thing going to go? Do we send in more men and make it a company fight, or do we back out?'" He was in constant communication with Lieutenant Colonel Johnston, keeping him informed "ops officer to ops officer."

Johnston was the decision maker, because the two commanders, Haslam and Mayer, were in Diwaniyah, out of communications range. After carefully considering the situation, he made the decision to pull Borneo out of the fight. "They [Borneo's platoon] were running out of ammunition, and Mahdi reinforcements seemed to be pouring into the area. All I could think about was there could be thousands of militia coming in behind them out of the Kufa and the Old City, and there's this little CAAT platoon caught right in the middle. So I said go ahead and disengage."

By this time, the QRF had arrived and added its firepower to the fight. "Within minutes of arriving, they had their force on the deck," the battalion after-action report noted, "and [were] effectively suppressing the enemy with overwhelming fire superiority." Thanks to the reaction force's suppressing fire, along with another AT-4 rocket blast that kept the enemy's heads down, Borneo's platoon slipped out smoothly, though not quietly; the team's guns blazed away as CAAT-Alpha withdrew. The QRF covered the withdrawal and then disengaged. It was estimated that during the roughly fifty-minute fight, the militia had fired dozens of 82mm mortar rounds, fifteen RPGs, and thousands of rounds of small arms. In response, CAAT-Alpha fired over six hundred MK-19 rounds, three AT-4 rockets, four hundred .50-caliber rounds, twenty 40mm grenades, and thousands of rifle and machine-gun rounds. The QRF, in the short time it was engaged, fired over 1,300 small-arms rounds. Borneo reported fifteen men from the Mahdi Militia confirmed dead and an undetermined number wounded. Lance Corporal Johnson's light wound was the only Marine casualty.

Newsman Phillip Robertson reported, "The crucial event had come on Monday . . . U.S. Humvees and Iraqi forces had fired on buildings near Muqtada al-Sadr's house and attacked al-Mahdi army fighters across the street. According to [Iraqi] witnesses, U.S. and Iraqi forces had come

Iraqi Resistance Report:
"U.S. Aggressors Launch Attack Towards an-Najaf, Clash with Jaysh al-Mahdi near shrine of Imam Ali"

In an-Najaf, U.S. invader troops battled Jaysh al-Mahdi fighters outside a cemetery near the Imam 'Ali Shrine, Iraq's holiest Shi'ite site. Battles erupted in and around an-Najaf on Thursday between U.S. invaders and Jaysh al-Mahdi forces. U.S. troops reportedly surrounded Jaysh al-Mahdi forces, as fighting raged with automatic weapons and mortars between the two sides. Columns of smoke rose over the cemetery on the edge of the city. U.S. helicopter gunships flew low over the battle zone. American spokesmen said that they would not go in to the city itself with its Shi'ite holy sites, in an effort to avoid arousing hostility. U.S. forces claimed that they had killed 41 Jaysh al-Mahdi militiamen in an-Najaf. Reuters also reported that U.S. aggressor troops had seized control of the office of the governor of an-Najaf. Earlier reports said that U.S. aggressor forces had massed tanks and armored vehicles as well as men north of the city of an-Najaf on Thursday, in apparent preparation for an attack on the Jaysh al-Mahdi in the city.

down the street several times before, but this would be the last straw and a deliberate provocation."

One of the eyewitnesses said, "The Americans are coming to provoke us and came four times before our people had permission to fire. They crashed through checkpoint barriers. The fourth time was yesterday. A woman died and a hospital was damaged. God will punish them."

Robertson went on to say, "One U.S. news story said the patrol that went by Sadr's house had become lost in the city, ending up there by mistake. Since a new unit was patrolling Najaf, this was a possibility. But, I believed, as other observers did, that the U.S. provoked the Mahdi army into an all-out war."

Mayer was very forthright in response. "We damn well were not going to let the militia run around 'our town' violating the law and openly brandishing weapons. So whether we started the fight or not, there was no way Najaf was big enough for the Mahdi Militia and U.S. Marines . . . [A] fight was inevitable!"

CHAPTER 5

Revolutionary Circle

FOLLOWING THE SHOOTOUT AT the maternity hospital on August 2, tensions between the Marines and al-Sadr's militia dramatically increased. At first, no shots were exchanged. "There was a kind of standoff," Major Moran explained. "We'd glare at them, and they would glare at us."

The militia, in fact, was gathering information before executing its next move. "We were getting reports of Iraqi police being captured, tortured, and

An Iraqi national guardsman shows a Marine from 1/4 an AK-47 magazine. The MEU's plan was to train the Iraqi National Guard for about four months and then combine forces to eliminate al-Sadr's Mahdi Militia from the city. *USMC photo*

released," Moran said, Their brutal militia interrogators wanted to know why the Marines had been sent to Najaf and why they wanted to attack the militia.

The police chief, Ghalib al-Jezairy, was high on the militia's hit list. "Many police have been beheaded," he said dolefully. "This is barbaric. They enter people's homes, and they kill the relatives of policemen."

The militia was convinced that the Marines were going to attack. "Truthfully," Moran said, "that wasn't really our plan. Our broad campaign plan was to try to maintain the status quo as best we could and to train the two Iraqi National Guard battalions at Najaf (the 405th) and Diwaniyah (the 404th)."

The Iraqi police were caught in a no-win situation. The Mahdi Army attacked them for cooperating with the Marines, who were not all that convinced the police did not have insurgent sympathies. The Iraqi government praised the police for holding the line against the militia, while

The Iraqi police shown here were outgunned and outnumbered. The Mahdi Militia targeted them, forcing the police to abandon any effort to uphold the law. The August 2004 battle was brought on by an attack on the main Najaf police station. *Defenseimagery.mil 040812-M-2306K-082*

journalists criticized them for human-rights abuses. Outgunned and with little support, the police developed a siege mentality, afraid to venture out of their compounds. The Najaf police chief's eighty-year-old father, elderly uncle, and nephew were kidnapped by al-Sadr's men. They threatened to kill the three men if the chief did not resign. He refused, and the gunmen killed the nephew and dumped his headless body in front of the police chief's house.

The deputy police chief said, "They kill officers just to take their money, their weapons, their uniforms, their IDs." He also accused the news media of false reporting. "It is all the fault of the media that we are being attacked,

Iraqi Resistance Report:
"Iraqi Puppet Police Force Disintegrates"

The U.S. Associated Press reported that it has become clear during the fighting in Iraq this week that the Iraqi puppet police have abandoned many of their posts and are now standing aside and watching the Resistance take the streets of Iraqi cities. This has led the American leadership to fear what the ultimate role of their puppet policemen might be. In an-Najaf, for example, puppet police on Thursday watched from their puppet police headquarters as a small truck carrying a dozen militia men supporters of Muqtada as-Sadr rolled in to take over, putting up no resistance whatsoever. One puppet policeman told the American Associated Press "we cannot intervene in what's going on at all. If his Excellency Muqtada as-Sadr issues an order we are obliged to carry it out and I am ready now to leave the [puppet] police if I'm asked to because we came here from the start on the basis of instructions that said we would be serving the city but now we have become targets."

In many cities of southern Iraq that have now come under the control of the Shi'ite militia run by Muqtada as-Sadr—known as the Army of the Mahdi—the puppet policemen have been compelled to stay in their places but not interfere in what is taking place, despite the fact that the U.S. occupation authorities were relying on the puppet police to preserve their "order" in Iraq for them. The puppet policemen had long complained that the American occupation troops did not trust them while the local population looked askance at them. Often they found themselves ordered to take up arms against their own kinsmen, a role many could not play. Recently U.S. General Martin Dempsey noted that in the predominantly Shi'ite district of Baghdad known as Madinat as-Sadr, three puppet policemen, one of them with the rank of colonel, had announced that they stood with Muqtada as-Sadr when the chips were down.

especially Al Jazeera and Al Arabiya. They are saying that the police are cooperating with the Americans and the Iraqi National Guard and attacking the Mahdi Army, and so the Mahdi Army attacks us."

The MEU continued to patrol. "We drove around the city," Colonel Haslam recalled. "We didn't see anything. It's like a switch was turned off."

However, Lieutenant Colonel Johnston's spine hairs continued to tingle. "We're going to have a fight on our hands," he warned. "I was pretty certain because there were a lot of bad guys in and around the exclusion areas." The MEU received intelligence from an Iraqi Special Forces platoon that infiltrated the ranks of al-Sadr's militia dressed in civilian clothes, while acting as true believers. The information they brought back verified the presence of large numbers of al-Sadr's supporters in the city. It was also used to target individual militia leaders, as well as pinpoint weapons caches and command centers.

The militia hit the Iraqi police stations, and when Marine security patrols responded, the militiamen fled back into the cemetery. "The operations tempo was increasing rapidly. The city was ready to explode," Lieutenant Colonel Mayer said. "The attacks against the police were getting bigger and more brazen."

Al Jazeera correspondent Amed Mansour reported, "The Iraqis who signed up with the police department . . . were generally viewed as traitors

Revolutionary Circle, named in honor of Iraqis who revolted against the British in 1920. It is the key intersection in the city, linking Najaf with Kufa via Route Hartford (east) and Karbala via Route Miami (north). *USMC Photo*

because of their willingness to cooperate with occupation authorities. Consequently, targeting these workers became fair practice for the insurgents. They were paying the price for being hated and distrusted by their fellow countrymen." The police were holed up, afraid to go out. They did not have any leadership, little training, and were outgunned by the militia.

Finally, in the early morning hours of August 5, the Mahdi Militia made its move. At 0200, it attacked the main police station near Revolutionary Circle, in platoon strength (thirty to forty men) and with mortars and small-arms fire.

Revolutionary Circle, named in honor of the Iraqis who revolted against the British in 1920, is located at the intersection of two main city roads, codenamed Routes Hartford and Miami by the MEU. It is the key intersection in the city, linking Najaf with Kufa via Route Hartford (east) and Karbala via Route Miami (north). When viewed from above, the circle compares favorably with a major interstate cloverleaf in the United States. The interior of the circle is built up approximately five feet and contains an ornamental, arched concrete ring. On the northwest side of the circle lies the Wadi al-Salaam cemetery. A six- to eight-foot wall, running the length of the cemetery, separates it from the highway. Two- and three-story buildings parallel the road on the southwest quadrant of the circle. The main Iraqi police station is located on the southeast side, immediately adjacent to the Old City. Finally, larger buildings front the circle on the northeast side. Tactically, the openness of the circle does not provide any cover from enemy fire.

The beleaguered police returned fire and held their ground. Governor Adnan al-Zurufi requested help from the BLT through the Marine liaison team located in the city hall compound. Al-Zurufi was afraid that the police station might be overrun, which would be a major political victory for the militia.

Lieutenant Colonel Mayer recalled, "At about 0300, we received a call telling us that the police station was under attack and to send American troops to relieve them." At the time, Mayer was not too concerned. "I was used to Iraqi officials crying that the world's falling. The militia was known to fire a few shots and return to the exclusion zone." However, just to be safe, he called out the reinforced reaction force consisting of Borneo's CAAT-Alpha, a platoon from Charlie Company mounted in trucks, and the battalion commander's vehicles, and fire-support vehicles. "We deployed out of FOB Hotel," Major Moran explained, "and drove south on Miami to the police station." The area was eerily quiet when they arrived. "We talked to the IPs [Iraqi police], and they told us through hand and arm signals

Governor Adnan al-Zurufi

Lieutenant Colonel Eugene N. Apicella was assigned to be the MEU liaison officer at the governor's compound, located on Route Hartford, between Kufa and Najaf. The compound was protected by the Iraqi police and national guard, as well as two platoons of Bravo Company. The Marines also manned the MEU's forward command element and the Joint Coordination Center, where a small cadre of the governor's trusted aides worked with them. Apicella estimated that he was located there for over two months. In that time, he got to know and establish an excellent working relationship with governor al-Zurufi. "One of the biggest advantages I had with the governor was that he speaks fluent English," he emphasized. "We did not have to work through an interpreter, which facilitated sharing of information. I talked with him numerous times a day about our battle plans—what was actually happening."

Despite their close ties, Apicella was reticent about disclosing everything. "I was still cautious to some extent, and I could tell Colonel Haslam was also. We were new in the area, and the governor was an unknown player, so we didn't know how much we could talk about without it getting out." However, Apicella said that as he got to know al-Zurufi better, "I felt confident enough that I could brief him in more detail, or relay information at the last moment. It ended up being a bit of a challenge because the governor might have questions, and I couldn't answer him or provide detailed information." Al-Zurufi was cut off from the outside world because he didn't have any means of travel. In addition, as a pro-government and coalition supporter, al-Zurufi was targeted for death, which was one of the reasons he left his family in the United States. He had formerly lived in Chicago and Detroit before returning to Iraq.

Apicella believed that the governor was not interested in personal gain, but rather had a "genuine love of the city."

"He was on a personal mission to get the city cleaned up from the Mahdi Militia and the other criminals that were plaguing it," Apicella said. "What more can I say?"

Lieutenant Colonel Eugene N. Apicella, executive officer, 11th MEU, was commissioned in 1983 and served in a variety of infantry assignments during his twenty years of service. *USMC History Division* and some broken English that they had been attacked by about a hundred Muqtada Militia firing AK-47s, RPGs and mortars. The police said they were OK and gave us a thumbs up." The reaction force mounted up and did a quick patrol through the city without incident and returned to the FOB about 0430 to bed down.

Two hours later, an extremely excited Governor al-Zurufi requested support for a second time. The militia had attacked again, in large numbers— perhaps in the hundreds—and threatened to overrun the police station. Lieutenant Colonel Mayer called out the reaction force.

"We're literally on our way back from the chow hall," Cpl. Calvert C. Wallace reported, "and the staff sergeant yelled, 'Get everybody, we've got to go [back]. They're under attack!'"

Lance Corporal Sanick P. DelaCruz remembered being "excited and nervous at the same time." Pfc. Heladio Zuniga was "happy we got to do something." The staging area became a scene of frenzied activity as heavily armed Marines scrambled to board their vehicles. Wallace's platoon commander, 1st Lt. Jeremy T. Sellars, recalled, "We were told that the police station was being attacked by the Mahdi Militia. We were going to roll into Revolutionary Circle, dismount, and secure the police station."

Within minutes, the reaction force was on its way, this time with additional force, 1st Lt. John F. MacDonald's four-vehicle light armored reconnaissance (LAR) platoon, 1st Lt. Lamar Breshears's 81mm Mortar Platoon acting as provisional infantry, and two platoons from Charlie Company. As the vehicles left the compound, Iraqis on the street waved and gestured good wishes. But as the convoy approached the Old City, ominous signs appeared. The streets were vacant, a clear indication that something was not right. In addition, Wallace saw "Al Jazeera with their cameras," another indication that something was about to happen. Al Jazeera had an uncanny habit of showing up just as a fight started.

Lieutenant Sellars's platoon dismounted some distance from the police station, farther away from it than he hoped. "As we got close to the circle, the Iraqis started disappearing," he said. "We had no idea what we were getting into." The battalion's plan called for elements of Charlie Company to secure the Iraqi police station and the southern part of the traffic circle, CAAT-Alpha and the 81mm Mortar Platoon to secure the north and east side, and the LAR platoon to picket the west side.

Borneo recalled, "We get to the circle, and everything is quiet, nothing's going on." He quickly deployed his vehicles to cover likely danger areas. Sellars's men moved in and set up in a perimeter, which incorporated the Humvees.

"We've been there for all of about three minutes," Borneo said, "when something burst in the air right in the center of the traffic circle, about two meters from my vehicle." The blast shook the Humvee, felling the gunner, and sent shrapnel into its side, leaving gouges in the metal.

"Obviously, the militia had fired [on] that target before," Sellers said, "because the first couple of mortar rounds landed right in the traffic circle, like right in the monument fountain where three of my new men had taken cover. 'Get the hell out of the fountain, you dumb ass!' I shouted. 'That was a mortar.'" The explosions finally registered on the men, and they sprinted across the street. Within seconds, snipers fired from within the cemetery area, west of the circle.

"Once we heard those first shots," Corporal Wallace said, "we're like, 'Well, there's no turning back now.'"

A few minutes later, the whole cemetery side of the road erupted—taking fire from small arms, automatic weapons, and RPGs—prompting the Marines to return a heavy fire. Private First Class Ryan D. S. Cullenward had an up close and personal encounter with an RPG. "I heard it go right over my head and heard the boom right behind me. I first thought, 'Whoa, I'm getting shot at.'"

A combined antiarmor team (CAAT) in action. *1st Lt. William Birdzell, USM*

An up-armored Humvee overlooks the Wadi al-Salaam cemetery. Note that the height of the wall enabled the vehicles to be in defilade while returning fire. The Marine is standing behind a TOW-missile launcher. *Defenseimagery.mil 040806-M-7719F-005*

Mortar rounds were also continuing to land in the circle. "Nothing that was real close," Sellars remarked, "but enough to keep our attention."

Corporal Wallace remembered, "We took mortar fire all day. When the first one landed, one of my Marines looked at me and goes, 'What was that?' I was like, 'Hold on,' because I thought it might have been an RPG. Sure enough, another one fell, and we were just like, 'Damn, those are mortars!'"

Many of the men in Sellars's platoon were not combat veterans. Sellars himself "had only a very, very few mortar rounds—maybe only two—land within fifty meters of me in the first war . . . [S]till, I knew what they were."

Fortunately, the militia mortarmen were relatively unskilled and did not adjust their fire. "All their shots landed right on the road," Borneo pointed out, "one short, one long, one right on, and fire for effect. There'd be lateral changes, but no deviations corrections. Later on, we started seeing better, more well-trained guys . . . [T]hey were actually pretty good mortarmen."

Lieutenant Thomas thought that "the mortars were probably the worst thing that we experienced in the entire fighting." He had read World War II veteran

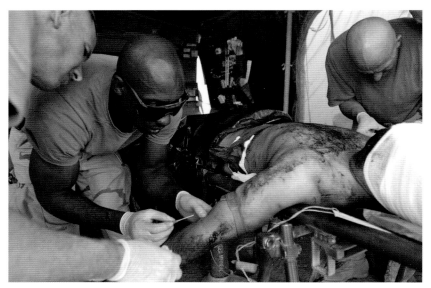

Medical personnel treat a badly wounded man in a field medical station. During the battle, casualties were generally evacuated by vehicle to a secure helicopter landing zone, where, if warranted, they receive further transport to a theater hospital. Speed was essential, because the first hour (known as the golden hour) of treatment determines the chances a patient has for survival. *Defenseimagery.mil 040819-F-1351B-007*

Poorly equipped Iraqi police arriving in an unarmored pickup truck. Note that some of the police have flak jackets while others do not have protection. In a shootout, the police were at a serious disadvantage. *Defemseimagery.mil 040812-M-2306K-076*

accounts describing mortar fire as horrific. "They [mortars] truly are," he emphasized, "because you don't know where they're coming from and where they're going to hit. You only hear them a split second before impact."

Cullenward echoed Thomas. "What stunk," he said, "was that we could see the mortar rounds being walked in on us. You're relieved when it hits somewhere else, but it's difficult, because it might have hit someone else." At one point, he was crouched behind a stone wall when a shell "landed just to the left of us, and our doc [corpsman] had to go to help a Marine that didn't make it."

Thomas remembered monitoring the radio when the casualty calls came in. "Shrapnel takes a man out," he remembered, "and the only thing you hear over the radio besides command and control information was the plaintive call—'MEDEVAC, MEDEVAC, MEDEVAC, WIA and KIA.'"

Sergeant McManus remembered rolling up to the police station and seeing "a lot of live and dead police in front of their headquarters."

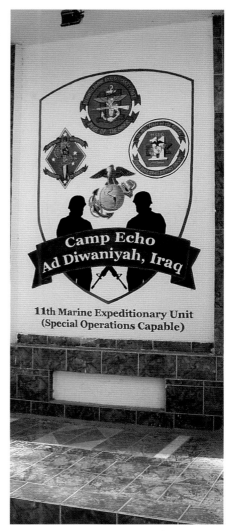

MEU logos at the entranceway to FOB Echo, Diwaniyah, Iraq. The MEU logo is at the top, while 1/4 logo is on the left and the Force Service Support Group logo is in on the right. *Maj. R. Bruce Sotire, USMC*

He said, "We noticed forty or fifty policemen in different uniforms walking down the road." The sight was somewhat unnerving because the Marines weren't sure the policemen were friendly. "There were no American personnel with them," he said. "They looked like they

Captain R. Bruce Sotire, commanding officer, Alpha Company. The aggressive leader of the battalion's raid company, he had inculcated that same spirit in his men. They were proud of their company slogan, "Alpha Raiders." *Maj. Michael S. Wilbur, USMC*

were ready to get into the fight, but they didn't get into the engagement that followed."

First Lieutenant Seth Moulton said, "The Iraqi policemen were incredibly relieved to see us. They were pretty bewildered and undertrained, maybe not super motivated, and would get easily flustered. There was one point when one or two of the Iraqis got shot. It really hit them pretty hard."

As McManus's platoon dismounted, they started receiving "a lot of small-arms fire," and that's when they took their first casualty. Corporal Jesus E. Alveres-Garcia was hit by a mortar and suffered multiple shrapnel to his legs and abdomen.

The BLT "immediately recognized that this was a pretty sizable enemy attack using combined arms," Moran said. "We started to ramp up the different assets we had available to us." Mayer discussed the situation with Haslam, who agreed to reduce the force at FOB Echo in Diwaniyah and send them to Najaf. At that point, it was estimated the BLT was facing 3,000 to 4,000 militia.

Alpha Company, 1st Battalion, 4th Marines, commanded by Capt. R. Bruce Sotire. The company's nickname and slogan, Alpha Raiders, was earned during its workup prior to leaving the United States, when it trained as the battalion's raid company. During the fight in Najaf, Alpha Company fought with two infantry platoons. Here, members of the company are "crapped out"—taking a break. *Maj. Michael S. Wilbur, USMC*

"The call from the CO [Haslam] came in about 1000 to mount up elements of the BLT and to leave a skeleton security element at FOB Echo," Lieutenant Colonel Apicella recalled. Captain Steven O. Wallace's Weapons Company headquarters, 1st Lt. Scott A. Cuomo's CAAT-Bravo, and Captain R. Bruce Sotire's Alpha Company (Alpha Raiders)—"a superb rifle company," according to Lieutenant Colonel Johnston—were told to saddle up.

First Lieutenant Richard Zjawin recalled, "Captain Sotire disappeared into the command post to the get the word. He returned and told us that there was a fight in Najaf, that a Huey had been shot down, and Charlie Company was heavily engaged."

Sotire said, "I was told we better get there quickly. We rounded up the company, except for ten or fifteen men who remained behind as security for the compound." (At the time, Alpha Company consisted of only one hundred men because one of its rifle platoons was attached to the Maritime Special Multi-Purpose Force.) As the company assembled, Sotire scrambled

A squad of Marines in the back of a seven-ton truck. The unarmored trucks were vulnerable to RPGs and VEBIEDs (vehicle-borne improvised explosive devices). Alpha Company depended on the trucks for transport to Najaf. *Maj. Michael S. Wilbur, USMC and Maj. R. Bruce Sotire, USMC*

to find a map of Najaf. "I finally got my hands on a map that we found tacked to a wall. At the time, I did not have any expectation that I was going into battle. I was certain I was going to FOB Hotel to get briefed on the situation." Sotire did not have direct communications with the battalion because of the distance between the two locations.

Within a short time the convoy, a mixture of seven-ton trucks and armored Humvees, was on its way to Najaf, a two-hour trip. "I didn't have a vehicle," Lieutenant Colonel Apicella said, "so I jumped in with Major Hollahan [battalion executive officer]." The convoy reached the edge of the city by mid-afternoon. "We were finally within radio range of the battalion, and I was surprised to hear Major Moran directing a fight. I also saw helicopters shooting, so I was able to gain some situational awareness." Moran directed Apicella and his convoy to pull off to the side of the road and standby for further instructions.

"At this point, six buses full of young men drove right by us," Apicella recalled, "and I'm thinking, where the hell are they going? They're looking at us, and I thought, 'I can't believe this is happening. They're going to reinforce the city.' We probably ended up killing them in the following days."

One of the men that Apicella observed might have been Abbas Fadhel, who Philip Cockburn described as "a twenty-four year old member of a Mahdi Army company [who] volunteered with a group of other fighters in Sadr City to go to Najaf to take part in the second battle for the city." Fadhel, who had some military training, "knew how to use a Kalashnikov [AK-47] and a PKC [Russian-made light machine gun]." The group journeyed

The wall around the cemetery provided convenient protection for the Marines. The man in the foreground is firing an M-60 machine gun. *Maj. Michael S. Wilbur, USMC*

partway to the city by car, but the driver got cold feet. Fadhel and his friends were forced to hitchhike and go "shanks mare" for the rest of the trip. Fadhel ended up in the Wadi al-Salaam cemetery and "stayed in the crypts and fought from there."

Revolutionary Circle was an obvious militia-registered mortar target, so Borneo moved his platoon to firing positions on the eastern wall of the cemetery, along Routes Miami and Hartford. The wall happened to be just the right height to allow the gunner to fire over the top, while the vehicle remained protected by the masonry. The platoon quickly became engaged. A force that was at least platoon sized was firing at them with automatic weapons, mortars, and RPGs. "We were engaging targets, and they were engaging us," Borneo recalled. "We were trying to figure out what was going on." CAAT-Alpha laid down a tremendous amount of fire from its

First Lieutenant John F. MacDonald III, commander of the battalion's light armored vehicle platoon.
USMC History Division

crew-served and individual weapons and within five minutes had suppressed most of the enemy in their sector, except for scattered sniper fire.

Despite the mortar fire, Section A of the LAR platoon stayed in the circle, while Section B moved north on Miami to gain a better firing position behind the cemetery wall for their 25mm chain guns. The powerful 25mm automatic cannon could fire 200 rounds per minute and penetrate a concrete wall over a foot thick, and the rounds played havoc with the militiamen seeking cover behind the cemetery's brick and mortar structures. "They just tore the enemy up," according to Sellars. "They [those firing the cannon] could see them [the militiamen] better because of the height of their vehicles." Lieutenant MacDonald's scouts dismounted to provide security for the vehicles. As they deployed, one lance corporal spotted and killed three militiamen maneuvering through the graves, at a range estimated to be 400 meters.

Sniper fire forced Lieutenant Sellars and his platoon to take cover behind a low wall. "The shots were fairly close," he remembered, "but not super accurate." Suddenly, an RPG exploded close to one of his men, striking the Marine in the hand.

"Sir, I've been hit!" the man exclaimed.

"Shrapnel almost took his pinky finger off," Sellars observed. "He's bleeding and shaking a bit." The officer thought, "Oh, great, he's going into shock." Sellars tried to calm the wounded man. "Oh, it looks like it'll be OK," he said. "Go see the doc. Everything will be fine."

As bullets continued to impact the wall, Sellars spotted several piles of bricks that he thought could be used to build even more protection. "Start moving those bricks," he told his men. "They [the bricks] turned out to be made of chalk. They look like they're going to weigh five tons and really only weigh five pounds. The darn things ended up being more concealment than cover."

The LAR platoon was positioned in front of Sellars platoon. "They could see the enemy better," Sellers remarked, "so they were actually doing better engaging them. We were just shooting bad guys here and there." His platoon maintained its position at the corner of the circle for several hours before being told to secure the back of the police station. "I swung around and swept through a large, open field that led to a power transfer yard that had a large, heavy-duty fence around it," Sellars explained. "Four of us pushed through and searched several buildings. I put two designated marksmen on top of one of the buildings, and they engaged some guys who were trying to flank us."

As the fighting raged, Charlie Company's forward air controller (FAC), Capt. Randy Gibbons (call sign Chimp), requested close air support (CAS); however, getting permission was a constant problem. "I remember the first time we tried to clear fires," Colonel Haslam said, "It was like, 'Oh, you can't drop in the cemetery, it's an exclusion zone . . . disengage.'"

Major Glen G. Butler, Marine Medium Helicopter Squadron 166 (HMM-166), was equally frustrated because the airspace was so restricted. "The whole area surrounding the shrine and up into the cemetery was off limits for us," he explained. "We couldn't fly near it, despite the fact that we were getting intel that the militia was stockpiling weapons inside the cemetery. It was a safe haven for them. We were frustrated that a large part of the city was an exclusion zone."

The cemetery and the Old City were in the exclusion zone that had been agreed upon after the fighting in May. Returning small-arms fire was authorized because the enemy was using the exclusion zone to attack friendly forces, but using artillery and air support was a different issue entirely. Initially, every target had to be approved by higher headquarters, and obtaining permission was a slow and time-consuming process. At times, it would take twenty to thirty minutes for a target to be approved. Borneo was frustrated by the restrictions. "At the time, you're like 'Screw that, let's just drop a five-hundred-pound bomb and level the place.'"

Colonel Haslam pressed for approval. "I've got targets in there," he emphasized, "and Marines are getting shot at." Permission was finally granted to approve some targets.

"When Colonel Haslam wasn't clearing fires, I did, as quickly as I could," Apicella explained, "It really killed me, as an infantryman, that every fire mission that was going to be run had to be cleared at the MEU level." The BLT was required to call in the grid coordinates of the target so they could be verified. "I quickly identified what they [BLT] wanted to shoot and where it was located. Many times, I just felt like it was taking too long," Apicella said.

Lieutenant Colonel Mayer was also upset with fire-support procedures during the early days of the operation because it "was not clear who had the authority to approve fires. He recalled, "[I]t wasn't battalion, nor the MEU or Conway [Lt. Gen. James T. Conway, MEF commander]. It was at the MNF-I [Multi-National Force, Iraq], General Casey [Gen. George W. Casey] level. There were nights when we needed help to suppress enemy fire, and it was rumored that there were officers up there who did not want to wake General Casey to clear fires."

The exclusion zone provided the militiamen a safe haven. They could set up their mortars and maneuver against the Marines with impunity, as long as they were in the zone; however, once there were Marine casualties, all bets were off. "Colonel Haslam gave us permission to fire back into the cemetery," Mayer explained, "We also reduced the exclusion zone down to 1,200 meters around the Old City, including the Ali mosque. Everything outside that circle became a free-fire zone."

Marine Medium Helicopter Squadron 166 (HMM-166, Sea Elks) was tasked to provide Cobra and Huey gunship support. A mixed section of helicopters, a UH-1N Huey and a AH-1W Cobra, maintained a thirty-minute strip alert at FOB Duke, a few minutes flying time from Najaf, when the request came through. Captain Stephen "Slade" Mount, the pilot-in-command of the Huey, was also the section leader.

"We were in the ready room at about 0800 when the ODO [operations duty officer] got a call from the MEU," he recalled. "Wombat [Capt. Carl Lowe, battalion air officer] wanted us to fly over the [police] station and through town from north to south, parallel to his route. We could tell it was getting 'exciting' down there because the tone of Wombat's voice went from frustrated to . . . really anxious!" The helicopters immediately launched and checked in with the battalion air officer, who cleared them to make firing runs west of the road, in the eastern part of the cemetery, without waiting for additional clearance.

Initially, the helicopter crews could not see anything to shoot at. "I don't know if the bad guys were hiding because we showed up," Mount said, "or if they just weren't there." The helicopters made a couple of passes and then reset east of the city in a holding pattern for a few minutes. "Wombat cleared us back into the southern part of the cemetery," Mount recalled, "where there were two covered, open air structures." He made a pass, but didn't see anything.

Marine Medium Helicopter Squadron 166 (HMM-166, reinforced). The helicopters in the
foreground are Huey gunships. The ones in the background are CH-46 transport helicopters.
Lt. Col. Glen G. Butler, USMC

The Cobra, piloted by Capt. Dale R. "Amish" Behm, fired at a few
fleeting targets, but did not see any enemy concentrations. "We pulled
off to the right," Mount said. "It was about that time that the entire
southeastern corner of the cemetery lit up! My gunner, Cpl. Teodoro
Naranjo, returned fire with his .50-caliber and, as we rolled out of the turn,
Staff Sgt. Patrick O. Burgess started firing the minigun." The Cobra popped
up as the Huey pulled off the target and fired two TOW missiles into a
storage point. "A terrific shot," Mount exclaimed.

The two aircraft made several more passes, in which "things got worse,"
Mount recalled. "The guys on the ground tried to give us directions to a
mortar position that was firing at them from a gas station. We could see
occasional flashes from gunfire and RPGs . . . small puffs of smoke when the
rocket exploded . . . but we still couldn't make out where it was." As Mount
pulled the aircraft into a hard right turn, a piece of metal pierced his helmet
visor, went through the bridge of his nose, and exited out his right eye.

"Reflexively, he yanked back on the cyclic," Major Butler said, "putting
the helicopter in an extreme nose-high attitude, which bled off air speed . . .
not a good thing."

Behm was "perched" above and behind, waiting for Mount to pull off
the target before starting his own run. "Suddenly, his aircraft pivoted about

Marine Medium Helicopter Squadron 166

Marine Medium Helicopter Squadron 166 (HMM-166, reinforced) was a Marine composite helicopter squadron consisting of:

- Marine Medium Helicopter Squadron 166 (HMM-166)—twelve CH-46 Sea Knight helicopters
- Detachment Marine Aviation Logistics Squadrons 13, 16, and 39
- Detachment Marine Air Control Group 38
- Detachment Marine Heavy Helicopter Squadron 465 (HMH-465)—four CH-53 Super Stallion heavy-lift helicopters
- Detachment Marine Attack Squadron 211 (VMF-211)—six AV-8B Harriers
- Detachment Marine Light Attack Helicopter Squadron 169 (HMLA-169)—four AH-1W Super Cobra attack helicopters and three UH-1N Iroquois helicopters
- Detachment Marine Wing Support Squadron 37

Major Glen Butler recalled, "The LZ [landing zone]/flight line we built at [FOB] Duke was fairly small, so initially we only had a few skids and a medevac Phrog [CH-46 nickname] or two there. After the fight in the cemetery started, we crammed many more aircraft into Duke." The bulk of the squadron stayed at Al-Asad, including the Harriers, which maintained a thirty-minute strip alert to provide close air support.

Cobra pilot Capt. Dale Behm remembered, "When we first arrived, we couldn't fly over the cemetery because we weren't supposed to antagonize the militia, even though we could see them lug things into it [the cemetery]. We knew they were exploiting the exclusion zone." The squadron's mission was to provide direct support of the ground force. "We flew in mixed hunter-killer team consisting of a Cobra and a Huey," Behm recalled. "We developed a working relationship between the two. The aircraft in front would engage the target, while the one in the rear covered him. The tactical lead was passed back and forth to whoever had the best situational awareness."

Major Butler pointed out, "Just about every helo there was returning to Duke with multiple bullet holes and often severe battle damage."

FOB Duke had an earthen berm around it for protection, which caused problems for the fully loaded aircraft. "The heat, low power, and full ammunition load made it difficult to get over it," Behm recalled. "We had to drag the skids along the dirt/gravel runway to get in the air."

Major Butler said, "We were always taking off at maximum gross weight, so it was challenging getting the birds airborne. Fortunately, Najaf was only about seven minutes away, so we didn't need to take tons of fuel."

We would actually go Winchester [run out of ammunition] before we ran out of gas." The Hueys were armed with a .50-caliber machine gun on one side; a GAU-17, 7.62 minigun on the other; and seven to fourteen 2.75-inch high-explosive (HE) rockets. The Cobra generally carried two Hellfire missiles, two TOW antitank missiles, a rocket pod, and a 20mm cannon with two hundred rounds of ammunition.

The squadron worked out a system where the helicopters would refuel without shutting down ("hot refuel"), saving valuable time. While refueling, one of the pilots would continue to talk with the FAC to maintain situational awareness. In addition, the aircraft would also be rearmed. Captain Behm remembered Captain Edwards, who supervised the ordnance section. "He had a boonie hat [a wide-brimmed military hat], who we called the Mad Hatter. After taxing into the refueling area, we gave him a slip of paper with our ordnance needs, and he would pass it to the ordnance crews to rearm the aircraft." Captain Edwards received the Bronze Star for his around-the-clock heroic efforts.

Marine Medium Helicopter Squadron 166 (HMM-166), known as the Sea Elks, provided gunships (Huey and Cobra), logistics (CH-53 heavy-lift helicopter), and casualty-evacuation (CH-46 medium helicopter) support. *USMC*

A TOW missile shot on a Mahdi Militia mortar position by a Cobra gunship flown by Capt. Jason "Frenchy" Grogan on August 10, 2004. The golden dome of the Imam Ali mosque can be seen in the background. *Lt. Col. Glen G. Butler, USMC*

the tail and went nose high," Behm recalled. "I'm riveted on it. He went up about two hundred feet and started to slide backwards, and I thought, 'Oh, my God!' It's the worst thing I've ever seen."

Captain Andrew "Smithers" Turner, Mount's copilot, grabbed the controls and pushed them forward, forcing the aircraft into a severe nosedive. "I attempted to regain the lost air speed," Turner explained. "My intent was to scoop out the aircraft as we approached the ground and fly up and away from the deck." Unfortunately, the aircraft continued to fall.

"At the last possible minute—fifty feet off the ground," Butler said, "he pulled back and leveled the aircraft just before it hit."

This was the second crash that Turner had been involved in. "I thought, 'This can't be happening to me again,'" he said. "The helicopter hit the deck, spread the skids, bounced high in the air, hit the ground again, and came to a sliding stop just prior to hitting a telephone pole." The irony of the crash was that it hit right next to an Iraqi hospital on the edge of the cemetery.

The dazed crew scrambled out of the badly damaged Huey and took cover, as small arms zipped overhead. "I remember that I was wrestling with the harness with my left hand and trying to hold my face together with my right hand," Mount explained. "I kind of fell out my door, and Staff Sergeant Burgess caught me."

Corporal Naranjo moved to a cinderblock wall and set up security, while Captain Turner ran to the Iraqi hospital for help. "I made my way through the entrance and discovered five Iraqi men sitting in the room," Turner remembered. "Now imagine someone in full flight gear, helmet on, visor down bursting into your office pointing an M-16. This shock, combined with the language barrier, made communications somewhat interesting." However, Turner was able to make them realize what was going on. "They rushed to assist us," he said, "bringing out an ambulance for Mount."

Meanwhile, Burgess dragged Mount clear of the helicopter as the pilot fumbled with his pistol. "For whatever reason," Mount said, "I had managed to pull it from my holster and was trying to rack a round into the chamber with just my left hand, while I was holding my head with my right. It turned into a slippery, bloody mess." In the process, Mount accidentally ejected the magazine.

"Burgess just kind of got exasperated with me," Mount chuckled, "so he fished another magazine from my vest, slapped it in, chambered a round, and stuck it back in my hand." Burgess helped Mount to the hastily prepared defensive position behind a brick wall. Naranjo covered them with his weapon and a machine gun that he had brought from the helicopter.

"I loaded the M240 [machine gun]," Burgess said, "And prepared to defend the position."

A thousand meters away, Lieutenant Borneo saw the helicopter "pull up, nosedive, and crash." From his vantage point, he thought it went down right in the middle of the cemetery. "I'm thinking we're going to be fighting our way through to it, in a *Black Hawk Down* scenario." He leaped into action and sped to the scene with reinforcements in the form of an LAR section and two vehicles from his own platoon. "We were there within two

Personal Security Detachment

The personal security detachment (PSD) was formed in April 2004, immediately after the battalion received the deployment notification. During the fight in Najaf, its mission was to provide security for the battalion command group and casualty evacuation. The PSD consisted of fourteen Marines—one lieutenant, six corporals, one corpsman, and six lance corporals—mounted in two Humvees, a high-back Humvee, and the battalion commander's vehicle.

Lieutenant Billy Birdzell, PSD commander, said, "After we formed, I contacted the U.S. Secret Service in L.A. for assistance. A special agent told us how they protected the president . . . and we tailored our tactics in the same manner." Birdzell's team also developed a special shooting package, and "we got to shoot lots of M-16 and pistol rounds."

to three minutes," he explained. His reaction force arrived in time to prevent several Iraqis from attacking the helicopter's crew.

The battalion Command Chronology noted: "Lieutenant Borneo killed one MM [Mahdi militiaman] preparing to fire an RPG at his vehicle from a range of 75 meters with his M-16. Lance Corporals [Erik] Smith, [Christopher] Abner, and [Brad] Kidder killed a fire-team that was moving towards the adjacent aid station where the helicopter crew had moved." Mount remembered that "the volume of fire increased almost exponentially." The rescue force laid down a heavy volume of fire to keep the advancing militiamen at bay.

First Lieutenant William Birdzell, along with corporals Carlos Rochel and Xavier Cobb from Colonel Mayer's personal security detachment (PSD), arrived at the same time as Borneo. Birdzell positioned his Humvee with the two corporals south of the crash site for additional security and then went looking for the helicopter crew.

"Lieutenant Borneo and I looked around the helo, but didn't see anyone," Birdzell recalled. "We moved north and found the crew taking cover in a small building."

Mount was startled when "a corpsman hopped over the wall and started checking me out. While he looked me over, he asked me questions . . . trying to get a sense of how badly wounded I was. Then he rolled me over and jabbed me with a morphine shot. It really hurt. In fact, it really, really hurt!"

As the corpsman administered aid, Borneo "brought up the ambulance from a not-so-willing Iraqi guy."

Birdzell recalled, "Captain Mount's face was bandaged, and he was lying down. I asked him if he could move his feet because I thought he might have a spinal injury. He said he was fine. I helped him to his feet (he was effectively blind at the time because the bandage was wrapped around his head) and guided him toward an ambulance." Mount was loaded in, and Borneo then had one of his men drive it, while another provided security. Two of his Humvees provided additional security. In less than ten minutes, they reached the aid station at FOB Hotel, where Mount was stabilized and evacuated by helicopter to a larger field hospital and then back to the United States for more advanced medical treatment. (Captain Mount remains on active duty. After recovery, he was sent to the naval postgraduate school in Monterey where he earned a masters degree in operations research. Mount is currently stationed at Quantico, Virginia, and serving as an operations research analyst at the Marine Corps Systems Command.)

Despite the danger and a back injury, Staff Sergeant Burgess ran back to the helicopter to help extinguish a small fire and collect the classified radio equipment, which the PSD Marines had begun taking out of the helicopter.

"Staff Sergeant Burgess, Corporal [Marshall] Medrano, and I began taking apart the Huey's radios. Sensitive communications equipment was scattered throughout the aircraft," Birdzell recalled. At the time, he and Staff Sergeant Burgess were in the nose, facing each other. "A sniper's bullet passed right between us—a very close call," Birdzell said. "I did not know what our security situation was, so I shot all the comm [communications] gear with my rifle. Later, a major from HMM-166 approached me exclaiming, 'Some asshole shot up all the comm gear!'" Lieutenant Birdzell realized that discretion was the better part of valor and remained silent. His men also "rescued" the weaponry and anything else that wasn't nailed down. "Our .50-caliber broke during the battle," Birdzell said. "So we modified the helo's machine gun to fit on our Humvee and used it for two days before having to give it back. The battalion executive officer yelled at me for stealing it . . . but we didn't think HMM-166 needed it any longer."

With visions of Mogadishu in the back of his mind, Lieutenant Colonel Mayer deployed the mechanized quick reaction force (QRF). "I wasn't going to let any of the militia show up on Al Jazeera dragging a Huey through the streets," he emphasized.

The QRF, Lt. Russell L. Thomas's four M1A1 Abrams tanks, and an infantry platoon from Bravo Company embarked in amphibious assault vehicles (AAVs), roaring out of FOB Hotel's gate. "We hauled ass down to Revolutionary Circle to support the Marines taking fire along [Route]

Miami," Thomas exclaimed. "That's when the stuff really hit the fan! I had an 82mm mortar round explode between my first and my tank." He split the four tanks into two sections; one section and the AAVs engaged mortar positions north of the traffic circle, while the other section took on ten to fifteen militiamen firing automatic weapons near the Iraqi police station. Thomas was pretty frustrated with the rules of engagement. "We could see truckloads of military-age males coming into the exclusion area. I asked several times to engage, but, as they weren't showing hostile intent, my request was denied. I think it gave them time to build up their forces."

Overhead, a section of skids (a Huey and a Cobra) made a run on the south side of the cemetery. Major Glen Butler piloted the Huey. "I put the Cobra wingman out front, which we often did, so I could cover their pull-off

Staff Sergeant Patrick O. Burgess mans a .50-caliber machine gun while running a close-air-support mission over the Wadi al-Salaam cemetery on August 8. Burgess survived an earlier helicopter crash with only a wrenched back. *Lt. Col. Glen G. Butler, USMC*

with my door guns." The FAC radioed the nine-line close-air-support request as the section flew in at rooftop level from south to north over the Old City.

"It was the first time I had the pleasure of hearing enemy gunfire," Butler recalled, tongue in cheek. "It was coming from the rooftops and buildings just below us. We didn't see any tracers, just heard the sound like Rice Crispies—snap, crackle, and pop!" As the section approached the cemetery near Revolutionary Circle, they were cleared "hot" by the FAC. The Cobra, piloted by captains Mike "Hasty" Swift and Jason "Frenchy" Grogan, popped up from their rooftop altitude to 300 to 400 feet.

"As soon as they initiated that pop," Butler explained, "my crew chief screamed, 'RPG, RPG!' There were big red tracers everywhere. Very surreal.

A Cobra gunship piloted by Capt. Jason "Frenchy" Grogan launches a rocket attack on the Mahdi Militia positions in the Wadi al-Salaam cemetery on August 8, 2004. The smoke in the upper right is from the army's 1st Battalion, 5th Cavalry Regiment, who are also firing into the cemetery with its armored vehicles. *Lt. Col. Glen G. Butler, USMC*

Captain Duane T. Fosberg, the battalion logistics officer. Fosberg was instrumental in recovering a downed Huey gunship so that its crash would not become another *Black Hawk Down incident. USMC History Division*

I felt like I was watching a slow-motion car crash." His door gunners hosed the area with their machine guns while both helicopters yanked and banked in an effort to keep from getting shot down. "I remember one very distinct moment," Butler recounted. "I looked at my copilot, Capt. Keith Thorkelson, and saw him leaning back as far as possible, like he wanted to melt into the seat. I glanced out and saw a huge glowing baseball heading directly for us. It streaked right by, seemingly inches away." To add insult to injury, the Cobra's weapons system jammed, leaving it defenseless.

Mayer radioed the battalion logistics officer, Capt. Duane T. Fosberg, to work out a plan to recover the downed Huey. Fosberg used a tank recovery vehicle, two seven-ton trucks, and a thirty-ton civilian crane for the effort. The crane was commandeered from FOB Hotel's construction firm and driven by a Marine who had never operated one before. Mayer admitted privately, "I found out later that even though the crane was not supposed to leave the compound, the KBR [Kellogg Brown and Root] manager let him have it."

Staff Sergeant Burgess had already dismantled the helicopter and separated it into two pieces, which made lifting them onto the truck beds much easier. As the crane operator nonchalantly went about his work, small-arms fire pinged off the steel boom. Sergeant McManus provided security for the operation. "My squad went into a building overlooking the crash site. The Iraqi family wasn't too happy with us setting up on the roof of their house. We stayed there until we started receiving some pretty heavy fire."

McManus's team did not suffer any casualties; however, an LAR scout team was not so lucky. An RPG impacted their rooftop position, spraying shrapnel, wounding all three team members—two seriously.

McManus's squad was ordered to escort the recovery vehicles back to the FOB. "The second we started off, we started receiving fire," he recalled, "sometimes pretty sporadic and sometimes pretty heavy at

Wreckage of the Huey shot down over the Wadi al-Salaam cemetery on August 5. The pilot was wounded, but the rest of the crew survived the crash. The helicopter was dismantled so it could be evacuated from the crash site. *Lt. Col. Glen G. Butler, USMC*

some points." The entire operation took about four hours and cost the battalion one man killed in action during an ambush on the way to the recovery site.

The loss of the Huey caused a significant change in the rules of engagement. "We started doing gun runs and shooting TOW missiles into the cemetery," Borneo recalled. "We also started getting artillery missions approved. In the long run, it turned out to be the right way to fight. But at the time, it was frustrating."

CHAPTER 6

Reinforcements

B Y MID-AFTERNOON, THE REINFORCEMENTS from Diwaniyah had arrived after an eventful interlude. "They'd been ambushed a little bit just south of Najaf," Major Moran said.

Lieutenant Colonel Apicella described the scene: "We were waving at people, and the Iraqis on the side of the road were waving back. And maybe just at the southernmost edge of the Old City, people quit waving. About 100 to 150 meters beyond, the whole left side of the street just erupted in gunfire!" The Marines immediately returned fire. "They just started hosing down the buildings on their left," Apicella said. "Like you're driving down the road—twenty to thirty meters apart—and it's just point and shoot, back and forth . . . [I]t's one of the most surreal things I've ever seen in my life!" Two heavily gunned CAAT-Bravo Humvees turned head-on into the buildings and unleashed a furious fusillade of .50-caliber machine-gun fire. The heavy volume of Marine fire quickly suppressed the militia gunmen, allowing the convoy to proceed through the ambush. Just before reaching the city, it stopped to wait for orders.

While waiting on the side of the road, Captain Sotire was called by Major Moran and told, "You're the main effort. Conduct a passage of lines and go into the attack, immediately!" Sotire recalled, "Hearing those words after years of training for combat was almost surreal. I had no expectation of going into battle, and I only had ten minutes to formulate a plan!"

The battle-damaged Old City. Fire in the background caused by an air strike. *Maj. Michael S. Wilbur, USMC*

He quickly called his three platoon commanders to his location to brief them. "I'm formulating a plan for the attack," he recalled, "but the platoon commanders didn't realize that we'd soon be shooting and started a sidebar dialog." The company executive officer (XO) barked at them for not giving the commanding officer their undivided attention. Sotire just looked at the XO, for they were the only two who understood the gravity of the situation. The XO had seen combat; the other three lieutenants were inexperienced, but that would soon change.

Captain Sotire spread the only map in the company on the hood of a Humvee. "I briefed them on the attack by pointing out the key terrain—the road network, the cemetery, the objective, and other features that stood out," he said. The scheme of maneuver seemed to emerge from the map. Fortunately, there were natural lanes in the cemetery that made it easy for Sotire to assign sectors to each platoon. Thanks to months of hard small-boat-raid training, the company was ready to go into high-intensity combat within five minutes. Sotire described the readiness as recognition tactics: "After a certain amount of small-unit training, the degree of understanding leaders have with their subordinates in a rifle company is remarkable. The small-unit leaders do not need much direction. I had some of the best squad leaders I have ever experienced in the Marine Corps. All they needed were simple graphics, a clear task, and purpose . . . and they were ready for action."

After hurriedly completing the brief, Sotire got the convoy on the road and started toward Revolutionary Circle. "I met the Weapons Company commander," he said, "and he told me to watch out, everybody's getting ambushed on the circle. And sure enough, we did—small arms, RPGs, and accurate mortar fire." The company passed through the heavy fire without any casualties. Sotire remembered a militiaman shooting from a roof who got hit with a .50-caliber bullet and was flung off the three-story building.

The convoy made its way to the battalion forward command post, which was tucked into the trees on Route Miami. Apicella remembered watching as Major Hollahan and Lieutenant Colonel Mayer nonchalantly discussed the tactical situation. "It's crazy," he recalled. "I mean there were rounds flying everywhere! There were snipers on top of the police station, cranking off rounds and taking out guys [militiamen] on the rooftops. There were Apaches [army helicopter gunships] making gun runs and the constant crack as tons of AK-47s fired at them from the militia-held area."

Apicella took cover behind a brick wall as mortar rounds detonated. "A couple of RPG round flew over and exploded on the other side of the wall," he recalled. "And there's John Mayer standing outside his Humvee, calmly speaking on his radios." Unbeknownst to the three men, an army Apache helicopter approached their position. "They fired Zuni rockets," Apicella recalled, "which scared the hell out of us because we couldn't hear them starting their gun run. Everybody in the command group jumped when the rockets went off."

As the reinforcements came up, they were directed into a firing line along Route Miami. "We positioned Alpha Company [led by Sotire] from the south side of the amusement park," Moran pointed out, "all the way down to the intersection of what became known as Diagonal Road. Weapons Company [81mm Mortar Platoon, led by 1st Lt. Lamar Breshears] had the middle portion of the battlefield from the intersection of Diagonal Road and Miami all the way down to Revolutionary Circle. Charlie Company [led by Capt. Matthew T. Morrissey] maintained its positions in the Iraqi police station." The battalion positioned the reconnaissance platoon [led by Capt. Stephen A. Kintzley] on Alpha Company's right flank, making it the northernmost unit. Bravo Company's 1st Platoon [led by 1st Lt. Jay Lewis] held the extreme southern flank, tying in on Charlie Company's left. The battalion extended in a line from north to south, facing the cemetery, the main militia defensive positions.

Mayer relocated his command post "further up, more abreast of the cemetery," according to Lieutenant Colonel Apicella, who followed along in another vehicle. "We passed the troops . . . [R]iflemen and dismounted LAV crewmen . . . were spread out along the wall, engaging individual targets. A couple of tanks blocked Revolutionary Circle, denying militiamen the ability to come out of the Old City."

One of the most surreal things Apicella observed was an amusement park in the northern part of the cemetery. "There's a Ferris wheel in there, and it's slowly turning." He turned to an officer and pointed it out.

The officer nonchalantly replied, "Ya, it'll turn for a while and then stop."

Apicella thought it was bizarre. "All those Marines in the middle of a gunfight, and here's this big Ferris wheel going round and round on the other side of the cemetery wall."

By happenstance, the cemetery wall served as the demarcation line between the two forces, as well as a protective barricade for Mayer's Marines. "They had the AAVs [amphibious assault vehicles] and LAR vehicles sitting up on that wall," Corporal Wallace recalled, "and they were just shooting into the cemetery." Militia snipers kept up a steady, but largely inaccurate, fire. One of them made a fatal mistake when he allowed himself to be spotted by two alert TOW missile gunners. Another gunner destroyed a militia RPG and sniper position with several bursts from his MK-19 automatic grenade launcher. An entire squad of militiamen was wiped out by CAAT-Bravo when they kept popping out of the alleyways to fire RPGs and rifles.

The fight was not all one sided. Hospital Corpsman Sanchez was wounded in the shoulder and upper arm, but refused to be evacuated. Sergeant David R. Stegall was perhaps the luckiest Marine on the gun line when an RPG landed ten meters from him, failed to explode, glanced off the road, and sailed over his head.

As more and more enemy gathered in the cemetery, Captain Lowe directed helicopter gunships against their positions and assembly areas. Major Glen G. Butler piloted one of the gunbirds. "I was shot at on the first run. I didn't realize it at first. I just heard a kind of like Jiffy Pop and the crackle sound. We had our helmets on, but I could hear the distinct crackle. My copilot and I just looked at each other quizzically, as if to say, 'They're shooting at us. We're getting shot at!'"

On the second run, Butler put the Cobra in the lead. A wall of red tracers seemed to be "coming from everywhere . . . every tombstone." Then the Cobra's weapons system jammed. As it broke away to escape, Butler flew in. "At this point, we were just trying to survive," he recalled. "My gunner on the left side, Corporal Hail, started shooting with a .50-caliber and basically sprayed into that cemetery." Luck was with them, and both the Cobra and Butler's Huey escaped.

By this time, Sellers's platoon had relocated about 1,500 meters north of the police station. "It's getting into afternoon, and it is hotter than hell," Sellers remembered. "The guys aren't doing too good on water at this point." Temperatures reached 120 degrees Fahrenheit or more in the shade, and the men were running out of water.

"I remember . . . our radio operator and one of our team leaders . . . ran all the way back to the trucks, which is probably 400 meters," Corporal Wallace recalled. "It doesn't sound far, but when you've got a full combat load and people shooting at you, it's a long way." Mayer was proud that despite the heat and lack of water, his battalion did not suffer a single heat-exhaustion casualty.

However, it took some rather unorthodox procedures to keep heat casualties from happening, particularly in the tank platoon, which had to fight with the hatches buttoned up. The inside of the tank was like an oven—more than 140 degrees Fahrenheit. "My Marines couldn't drink water fast enough, and they'd be physically exhausted and dehydrated," Lieutenant Thomas

Major Glen G. Butler's flight crew posing beside their Huey gunship. Note the GAU 7.62-caliber mini-gun. *Lt. Col. Glen G. Butler, USMC*

Iraqi Resistance Report

Fighting resumed in an-Najaf between the U.S. aggressor forces and the Jaysh al-Mahdi militia loyal to Shi'i religious leader Muqtada as-Sadr. Hundreds of residents of the city have begun to flee the usually crowded streets in the center of the city. Shopkeepers rushed to close the shutters on their stores and women and children hurried out of the line of fire.

explained. "I had some Marines, a couple of gunners, who passed out or threw up from sucking in the fumes from firing the weapons." Thomas had the platoon corpsman insert IVs into the tankers' arms. "We'd be good for about four hours, and then we'd have to go back and get more fluids," he said rather matter-of-factly. "It sucked being in a seventy-ton tank in that heat, but we knew that there were Marines out there in the cemetery that needed help."

With his battalion aligned along the cemetery wall, facing the militia defensive positions, Lieutenant Colonel Mayer devised a plan to attack into the burial ground to eliminate enemy resistance. "We had been talking to the MEU [led by Haslam]," Moran said, "who had received approval to commence the attack at 1800." The plan was pretty straightforward, Moran explained. "We'd attack to clear the cemetery from east to west, eventually turning to attack south onto the ring road, facing the built-up structures that surrounded the Imam Ali shrine and the Old City." The three assault elements—Alpha Company on the north, the 81mm Mortar Platoon in the center, and Charlie Company on the south—were each given its own sector and a limit of advance. They were to maintain lateral contact to ensure the enemy did not get between units and to prevent friendly fire incidents.

Mayer said the plan sounded simple except "the dense tombs, catacombs, and tunnels made tactical control extremely difficult. It was just like combat in a built-up area—the worst kind of fight."

Moran echoed Mayer's comment. "Maneuver was difficult," he said. "There were so many different angles for the enemy to attack us from. We were really fighting a three-dimensional battle."

The battalion was initially plagued by problems maintaining contact among units, as individual Marines tried to work their way through the densely packed graveyard under heavy fire. It was difficult, if not impossible to maintain straight lines. Unit leaders often found their men engaged from more than one direction. The battle quickly became a fire-team leader,

Battalion Operation Order

Prepared and issued by Maj. Coby Moran
Mission: BLT 1/4 attacks to seize key terrain in Najaf cemetery in order to prevent Mahdi Militia dominance of Najaf.
Concept of Operations: Three-company attack in zone from current line of departure. Weapons Company supports with screening and attack by fire operations.
Concept of Fires: Use rotary-wing (helicopters)/close air support in conjunction with indirect fire to combine arms and prevent damage to friendly aviation. Sequential arms are not preferred.
Tasks:

- Charley Company (main effort) attacks to seize BLT Objective One, establishes a defensible base in vicinity of Najaf's Old City. Attach tank and LAR platoons.
- 81mm-Mortar Platoon attacks to clear in zone in order to facilitate main effort attack.
- Alpha Company attacks to clear zone in order to destroy Mahdi Militia in northern cemetery.
- Weapons Company screens Route Miami to east along BLT zone. Screens Route Hartford to the south. Controls Revolutionary Circle to prevent enemy flanking attacks on main effort.
- Coordinating Instructions:
  Time of Attack: 0530
  Direction of Attack: West
  BLT Objective: Building Complex MA 358403
  Phase Lines: Alzado, 36 Easting, Dicy Road
  Limit of Advance: Route Alzado
- Amphibious Assault Platoon provides sections for armored ambulances, armored supply, and mechanized infantry.
- Light Armored Reconnaissance Platoon screens BLT northern flank.

stand-up, close-quarters fight, pitting man against man.

The militiamen knew the area like the back of their hands and were able to maneuver freely against the Marines, who did not have the same knowledge of the terrain. The militia had prepared extensive defensive positions and ammunition caches in the "shantytown," as Lieutenant Thomas called it. "Tombs rose high in the air, giving the enemy a perfect view of the cemetery," he added.

Mayer said one had to see the cemetery to believe it. "Huge one- and

Many of the tombs had underground burial chambers, where the militia stored weapons and ammunition. At times, the fighters themselves took shelter from the American air attack in the chambers, and used them to move through the cemetery and come up behind the Marines. *Defenseimagery.mil 040806-M-7719F-001*

two-story mausoleums, crypts that go down into blackness, where bodies lay on shelves, . . . skulls sticking out, and the stench of the dead in the air and in the dust. The whole place is horrific!"

By mid-afternoon, the MEF commander, Lt. Gen. James T. Conway, approved the attack, to kick off at 1800. The order was passed down the chain of command. Charlie Company's Lieutenant Sellers recalled, "Hey, you're going to get on line, and you're going to go west 3,000 meters." He remembered thinking sarcastically, "Oh, of course, why not? That sounds like a plan! That's a great idea. We'll just make our way through the cemetery, where no American has been in a long, long time." He passed the word to his platoon.

"I remember the lieutenant saying, 'Start moving forward on line,'" Cpl. James T. Jenkins recalled. "Our platoon and all the other platoons moved forward on line and started clearing the tombs."

Lieutenant Moulton recalled, "At this point, we did not know if the cemetery was full of militia[men] hiding out in camps or . . . just a place they kept some mortars. I knew it wasn't a New England cemetery, like where I grew up, but we had absolutely no appreciation for what it was really like. Going into the cemetery right then and there was pretty daunting." In retrospect, Moulton was disappointed about the lack of information. "It's pretty shocking that we weren't given some basic intelligence on what it would be like to just take a step into there . . . There were tombstones all on top of each other. In any ten-foot-square area, there were a hundred places for them [the enemy] to hide. You were literally walking over and through the graves, and there were mausoleums, little rooms, and lots of cellars that you could walk down into. It was the perfect defensive position."

CHARLIE COMPANY, 1ST BATTALION, 4TH MARINE REGIMENT

Captain Morrissey's Charlie Company kicked off the assault on schedule and swept through two factories and the tombs around them. The company encountered little resistance, but "ran out of flashbangs [nonlethal stun grenades] in the first ten minutes," according to Corporal Jenkins.

After moving a few hundred yards, Sellers's platoon started to lose contact with the Bravo Company platoon.

"We started to buckle in the center," Sellers explained. "The buildings that I had in my area were taller catacombs, which made it more of a pain in the ass and slowed us down. Bravo had smaller tombstones and made steady progress, but when we got into those thicker buildings, we started

Charlie Company's attack into the city moved along Diagonal Road. Lieutenant Colonel Mayer's command vehicle is on the left, Charlie Company's is on the right, and Team Tiger (1st Lt. Russell Thomas's tanks) are in front. *1st Lt. William Birdzell, USMC*

Even the bravest man was hesitant to climb down into the darkened burial chambers within the cemetery. Throwing a flashbang or fragmentation grenade into the chamber then following it on foot was the preferred method for entering one of the macabre chambers. *Tip of the Spear, U.S. Army Small-Unit Action in Iraq*

losing contact." Sellers told his men on the left to keep up with the Bravo platoon, then worked his way over to the right flank, where he found his men hanging back to stay even with Charlie's 3rd Platoon. He said that after checking on them, he went back to find his other squad. "But they were so far behind that I kind of found myself stuck in the middle with about three other guys," he recalled.

By this time, the company came under a hailstorm of RPG, machine-gun, sniper, and mortar fire. "It was the heaviest fire I've ever encountered, period!" Sellers exclaimed.

"We had three or four different firefights going on," Jenkins recalled. "My squad was in a firefight. Corporal Wallace, one of my team leaders, and Lieutenant Sellers—they're off to the right in a firefight."

Sellers collected another four men, who had somehow gotten separated from their squad, and moved forward. "I had a squad ahead of me and seven Marines with me," he recalled, "and we're kind of snooping and pooping up to where the enemy is probably going to be." Jenkins thought they were within ten meters of the enemy. "We could hear them," Sellers said, "and we could smell them. We just couldn't see them." One of his men stuck his head around a tomb and had a bullet strike the wall two inches from his face. "He was a chubby kid, and his face had that scared fat-guy look," Sellers related humorously. "Get out of the way, I yelled . . . [A]nd he got out of the way." The same thing happened to Sellers. "It was the first time that it ever dawned on me that I could get killed," he said.

Private First Class Anthony Perez was in the 1st Platoon, Bravo Company. "I remember being right next to Lieutenant Lewis as he was talking on the radio," he said. "I could hear the enemy talking about thirty meters in front of us. I whispered, 'Sir, I can hear them. They're right in front of us.' He looked at me and said, 'Well, go in there and get 'em!' I remember looking at him and thinking, 'Are you fucking kidding me?' It was pretty funny because I knew he didn't expect me to take them on all by myself. I think it was just the first thing that came into his head."

Within minutes, mortar fire wounded three Marines. First Sergeant Justin D. LeHew immediately moved to their location, directed treatment, and evacuated them to the rear. His actions were officially cited:

> First Sergeant LeHew left his position of cover . . . to the impact site to direct company corpsmen . . . [M]ore mortar rounds impacted and he stood completely exposed. When complete he moved approximately 500 meters to the company's combat trains staging point, where on 3 separate occasions, he directed the fires of the vehicle mounted weapons against enemy snipers and militia attempting to penetrate the rear lines of the company. For the next six hours, he repeatedly moved back and forth under the crack of sniper fire and mortar explosions to communicate the enemy situation and the status of the Marines to the company commander.

First Sergeant LeHew, who recieved the Navy Cross for heroism in Operation Iraqi Freedom was awarded the Bronze Star with the Combat Distinguishing Device for heroic achievement during the twenty-two-day battle.

The fighting was close, an infantryman's slugfest. "You could actually see them [the militiamen] when our Cobras and Hueys flew over," Wallace recounted. "They'd come up on top of the tombs and start shooting . . . so we just picked them off."

Jenkins said that he killed at least five. "I'd take the red or black masks off their faces and break their weapons so they couldn't be used again."

Sellers nominated Jenkins for a Bronze Star for "jumping up on a tomb and shooting four or five bad guys on the other side, like it was nothing—no big deal!" Another of his men crawled within fifteen meters of several militiamen crouched behind a large tomb. "Lance Corporal Izzo [Peter R.] kills a couple with a grenade," Sellers remarked. "He crawls back to our lines, and then went back out to throw another grenade." He is another Marine who Sellers recommended for a Bronze Star.

Corporal Wallace and several Marines—a mix of Jenkins's squad and Wallace's own—continued to work their way through the tombs. "It's so thick out there that I had a hard time squeezing through with my load-bearing vest and flak jacket on . . . particularly while rounds are coming at us!" Wallace said.

Wallace and his men got separated from the rest of the platoon during their advance through the closely packed gravestones. "When you come out from the side of one of those big mausoleums, whoever was on your left isn't there anymore. You can't see him, so by then we were just gathering whoever was next to you and saying, 'Hey, see me? Don't let me out of your sight. Stay with me.' That's pretty much how it happened," Wallace explained.

The advance continued through the forbidding graveyard, where every catacomb could have an enemy lurking inside or on a rooftop.

"[I]magine the scariest mountain town in the world, with local bad guys armed with guns, mortars, and RPGs," Sellers said. "And you receive an

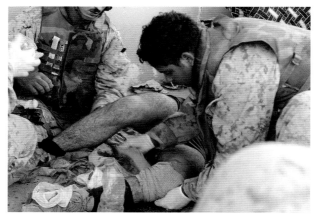

A navy corpsman administers first aid to a Marine wounded in the calf. Each platoon had its own "doc," whose practice ranged from aspirin giving to life saving—sometimes at the risk of his own life.
Defenseimagery.mil 041119-M-2583-075

Bronze Star Citations

Lance Corporal James T. Jenkins

For heroic achievement in connection with combat operations while serving as squad leader . . . in Najaf, Iraq from 5 August 2004 to 7 August 2004. His courageous actions enabled 1st Platoon to hold key terrain at the Iraqi police station and the Najaf cemetery despite a constant barrage of enemy sniper, RPG, and mortar fire. With his squad pinned down under intense enemy fire . . . Lance Corporal Jenkins moved along his lines to reestablish lines of communication with Bravo Company to his left flank. When he reached their position, four enemy militia located to his direct front began opening fire. Without regard for his own well-being, Jenkins jumped up onto an exposed catacomb and fired directly down at the enemy no more than 20 meters to his front. After killing these four enemy militia, Jenkins returned to his squad and directed the fire that killed four more enemy combatants. The following day, Jenkins killed two enemy snipers in a four story building approximately 300–400 meters from the company's defensive position . . . [H]is courage and actions while under intense enemy fire inspired the Marines under his charge and spearheaded the battalion's assault into a known enemy strongpoint. His courage reflected great credit upon himself and were in keeping with the highest traditions of the Marine Corps and the United States Naval Service.

Lance Corporal Peter R. Izzo

For heroic achievement in connection with combat operations while serving as fire team leader . . . in Najaf, Iraq from 5 August 2004 to 7 August 2004. With his squad pinned down under intense enemy fire in the Najaf cemetery, Lance Corporal Izzo maneuvered within fifteen meters of the enemy and launched two hand grenades that killed four enemy to their direct front. The following day Izzo killed three enemy snipers in a four story building approximately 200–300 meters from the company's defensive position with his accurate M203 fire. His courage and actions while under intense enemy fire inspired the Marines under his charge and spearheaded the battalion's assault into a known enemy strongpoint. His courage reflected great credit upon himself and were in keeping with the highest traditions of the Marine Corps and the United States Naval Service.

Lance Corporal Peter R. Izzo holding a Bronze Star, awarded for his bravery in action on August 5. His citation notes that he braved heavy fire to eliminate several enemy fighters and spearheaded his squad's assault. *USMC photo*

order to get on line, walk three thousand meters at dusk, with the sun in your face. It's a nightmare of monumental proportions."

Sellers's platoon fought its way through heavy fire approximately 100 to 150 meters past Diagonal Road. "At this point, we're taking casualties— myself and Lance Corporal Izzo," Jenkins recalled. "I guess it was an RPG or a grenade that hit the tombstone. It burned through my camis [camouflage uniform] and burned me a little bit on the face. Izzo got hit in the hand and neck, but nothing major." Jenkins and his men lacked communications and did not have any idea what was going on, but they continued to fight.

"It was kind of scary," Jenkins admitted. "Where's everybody at?" he thought to himself. "I kept running over to the Bravo platoon to use their radio." He was finally able to contact Morrissey, who told him that he had one minute to get out of the cemetery before it was hit with an artillery barrage. "We can't get out," Jenkins exclaimed, "we're in a fire fight, and if we pull back, the enemy will just pick us off."

Corporal Wallace and two other Marines were separated from the platoon. "We're walking around in there," he explained. "We're picking up Marines left and right—find a lost man over here, he's by himself. So we're snatching Marines up, and we're taking fire the whole time, returning fire the whole time." Wallace led the group back to the platoon sergeant's location. "The next thing I know, one of the men looks behind us. He's yelling to get down. I look up, and . . . we see rounds coming from behind us." Just at that point, Wallace said, "The lieutenant [Sellers] comes trotting over shouting, 'Hey, we've got artillery coming in, like in no time at all. We need to get out of here.'"

Sellers pulled half the platoon back to the wall—minus Jenkins and his men—and told everyone, "I don't have half of my platoon!"

Jenkins was still in the cemetery and in danger of being cut off by the advancing militiamen. "They're coming toward us," he recalled, as his men poured out a torrent of fire. "We threw grenades and finally got them off our back." Jenkins yelled to his men that they had to get out of the cemetery. "We bounded back," he said. "I'm stopping every twenty feet to get head counts to make sure everybody's accounted for." The militiamen threw everything at the Marines as they pulled back—mortars, RPGs, and sniper fire—and reinfiltrated the cleared area.

"The Iraqis are coming up from the tombstones, and we're picking them off," Jenkins exclaimed. "I kid you not; my fourteen guys killed at least a hundred." Despite the heavy fire, they made it back to the road without further casualties. The platoon had only four slightly wounded. "It's amazing that I came out of that maze of crap with nothing but superficial casualties," Jenkins said.

Bravo Company's attached platoon was not so fortunate; a mortar round wounded Lieutenant Lewis and several of his men. "Bravo was getting torn up," Jenkins recalled sadly, "taking RPGs, freakin' sniper fire—everything. They had four casualties."

Private First Class Perez recalled, "I was lying flat on the ground next to Lieutenant Lewis and two others when all of a sudden, about twelve to fifteen feet away, there was an explosion. I remember seeing a bright ball of white light with what looked like a thousand needles shooting from it." All four were wounded by shrapnel, but Lieutenant Lewis took the brunt of it. "A flood of pain hit me," Perez said, "and I knew that I had been hit. I frantically checked myself . . . [T]here was a lot of blood, and something dangled in front of my face. I thought it was my nose that had been peeled off from the blast. I reached up and found it was my NVGs [night-vision goggles] that had blown off my helmet. Thank God!"

First Sergeant LeHew sprang into action. According to official correspondence: "Without hesitation, he assembled his casualty collection team and ran north along the company's lines under heavy enemy fire. Not knowing how far away the adjacent unit was, they pushed on alone, until they came upon the wounded Marines. Still under a barrage of mortar and machine

gun fire, LeHew supervised the treatment and immediate evacuation of the casualties, allowing the attached platoon to continue the fight."

Sergeant Joey W. McBroom was cited for assisting with the evacuation and for "repositioning his squad to prevent any further injuries from enemy mortars." Says his citation: "When an adjacent platoon took a direct hit from enemy mortar fire,

Sergeant Joey W. McBroom was awarded the Navy Achievement for assisting with the evacuation of several wounded Marines and for maneuvering his squad to protect an exposed flank. *USMC photo* he supervised the evacuation of the injured Marines, and maneuvered his squad to protect the company's flank."

With the platoon commander out of the fight, Staff Sgt. Robert Willis, the platoon sergeant, immediately took command and brought up the squad leaders to brief them. At that point, another mortar round exploded. "It landed at our feet," Willis said, "and hit my corpsman, my radio operator, and one of my squad leaders about twenty-five meters behind us."

Staff Sergeant Ian Bonnell was some distance away when he heard someone yell, "Incoming!" He was amazed to see Father Paul Shaughnessy, the battalion chaplain, strolling toward him like he didn't have a care in the world. "I remember looking over, and the chaplain was walking up and down the lines and it [explosions] wasn't even fazing him. A round would go off and blow up, and he'd turn around and look and start walking that way to make sure everyone was OK."

Lockheed AC-130H Spectre Gunship

The Lockheed AC-130H Spectre gunship is a heavily armed ground-attack aircraft manned by a crew of thirteen. It incorporates side-firing weapons integrated with sophisticated sensors and navigation and fire-control systems to provide precision firepower or area-saturation fire. Its armament consists of 7.62 miniguns, 20mm Vulcan cannons, and a 105mm howitzer, which can fire six to ten 50-pound shells a minute. The AC-130's optimum altitude in Najaf was somewhere between seven and nine thousand feet, which allowed its sensors to positively identify armed militiamen.

Lockheed's AC-130H Spectre gunship, call sign Basher, was loved by Marines because of its awesome firepower and ability to detect the enemy with its sophisticated sensors. Basher's female weapons officer endeared herself to the Marines. *Defenseimagrey.mil 070305-F-4684K*

Charlie Company established defensive positions on the road for the night. "After the sun went down," Wallace said, "the C-130 gunship came in there and just pounded the whole area in front of us all night long." It was the first time the battalion observed the AC-130H Spectre gunship (call sign Basher) in action.

"That night they worked over the cemetery," Moran said, "as the militia were doing a lot of their resupply, moving men and vehicles around."

Mayer was ecstatic. "The Mahdi Militia learned not to mess with the AC-130 . . . [D]on't come out, don't fire, don't do anything, just hide!"

The Marines were enamored with the female crewman who spoke on the radio. "I'm not sure who she is," Mayer commented, "but I'm going to give her a coin, a T-shirt, and a battalion guidon if I ever meet her, because she's calm and cool. She taught us the magic way of fighting."

Mayer estimated that the aircraft killed hundreds, including the militia command group that controlled the fight in the cemetery. "The militia would fire at us, betraying their position," he said, "and then we would destroy them with the AC-130."

Corporal Jenkins was more succinct in his recount. "The AC-130 was killing everybody!"

In addition to using Basher, the battalion ran several close-air-support missions. "We'd received a report from a walk-in intelligence source," Moran explained, "who told us where a key enemy communications and assembly area was located. It was supposedly filled with Iranians, which was never confirmed, and we were able to drop four bombs on them that night. The next morning, the source told us the bunker had collapsed and trapped up to twenty enemy fighters in it."

DelaCruz remembered "taking fire from a building that had been firing at the 81mm Mortar Platoon all day long. Suddenly, the whole building just went boom! Someone had called an airstrike in on it."

The strike had been coordinated and controlled by Captain Carl Lowe, call sign Wombat. Moran commented, "He was running with me in the CO's vehicle, and we spent a long day and night controlling the fixed wing and AC-130 fires."

81MM MORTAR PLATOON, 1ST BATTALION, 4TH MARINE REGIMENT

Lieutenant Breshears's 81mm Mortar Platoon was designated a provisional rifle platoon of two twenty-five-man sections, each reinforced with a medium machine-gun squad and given the middle sector of the battalion's

Lieutenant Colonel John L. Mayer sits in the front seat of his up-armored Humvee, studying a map of Najaf, while Capt. Coby Moran talks on the radio. The two traveled throughout the battle space, keeping their fingers on the pulse of the battalion. They traveled with a small security detachment under the command of 1st Lt. William Birdzell. *Maj. Michael S. Wilbur, USMC*

advance. At 1800, the platoon moved forward to support Charlie Company's right flank. However, the maneuver left its own flank exposed because of the numerous buildings between it and Alpha Company on the right.

"I didn't want to go in there," Staff Sgt. Ian Bonnell said. "[W]e're on a wall, and we're taking all the fire in there. And I just kept thinking to myself, 'We're gonna have to go in there.' It played out pretty much how I expected it . . . close-in fighting, getting up close and personal with people."

Breshears encouraged his men. "I told them this is what you've been preparing for your entire Marine Corps career . . . [L]et's go get 'em!"

The platoon made good progress until it reached Diagonal Road, about 200 meters from its starting point.

"We crossed a two-lane road and started receiving some small arms fire," Sgt. Jason McManus recalled. "The fire was coming from in front of us, so we kept pushing, clearing the tombs as fast as we could." Enemy fire intensified as Breshears's platoon maneuvered through the broken terrain of tombs and mausoleums. "They were not the tombstones we were familiar with," McManus explained. "These were about a foot by a foot square and sticking up about waist high, with some weird monuments on the top."

Within another 150 meters, the platoon encountered a well-prepared, platoon-sized defensive position. A pitched battle quickly developed—one

First Lieutenant Lamar Breshears, commander of the 81mm Mortar Platoon, led his men into the cemetery as infantrymen and soon found they were up against a platoon-sized enemy position. The fight developed into a slugfest at close range. *USMC History Division*

that threatened to overwhelm the senses. "When you have that many people, that many rifles, that many machine guns, explosions, and rockets being fired," Breshears said, "it's deafening, it's a dull roar." There were no front lines, no fixed positions, he recalled. "They started coming out of the crypts," Breshears said. "It was like a video game. They pop up, fire a couple of shots, and drop back down. You only see them a second or maybe two. They were armed with AK-47s, light machine guns, rocket-propelled grenades."

The fighting was as close as twenty feet. "You could smell them and their living spaces, that sort of thing," Breshears remembered. "I saw two who were in their midtwenties. They were just young males fighting for what they believed in." The fighting was so close, the two sides exchanged taunts and verbal insults as they tossed hand grenades back and forth.

"We were pretty short on grenades," McManus said. "I had two, and another guy from my squad had two as well. I told my guys to stay tight so we could clear individual crypts that popped up." He continued to lead his squad forward. "We started being engaged by indirect RPG and small-arms fire. Bullets ricocheted off the hard-packed mud and bricks," McManus recalled. "I could tell that the rest of the platoon was heavily engaged further down to my right. We started to get split up a bit." McManus's team checked two more crypts, which turned out to be empty. "We made it up to a point where we saw the section from 81's pinned down about twenty meters to our right," he said.

By now darkness was approaching. Breshears received word over the radio to pull his men back to the Diagonal Road. He had his second section pull back, while he went alone in search of the missing first section in the gathering darkness. He had lost contact with the section in the confused fighting and was unable to pass the word about the withdrawal. Despite the heavy fire, he managed to work his way through the maze of tombstones and reach the section, which was pinned down in a small perimeter. The withdrawal of Alpha and Charlie Companies had left the section isolated and exposed to enemy fire from three sides. Breshears attempted to bring in artillery support, "but the mission was denied because it was too politically sensitive to fire it in the cemetery," he wrote in an after-action report.

One of the section's squad leaders, Sgt. Yadir Reynoso spotted a team of militiamen working their way through the jumble toward the embattled Marines. Quickly reacting to the threat, Reynoso took a hand grenade, pulled the pin, and lobbed it into the enemy formation. After the explosion, three militiamen lay motionless on the ground. He pointed out four others to another Marine, who blasted them with an AT-4 antitank rocket.

Reynoso kept the enemy under fire with his rifle, hoping to pin them down long enough for the men to withdraw. As he rose to fire, a burst of fire hit him in the neck and face, killing him instantly. He fell some distance from the small perimeter. The section leader, Staff Sgt. Bonnell, concerned that he would lose more men if they attempted to reach the body, told them to hold their position until they gained fire superiority. Lance Corporal Justin C. Vaughn ignored the order and moved forward under heavy fire to retrieve the mortally wounded Marine.

"With machine gun and small arms rounds impacting directly on his position," the battalion after-action report noted, "Vaughn stripped Sergeant Reynoso of his flack jacket, helmet, deuce gear and weapon, lifted the body in a fireman's carry, and ran across fifteen meters of rough terrain back to his section's position." After placing Reynoso's body on the ground inside the small perimeter, Vaughn retraced his steps to retrieve Reynoso's equipment and weapon so it would not fall in enemy hands.

Under cover of darkness, the section was finally able to withdraw. Lance Corporal Vaughn carried Reynoso's body over 150 meters until he collapsed from heat exhaustion. The battalion noted "Many Marines believed that the restrictive fire support restrictions caused Sergeant Reynoso's death. The incident caused immediate and lingering bitterness." His death also brought about a quick easing of restrictions that led to "almost immediate facilitation of fire mission approval and reduction of restricted areas from 1,000 meters around the mosque to 300 meters."

Lieutenant Colonel Johnston was quoted as saying, "If higher headquarters is slow in approving a critical fire mission, I will approve it myself."

The 81mm Mortar Platoon was reunited on Diagonal Road, where it established defensive positions between Alpha and Charlie Companies. As they prepared the positions, two more Marines were put out of the fight, one with heat exhaustion and the other from shell shock when a mortar round exploded close to him. McManus recalled, "We fanned out, using the road as a buffer. There were a couple of guys who had some serious issues with the heat . . . [W]e were absolutely out of water; our CamelBaks were completely dry." Sometime during the night, the parched Marines were resupplied with water.

"Maybe I was just hallucinating from the heat," Pfc. Zuniga said half in jest, "but I swear I saw two ghosts."

McManus remembered, "There was no small-arms fire that night because there were Spectre-gun runs going on to our front pretty much most of the night."

The 81mm Mortar Platoon's furious assault had scattered the Mahdi force, accounting for twenty-eight enemy KIAs at the cost of one Marine killed in action and several slightly wounded. The battalion later determined that the enemy position had been the northernmost unit in a mutually supporting defensive line.

Silver Star Citation

Sergeant Yadir G. Reynoso

The President of the United States takes pride in presenting the Silver Star (Posthumously) to Sergeant Yadir G. Reynoso, United States Marine Corps for conspicuous gallantry and intrepidity in action against the enemy as Third Squad Leader, 81 millimeter Mortar Platoon, Weapons Company, Battalion Landing Team 1/4, Eleventh Marine Expeditionary Unit (Special Operations Capable), I Marine Expeditionary Force, U.S. Marine Corps Forces, Central Command, in support of Operation IRAQI FREEDOM ON 5 August 2004. Ordered to clear a 200-meter section of An Najaf cemetery, Sergeant Reynoso's squad engaged a reinforced platoon-sized enemy unit at ranges of 10 to 30 meters and was immediately pinned down by a heavy volume of rocket-propelled grenade and AK-37 fire. Sergeant Reynoso responded by throwing a fragmentation grenade that eliminated three insurgents, destroying their position. He then directed the fires of an AT-4 rocket team on a pocket of four insurgents, destroying their position and all personnel. While providing suppressive fire against the enemy to enable his squad to withdraw from its position and maneuver against the enemy, Sergeant Reynoso was mortally wounded. Sergeant Reynoso's bold leadership, wise judgment, and unyielding dedication to duty reflected great credit upon him and were in keeping with the highest traditions of the Marine Corps and the United States Naval Service.

ALPHA COMPANY, 1ST BATTALION, 4TH MARINE REGIMENT

Alpha Company was already to commence its assault when it received word to hold up. "We were about ready to go over the wall [the outer cemetery wall]," Sotire recalled, "When Coby [Moran] told me to shift to a different sector." Lieutenant Colonel Mayer decided that the battalion's attack frontage was too big and directed the companies to tighten it.

"We didn't have enough force," Moran explained. "At the time, we didn't have an idea how much frontage each unit could cover, so we moved Alpha [Company] south." Luckily, they had not become decisively engaged, and with the help of rotary-wing close air support, the company suppressed the militia's fire and pulled back to its vehicles. As enemy fire cracked over their heads, they climbed back into the trucks and moved about five hundred meters farther south.

"We had about an hour to get into position," Sotire noted, "which was good because it gave the company time to get ready."

Sotire also recalled, "It was unbelievably hot, and every time I leaned over the map, sweat literally poured off my face, threatening to destroy it."

As he continued the brief, an army Apache helicopter suddenly sent a stream of rockets into the cemetery.

"It came over the top of an LAV and let loose a volley of rockets," Moran recalled, "scaring the hell out of everyone." The battalion was excited about the gunship reinforcement, but quickly learned that the army's employment of helicopters was quite different that of the Marines or navy. "The Apache squadron is used to being its own maneuver element, with a separate area of operations," Moran noted, "and they didn't understand our CAS procedures."

The battalion called off the helicopters for the night, but the Apaches returned the next day and did good work. "Somebody at the MEU explained our procedures to them, and they were fine," Moran said.

Major Butler said, "The army guys were great. Many of them were experienced and easily became part of the team." The two units worked closely together. "We rapidly set up a plan," Butler explained. "We'd just go back and forth in hour-and-a-half flight increments—Apache followed by Cobra/Huey aircraft—to have twenty-four-hour CAS available. We essentially did that for three weeks."

Alpha Company's new position placed the 81mm Mortar Platoon on their left flank and Reconnaissance Platoon on the right flank, close to the amusement park with its conspicuous Ferris wheel. The company stretched in a line—1st Platoon, 3rd Platoon, and Weapons Platoon, in that order—from Diagonal Road to Route Favre, just south of the amusement park. Its objective was to attack and clear its sector to the north-south axis road that cut the cemetery in half, a distance of approximately 1,500 meters. Sotire established phase lines to maintain control and planned sectors of fire and on-call targets, but didn't fire because of the restrictions. He staged the company's vehicles—Humvees and seven-ton trucks—in a circle with a small security detachment of twenty-one men.

"They were positioned well," Sotire recalled. "It was easy to get into the cemetery with ammunition and to evacuate casualties." He left most of his machine guns with the vehicles, taking only three or four into the assault.

Sotire remembered the company jumping off in the attack and "crossing the wall just like something out of World War I." The sharp crack of small-arms fire, the heavy crump of explosions, and the sound of diving aircraft gave voice to the assault. The company advanced through a multistory industrial park that was surrounded by high walls. It was the same complex that had been the scene of the earlier fight. "Borneo had cleared them [the militiamen] out when the Huey went down," Sotire recalled, "and there was no enemy there."

Alpha Company pushed further into the cemetery maze. "It was unbelievable how bad it was, squeezing through the tombs, having to step over and on the crypts, through pretty heavy fire," Sortire said.

Moulton recalled, "Just simply walking twenty feet, you had to climb over walls and walk up and over the tombstones. Sometimes you would step on one that a mortar had landed on, so you were essentially . . . walking on bones and stuff. I wasn't freaked out by it, but it was definitely a little nasty.

"In any ten-foot-square area in this cemetery, there are a hundred places for these guys to hide. They could be anywhere in some tunnel or tomb and suddenly pop up and shoot. For all we knew, they could be shooting from right in front of us one moment and then pop up behind us the next moment."

Sotire echoed his comment. "I could see rounds impact around us, but it was hard to make out where it was coming from." A Marine close to him was shot directly in the chest and knocked down, but his small-arms protective-insert plate in his flak jacket stopped the bullet. "He jumped back up, saying, 'I'm all right!'" an amazed Sotire recalled.

Dozens of militia mortar rounds exploded in and around the company's formation; however, the closely packed tombs absorbed most of the shrapnel, much to the relief of the Marines. Moulton remembered, "There was a point where the insurgents started getting very, very accurate with their mortars. You would hear the distant pops of the mortar tubes firing off in the distance, and then a few seconds later you'd hear the rounds whispering through the air just before exploding. A lot of times, they'd just walk them right down our lines. All you could do was just get down between the tombs and hope one didn't land on you."

At one point Moulton, his platoon sergeant, and a corpsman were in one of the tombs. "A mortar hit right above our heads, skidded off the wall with a big thump, and landed smack on the ground in front of us," he recalled calmly. "It was a dud! We were lucky as hell, and we knew it."

Despite the protection provided by the brick tombs, there were some casualties. "As soon as the barrage ended, the next thing you heard was screams and shouts because someone's been hit," Moulton said, "The corpsman and others . . . would run down the line to try to take care of the wounded." The company gunnery sergeant, Richard S. Synovec, quickly responded with a security detachment and, despite heavy enemy fire, successfully evacuated the casualties.

To maintain control, Sotire and his small command group followed about twenty meters behind the 1st Platoon. "I could see about fifty to one hundred meters on either flank," he explained, "but as it got darker, I could only see a few meters ahead." Despite the limited visibility, Sotire felt he had good control and the company was moving well against the opposition. "There was no way the enemy was going to stop our attack," he exclaimed.

However, at one point, several snipers opened a heavy fire from three minarets that overlooked his lines. Sotire ordered his men to fall back so he could bring in an airstrike. "Due to the dense terrain, we had a tough time talking the aircraft onto the target. First Sergeant [Robert A.] Young, with a small security detachment, ran 200 meters forward and marked the target with a smoke grenade," he said. Helicopter gunships spotted the mark, identified the targets, and eliminated the enemy with rockets and cannon fire.

Alpha Company continued its advance and reached its limit of advance by early evening. It established a cigar-shaped defensive position, with the bulk of the company facing the cemetery.

The two antiarmor CAAT sections and the tank platoon patrolled along Route Miami from the police station northward to support the attack into the cemetery. "We were limited to what we could do in there," Borneo recalled. "We were pretty much relegated to screening the

The minarets were used by the militia snipers. Their height gave the snipers a tremendous advantage, as they could see the entire battlefield from these positions. Conversely, the minarets were conspicuous and easily targeted by Marine countersnipers and close air support. *Capt. Richard Zjawin, USMC*

flanks to make sure the route stayed open." However, they did engage targets of opportunity. "We put snipers on the roofs of several five-story buildings right off Route Miami," he said, "and were successful in eliminating several militiamen." While directing the fire of the LAR platoon, its commander, 1st Lt. John F. MacDonald, was wounded by a sniper and put out of the fight. His gunner, Lance Cpl. Michael J. Novak, spotted enemy reinforcements sneaking through the maze of crypts. He put them under fire with the vehicle's 25mm cannon and, over the next few hours, killed an estimated fifteen to twenty militiamen.

Major Moran remembered, "As nightfall came, the enemy posture increased a bit. We started seeing platoon-sized attacks all along the line. The companies reported twenty- and thirty-man counterattacks." The attacks soon petered out when Basher arrived on station.

A battalion report noted, "The plane targeted the enemy using infrared heat sensors. The scenario went: spot target, call AC-130 strike, plane picks out enemy's heat signature. Wham! A position, vehicle, building, or enemy in the open is no more." The Marines called the aircraft the "mad jackass" because of the distinctive sound of its 7.62mm Gatling guns.

Corporal Wallace remembered, "After the sun went down, the AC-130 gunship came in. It pounded the whole area in front of us all night long." The militia faded away and, for the most part, did not attack the battalion's lines. "It was pretty quiet. Every once in a while you'd hear a burst of AK fire, but other than that, it was quiet." The MEU after-action report noted, "HUMINT [human intelligence] indicated that the Mahdi Militia command element in charge of cemetery defense had been overrun, resulting in 130 enemy killed in action."

The battalion's line stretched from Route Favre, south of the amusement park, down Diagonal Road to Route Miami. However, it was not a solid defensive line. "Alpha Company was not tied in with the 81mm Mortar Platoon," Sotire admitted. "A gap existed." Fortunately, the enemy did not exploit it. The company was tied in with Reconnaissance Platoon on its right flank.

As the company settled in for the night, Sotire had time to survey his men—and himself. He had been worried all day about heat stroke, but his men had learned to drink plenty of water to keep hydrated. "Water intake was a high priority," Sotire said, "It was part of the culture of the battalion. The SOP in the company was to have the men piss in a bottle to see what color it was." At times drinking the water was difficult. "It was so hot," he recalled, "when it [water] was dropped off, it would burn my lips. I had to sip it or get burned."

A Marine light armored vehicle (LAV) is an eight-wheeled, amphibious infantry fighting vehicle. It mounts an M242 Bushmaster 25mm chain gun and two 7.62mm machine guns. It has a crew of three: a vehicle commander, gunner, and driver. *Defense.imagery.mil 040806-M-7719F-020*

CHAPTER 7

Once More into the Breach

CHARLIE COMPANY, 1ST BATTALION, 4TH MARINE REGIMENT

CAPTAIN MATTHEW MORRISSEY'S CHARLIE Company occupied a defensive line along Diagonal Road, facing west toward the Old City and the Imam Ali shrine. During the night, Morrissey received orders to commence an 0500 attack to battalion Objective One, a series of four- and five-story hotel and store complexes on the southwest corner of the cemetery, immediately adjacent to Ring Road, which surrounded the Old City. It was about as heavily urbanized an area as you can get in Najaf. Objective One was selected because it would give the battalion a good avenue of approach to penetrate the key east-west roads that led into the Imam Ali shrine. Charlie Company was designated the main effort and was beefed up with the Bravo Company platoon, the 81mm Mortar Platoon, and the tank platoon, giving it a pretty sizable force.

The company's tired men were roused well before dawn in preparation for the attack. "When we woke up, it's like 0430, and the sun wasn't even up," Wallace recalled. "We're beat, and so are the lieutenant and the staff sergeant." Very few of the men had slept the night before. "We [Wallace and Jenkins] rotated the watch all night long. We stayed awake, anxious to see what the next day was going to bring. We're sitting there thinking, 'What's going to happen next?'"

An up-armored Humvee cautiously moves through the cemetery as an air strike hits militia positions further ahead. Note the jumbled nature of the terrain. Without infantry support, the vehicles would be extremely vulnerable to RPGs. *Maj. Michael S. Wilbur, USMC*

Sellars gathered his squad leaders. "The lieutenant calls us over," Wallace said. "We all go sit around him, and he's like, 'OK, this is what we're going to do. The Abrams [M1A1 tank] is going to lead the way down Diagonal Road, and the platoon is going to follow behind.'" Sellars organized the platoon in a V formation, two squads up—Wallace's squad on the right, Jenkins's squad on the left—and one squad following in trace.

"Right then a machine gun opens up," Wallace said. "And it's like right in front of us, and all the 3rd Platoon opens up. And then the mortars started. We were like, 'Oh, crap, here we go again!' "

Charlie Company crossed the line of departure right on schedule. Sellars remembered "getting on line and pushing south-southwest down Diagonal Road behind the tanks."

"My platoon was up on the road," he said. "Lt. Seth Moulton's platoon [was] on the west side of the road, and the Bravo platoon on the east side."

One of the Bravo Marines, Cpl. Joshua Morris, recalled, "I was moving up and down my line of guys when I saw muzzle flashes coming out of a minaret window. I dumped over a half a mag [magazine] into the guy. The flashes stopped." To make sure the enemy fighter was dead, he directed Lance Cpl. Nathan Stocking to fire an M-203 round into the window. "It was the best shot I've ever seen," he said. The shooter never reappeared, and the platoon pressed deeper into the cemetery.

Corporal Morris ended up close to one of the roads, where he took a knee to catch his breath. "I looked down and noticed that I was kneeling on top of something buried in the ground," he said. "The thing had wires leading in and out in both directions." He stared at the strand for a few moments until he finally realized he was kneeling on an improvised explosive device (IED). As sniper rounds cracked overhead, he knew he had to do something quickly or risk the possibility of an explosion in the midst of his men.

"I made a bite in the wires and tried using my bayonet to cut them," he said. "My hands were too sweaty for a tight grip, so I had to wrap the wires around my hand, pull them taught across a rock by my foot, and whack away. I was covered with sweat, the adrenalin was pumping through me, and I damn near crapped myself . . . but I eventually cut through it."

At one point, Lieutenant Sellers went forward to coordinate his platoon's movement with Lieutenant Thomas via the tank-infantry phone, located on the back of the vehicle. "We decided that at the corner, I would take my platoon into the cemetery," Sellers recalled. As the platoon started into the maze of crypts, it came under fire from several hilltop buildings. "They're looking down on us. We were really pinned down, a lot of fire from rooftops—snipers and RPGs. The RPGs were horrible. I mean, they exploded about thirty to forty meters above our heads, like it was a fireworks show." Moran could see the RPGs. "They looked like a stream of smoke coming at me and had a sound like sizzling bacon—*shizz*, boom!"

Within minutes, the company was also hit by mortar fire. "That's what most of my casualties came from," Sellars said. "It was very effective . . . but my guys were just plain lucky. Most of [their wounds] were not serious." He had a pet theory regarding indirect fire. "It doesn't matter if you run or if you stay, the mortar is going to land where it's going to land. I think they're very ineffective—knock on wood—unless they land right on top of you."

However, a battalion report noted that the mortar platoon was not so lucky. "During the late afternoon, enemy mortars adjusted onto the 81mm Mortar Platoon's defensive line and accurately fired repeated barrages into the platoon for several hours. The platoon suffered five casualties, including Cpl. Roberto Abad who was killed by a direct hit on his position."

First Sergeant LeHew braved the enemy fire to supervise the treatment and evacuation of the casualties. In one instance, a report noted, "he bypassed the battalion casualty collection point and took it upon himself to personally evacuate a Marine with a sucking chest wound all the way back to the FOB where the wounded man could receive more intensive care."

The enemy also targeted the main supply route.

Bronze Star Citation

Sergeant Justin D. LeHew

The President of the United States takes pleasure in presenting the Bronze Star to Justin D. LeHew: "For heroic achievement in connection with combat operations against the enemy as Company First Sergeant, Company C, Battalion Landing Team 1/4, 11th Marine Expeditionary Unit (Special Operations Capable), I Marine Expeditionary Force from 5 to 27 August 2004, in support of Operation IRAQI FREEDOM II. While defending against a Mahdi Militia attack on Iraqi security forces, the Company came under intense mortar, rocket, sniper, and machine-gun fire at Revolutionary Square, in the heart of Najaf, Iraq. First Sergeant Lehew fearlessly moved about the battlefield to points of contact. On three occasions, he directed the fires of vehicle-mounted weapons against the enemy snipers and militia attempting to penetrate the real lines of the company. For six hours, he repeatedly moved back and forth under heavy sniper fire and mortar attack, ensuring safety and inspiring Marines. During the heavy fighting in the Najaf cemetery, he moved to assist in the treatment and evacuation of nine wounded Marines and three killed in action. His timely decision-making made the difference between life and death for two of these Marines. Throughout this 22-day battle, his decisive leadership and courage against a determined foe inspired the Marines under his charge and led the Battalion's assault deep into enemy territory. By his zealous initiative, courageous actions, and exceptional dedication to duty, First Sergeant Lehew reflected great credit upon himself and upheld the highest traditions of the Marine Corps and the United States Naval Service.

"All the intersections were registered for mortars," Borneo said, adding, "We would just stay out of them, and we would be all right."

On the second day, the militia brought a new weapon into play, the 120mm mortar, whose explosive power was vastly different from the 60mm and 82mm mortars it used on the first day. "We had a number of Marines wounded from the 60s, but they just don't shake the earth and blow you away like the 120s," Mayer recalled. "When the 120 mortars rain down on you, your respect for mortars goes way up. It's a life changing event!" The 120mm mortar seemed to be "deadly accurate." Many of the battalion's officers thought the heavy mortars were being manned by Iranians, but could not verify that. "The 120s were our greatest threat," Mayer said, "and they became our number one target."

Hospital Corpsman Benjamin Jensen recalled the first casualty he took care of:

A 120mm mortar hit, and I heard a Marine yelling. I ran toward him just as a second one hit and knocked me to the ground. When I got to the man, he was lying face down. "Get me out of here," he moaned. I rolled him over and saw bleeding. He was a little younger than me—maybe eighteen or nineteen. He started screaming in pain. I cut his cammies off. He had a lot of shrapnel wounds. The femoral artery was hemorrhaging. A big chunk of his ankle was missing. Shrapnel had blown through his other knee and shot through his elbow and into his rib cage. I used a tourniquet and pressure dressings to stop the bleeding and get him stabilized.

Jensen helped evacuate the seriously wounded man. "Just as I was coming back, another mortar hit," he said. "A sergeant in my platoon fell. I lifted his head, and my fingers kind of sank inside. A chunk of shrapnel had come through the back of his skull. He was dead before we got him out. Jensen suffered a great deal sorrow over the death of the sergeant.

"Everyone I treated, I knew. They're my friends," he recalled sadly. "It's tough to deal with losing them. You just try to get through it."

Sergeant McManus also vividly recalled the mortar fire: "At first they were about seventy-five to a hundred meters away from us, and then, all of a sudden, two rounds were right on top of us, which absolutely shook us up." He turned to see if everyone was OK. "The next thing I knew, I was slammed into a wall and actually fell into a crypt. I hit my chin on the base as I fell and ended up twisted and not being able to move." He lay on top of his rifle, with the muzzle jammed into his stomach, at the bottom of the stairs, about three feet underground. "I couldn't feel my legs and remembered thinking, 'Oh man, that really hurt!' I rolled over, and then realized I couldn't get up. And that's when it really hit me. My back started throbbing."

His men ran over to help him. "Hey, Sergeant, are you OK?" one yelled.

They tried to lift him out of the grave. "I had instant pain in my back that shot down my body," McManus said. "I thought my back was broken because I had absolutely no feeling in my legs." A corpsman was finally able to lift him out of the hole and place him on a stretcher. Heavy enemy fire prevented a vehicle evacuation, so he had to be hand carried out of the cemetery, which took almost an hour. "I was put in the back of a Humvee with another Marine who had a sucking chest wound," he recalled regretfully, "and evacuated to the FOB." McManus was air evacuated to the United States, where he underwent a long period of rehabilitation before being returned to duty.

In addition to being hit with the mortars, Charlie Company received fire from several snipers that were positioned on the rooftops. "They were hiding behind big advertisement signs and taking out our Marines," Lieutenant Colonel Apicella said. "We lost a couple of men." Lance Corporal Larry L. Wells from Sellars's platoon was one of them. "He was the only Marine that I lost in the whole battle," Sellars said. "He was shot in the neck and killed."

A report from Reconnaissance Platoon said, "The Militia made semi-effective use of snipers . . . [T]hey were obviously trained in the concept of urban hides and used them effectively by setting back into the buildings in the shadows away from direct observation. They may have used sheets and cloth to conceal their positions." The report also noted, "Enemy snipers are also coordinating their efforts . . . [O]ne sniper draws fire and when friendlies respond, another engages them from another direction."

The tankers were not immune to the heavy fire, either. Lt. Russell Thomas was hit in the arm by a piece of shrapnel. "I opened the hatch to assess the situation, and all of a sudden a mortar round hit to the left of our tank, and I was hit," Thomas recalled.

Lieutenant Birdzell and First Sergeant LeHew were in the road behind the tank when the mortar round exploded.

"I saw him [Thomas] go down in the hatch, and I knew he had been hit," LeHew said. "I got on the tank phone and confirmed he had been wounded."

Moran recalled thankfully, "It was a flesh wound that didn't hit any bone—a great injury."

Thomas was rather matter-of-fact about the injury: "My loader and gunner put a dressing on my arm. Within a few seconds, a corpsman and a first sergeant appeared and told me I had to go to the aid station for a tetanus shot."

LeHew recalled the incident somewhat differently. "I told Lieutenant Thomas to get his happy ass out of the tank so I could treat his wound. It was a clean wound, right through the meaty portion of his bicep. Good thing he was big boy."

Birdzell loaded Thomas in his vehicle and took him to the forward medical-battalion aid station, where he got a shot. Within half an hour, he was back in the fight.

The tanks continued down Diagonal Road toward an intersection with Route Hartford. "The biggest buildings in the city overlooked that intersection," Moran remarked. "As the tanks pulled up to it, every enemy shooter that had an RPG, a rifle, or mortar focused on them."

GBU-12

The Guided Bomb Unit-12, often called a smart bomb, utilizes a MK82 five hundred-pound, general-purpose warhead, which is guided by a beam of laser energy reflected off the target. According to the manufacturer, Raytheon, its circular error probable is only 3.6 feet (as one wag pointed out, it will not just hit a small building, but go through its window). The GBU-12 weighs over six hundred pounds, measures approximately eleven feet long and eleven inches in diameter, and costs $19,000. It has a range of more than eight nautical miles (14.8 kilometers).

Thomas exclaimed, "We took the most intense fire since we've been in Iraq! I could see rounds impacting on our tanks. There were so many mortars and RPGs raining down on us that I couldn't see my other tanks in front of me. I just can't adequately describe how much fire we were receiving." He estimated that in the first hour of the fight, his platoon saw more action than it did during the entire time it was deployed in liberating Iraq. "We were sustaining heavy impacts by RPGs and 120mm mortars. They were walking them onto our positions and firing for effect," he said.

The tanks were forced to stay on the road, making it much easier for the enemy to work up a firing solution. "The road became a linear target," Thomas said. "They used indirect fires in a superb manner; they would walk rounds right onto our tanks."

Thomas believed the militia's forward observers (FOs) were located in the seven-story hotels in the Old City. "That's where they had a position above the street, where they could look down on us," he recalled. "Their fire for effect was four to five rounds from two to five tubes that were zeroed in. We suspect they had FOs from Iran or some other country." But he was hindered in his response to the enemy fire: "Our rules of engagement required positive ID, so we would only fire when we had insurgents in our sights."

Individual fighters could not resist shooting at the steel monsters. "We could see the enemy come out, get down on one knee, elevate the RPG launcher forty-five degrees to maximize the range on the weapon, and fire," Thomas said. Those militiamen lucky enough to escape the deadly 7.62mm and .50-caliber return fire were targeted by the tank's 120mm gun. "If they took cover behind walls," Thomas related, "we would fire the main gun through it."

Because of the terrific heat, members of the tank platoon were rotated by section back to the rear. During one of the rotations, a one-hour gap

An M1A1 Abrams main battle tank, named after Gen. Creighton W. Abrams. Here, its main gun, a 120mm smoothbore cannon, persuades the militia that shooting at it is not a good idea. *Defenseimagery.mil 041210-M-8205V-027*

developed, during which no tanks were available. "I could see the militia charging our lines headed for the gap created by the missing tanks," Lieutenant Colonel Mayer recalled. "I directed my PSD [personal security detachment] to take the gun trucks and fill in until the tanks returned. I remember watching with great concern as enemy mortars, machine-gun fire, and RPGs impacted around the vehicles as they moved into position at the front of our lines. Thank the good Lord that none of the Marines were hurt."

Lieutenant Birdzell said tactfully, "None of my guys were too pleased with pretending we were a group of tanks while sitting on Diagonal Road while mortars landed all around us."

Corporal Wallace remembered taking constant sniper fire. "You couldn't poke your head up without getting a round impacting right next to you," he said. The Marines returned a heavy volume of fire. Wallace recalled pointing to a particular window where he saw a militiamen firing on them. "The SAW gunners just kept dumping rounds into the window."

Sellars was lucky enough to have a tank close by. "I got on the tactical radio and asked Thomas, 'Can you put a round through that bitch?' " Sellars took quite a bit of razzing for that communication faux paux, but under the circumstances, he was forgiven for the breach of radio discipline. The tank responded to his direction. "I'd just go, 'Window on the right, fire.' The tanker would say, 'Roger,' and he'd take the shot. If I needed to adjust, I'd

A 500-pound bomb blast. All the bombs dropped in Najaf were precision guided to eliminate collateral damage as much as possible. Massive firepower was used rather than risk American lives in an attempt to dig out the enemy. *Maj. Michael S. Wilbur, USMC*

say, 'Next window, right and down.' When we were done with that building, we'd shift buildings."

A large oil tank on the top of one building burst into flame. "We think a guy was shooting from behind it the entire time," Wallace remarked off-handedly. "After Lance Corporal Wells was hit, I felt almost a primal happiness that the building's on fire . . . I hope the guy cooked."

Borneo brought his CAAT section into play. "Charlie Company was getting pretty accurate sniper fire from inside the buildings," he recalled, "and it was stopping their forward progress." His up-armored Humvees moved in to provide support. "We started using the MK19 to mark the windows we thought the enemy was shooting from," Borneo said.

Charlie Company would observe and call in corrections. "OK, window to the left," the observer would call, confirming the target. "OK, that's the one," he'd say after a stream of heavy-caliber bullets hit it.

On one occasion, Lance Cpl. Daniel Barker shot a TOW missile right through a window 1,800 meters away, where a sniper was hiding. "A beautiful shot," Borneo exclaimed. "I can't tell you for a fact that the guy died, but I know that no more fire came from there. Another time, we noticed a guy with binoculars peering out of a window. He appeared to be adjusting fires. Every time we saw him pop his head up, a minute later mortar rounds hit us. We put another TOW into [his window], killing eight militiamen."

A sequence of photos showing the effects of five-hundred-pound bombs impacting on militia positions. *Maj. Michael S. Wilbur, USMC*

The objective Charlie Company had been assigned was more than it could chew. "The company was looking at having to clear out probably five or six multistory buildings in the face of massed enemy fire. It was a daunting task," Moran admitted. In the cold light of day, the battalion may have overestimated what the reinforced company could accomplish. "It was a funny phenomenon that when you look at the map," Moran explained "You don't really get a feel for the three-dimensional aspects of the battle-field. It's a perspective problem. What looks like [it] may be a company objective on a map is actually a battalion objective."

By afternoon, there was a degree of uncertainty about whether the attack should be fully prosecuted. "We're starting to realize that we were rapidly using up our combat power," Moran said. "We just didn't have the number of units to control the battlespace." The battalion decided to hold its positions and pound the buildings that overlooked their lines with airstrikes.

"We dropped some of them with five-hundred-pound bombs," Sellars noted.

Captain Gibbons, call sign Chimp, Charlie Company's FAC, brought in sortie after sortie of fixed-wing and helicopter gunship support. He was given the nickname "the Man," because of his ability to pinpoint targets. "If

Dust and debris boil up from the effects of a 500-pound bomb. Another bomb can just be seen in the upper left, heading for the target. *Defenseimagery.mil 041110-M-2789C-011*

he hadn't been with us," Wallace exclaimed, "we probably would have lost a lot of people. He leveled buildings right and left."

"Marine and air force aircraft, F-16s, F-15s, and Harriers dropped GBU-12 [Guided Bomb Unit-12] laser-guided five-hundred-pound bombs," Moran reported. The bombs' destructive power never failed to hearten the men on the ground.

"It's a great feeling," Wallace related, "when you know there could be thirty militiamen in a building, and you see that fixed-wing plane come in, drop his load, and the building just collapses. It was awesome!"

Not to be outdone, HMM-166 skids "were shooting everything," Glen Butler said. "Rockets, missiles, and bullets—sortie after sortie."

The MEU received a tip from an Iraqi that a certain building in the cemetery served as a militia command center and logistics point. A request was sent up the chain of command to hit the building with heavy air-delivered ordnance. The request was approved. Two aircraft swept in and dropped four one-thousand-pound bombs on the target. "The building was no more," the battalion report noted.

"The pilots were amazing at what they could do," Sellars recalled after watching the building pancake floor by floor. He related a story of watching one of his men lobbing 40mm grenades at a sniper, who was well out of range. "I'm heckling the guy, just as he shoots another grenade. Unbeknownst to us, an F-18 drops a five-hundred-pounder at the same time and levels the

Iraqi Resistance Report

Aws al-Khafaji, the director of the Muqtada al-Sadr office, reported that the religious leader was wounded during the American bombardment of a fortified position in which he was staying. After the attack, he was taken to an undisclosed location.

ش مهدينة أنتصر بأبن الصدر

A Mahdi Militia poster encouraging the faithful to fight for al-Sadr. The rumor that he had been wounded could not be verified, nor could his exact location during the fighting. Al-Sadr was convinced that the United States was targeting him. *Maj. R. Bruce Sotire, USMC*

building. The amazed Marine looked at his M-203 and then the building, probably thinking, 'This is one hell'va weapon!'"

Abbas Fadhel was a member of the Mahdi Army's Ahmed al-Sheibani company, which defended the cemetery. He recalled, "The bombing continued day and night. We saw the graves being demolished and our companions killed. We buried the martyrs without washing them because they were martyrs and the weather was very hot." (Muslims traditionally wash their dead before burying them, but there was little water in the cemetery, and bodies rapidly decomposed in the heat.)

He also told of how the militiamen were being supplied: "The water came in bottles, and our food was biscuits twice a day, though in that situation we did not have much appetite. I saw two cars come from Fallujah with humanitarian aid. We found that there was food on top and weapons underneath." Another member of Fadhel's unit pointed out that they used the cemetery because its size made it difficult for the Americans to find them.

The enemy units averaged between fifteen and seventeen men. They moved cautiously at night because they were afraid to reveal their positions. "We were not able to sleep at night, and our food, when we could get it, was very simple," Fadhel said. He described the intense street fighting: "We used snipers, mortars, and Katyusha rockets. The Americans stayed inside their tanks when we tried to hit them from many different directions. The Americans destroyed the shops and buildings, so Najaf became like a city of ghosts. Fighters that came from Fallujah were useful because they had also fought the Americans and were experienced in street-fighting tactics."

At one point in the battle, the militiamen were told that al-Sadr had been injured. "One morning a rumor spread that Sayyid Muqtada had been killed, and some fighters retreated, but others fought even harder," Fadhel said. "Then in the afternoon, Muqtada came and visited the fighters, his hand wrapped in a white bandage. He fought with us, and we saw him hold an RPG and fire it at the American tanks. He was always turning up during the battle, though he kept his movements secret. No one knew where he was going in the dark alleyways of the city. He used to give misleading hints about his movements to confuse the enemy, who unfortunately were not only Americans."

In an effort to take the pressure off his outgunned men, Captain Morrissey asked the Weapons Platoon and the LAR Platoon for support. CAAT-Alpha and CAAT-Bravo sections put the enemy positions under fire with their .50-caliber machine guns and TOW missile systems. The LAR Platoon joined in with its 25mm cannon and 7.62-caliber machine guns. The battalion report noted, "The additional firepower, along with the CAS and artillery support finally shut down the militia's RPGs, small arms and automatic weapons fire." The report also singled out the actions of three Marines: "Corporal Mazzola and Lance Corporal Carlsen silenced several sniper positions, while Corporal Cater, who had only minutes earlier had been shot in the shoulder, destroyed two machine gun bunkers with deadly accurate TOW shots."

In the close fighting, Cpl. Greg Confer came face to face with an armed militiaman that had been shooting at him. "The guy didn't move. He just stood there. It was him or me. I'm just pretty happy that it was me," he recalled gratefully.

Charlie Company was forced to go to ground, seeking cover behind the brick-and-mortar tombstones and mausoleums. "We actually ended up moving a little further back toward Diagonal Road, where we had a better defensive position," Wallace pointed out.

Thomas also pulled his tanks back to where they could support Charlie Company. In one notable incident, a tank round hit an air-conditioning unit on top of six-story building. The resulting explosion sent a huge fireball several more stories into the air. Thomas remembered thinking, "I'm going to be relieved!"

Instead of a rebuke, Mayer radioed him with an atta boy: "Good shot, well done." Thomas also received a rousing cheer from the Marines around his tank.

ALPHA COMPANY, 1ST BATTALION, 4TH MARINE REGIMENT

Alpha Company jumped off on schedule and by 0900 was deep in the cemetery. Moran said the company used "a good combination of maneuvers to identify enemy positions, make contact, back off, fix them in place with machine-gun and mortar fire, and then destroy them with aviation."

At one point, however, the company ran into a militia man with a machine gun in a minaret. Sotire recalled, "It was right in the middle of the

An AH-1W SuperCobra attack helicopter flying over the cemetery. It is armed with four Hellfire missiles, two TOW antitank missiles, a rocket pod, and three to four hundred rounds of 20mm ammunition—a formidable weapons platform. *Defenseimagery.mil DM-SD-04-16323*

Bronze Star Citation

Gunnery Sergeant Richard S. Synovec

Heroic service while serving as Company Gunnery Sergeant, Company A, Gunnery Sergeant Richard S. Synovec performed his duties in an exemplary and highly professional manner. He frequently exposed himself to direct and indirect fire while conducting combat resupply, casualty evacuation and detainee processing. Additionally, he provided combat leadership and firepower on the front lines by directing vehicle mounted heavy and medium machine guns to cover the unit's movements, isolate the enemy, and attack by fire as he assisted in the destruction of a strongly held enemy position that resulted in several enemy casualties. His noteworthy accomplishments, perseverance, and total devotion to duty reflected great credit upon him and upheld the highest traditions of the Marine Corps and the United States Naval Service.

---

company—shooting right at me—and we couldn't get by." He reviewed his options: set up a base of fire and try to get close enough to knock out the gun, or pull back and hit it with air strikes. Sotire chose the second option. "We hit it with Cobras, TOWs, and rockets and destroyed the position." The company moved on, clearing the cemetery as it advanced.

"A big figure in this battle was our chaplain, Father Paul Shaughnessy, a Catholic priest," Moulton recalled. "He was in the cemetery with us, constantly walking up and down the lines, encouraging the Marines, completely unfazed by the rockets and mortars. He was exactly like the chaplain you see in World War II movies."

Alpha Company's FAC requested an air strike in front of the company's position. Sotire approved the mission, provided it was parallel to the line of advance—standard operating procedure in case the aircraft dropped short. "The FAC said, 'I got it, I got it,'" Sotire remembered. "I saw a fire team go into a building about fifty meters ahead of me, when suddenly a helicopter gunship comes right over my shoulder. The FAC yelled, 'Dry run, dry run!'" into his radio. It was too late. The helicopter opened fire with its cannon. "Abort! Abort!" Sotire yelled at the FAC, hoping it was in time to stop the helicopter's wingman from making the same mistake. In the depths of despair, Sotire suddenly observed the fire team stumble out of the partially destroyed building. "What the hell hit us!" one exclaimed, woozy and shaken from the close call. Sotire strongly counseled the FAC, who "became much more cautious" afterward.

An aerial photo of the escarpment, with the Imam Ali shrine in the background, after an airstrike causes a large building fire. The dry lake is in the foreground. *Lt. Col. Glen G. Butler, USMC*

By that evening, Alpha Company had reached its limit of advance. As it pushed farther into the graveyard, Gunnery Sgt. Richard S. Synovec kept supplies moving forward to maintain the momentum of the attack. On one of his supply trips, he spotted a suspicious-looking circular shape in a stone wall. He pointed it out to Sotire, saying, "Is that what I think it is? I think we need to recon this by fire."

Sotire watched as Synovec pulled out an M-203 grenade that had "Have a nice day" and a smiley face drawn on it in black magic marker. Synovec fired, and the grenade arched behind the wall and exploded. A wounded enemy combatant staggered out with his hands in the air. Upon inspection, the dark circular shape turned out to be the mouth of a 106mm recoilless rifle that was pointed down the company's axis of advance. Synovec's vigilance and shooting skill undoubtedly saved Marine lives.

RECONNAISSANCE PLATOON, 1ST BATTALION, 4TH MARINE REGIMENT

Captain Steve Kintzley's Reconnaissance Platoon anchored the battalion's right flank in the amusement park on the north side of Route Favre. During the assault into the cemetery, the platoon kept pace with Alpha Company. The battalion after-action report noted, "The platoon came under hostile enemy mortar, machine gun, and small-arms fire. Close air support (CAS) was precisely employed on several occasions by the Alpha Company FAC to effectively assist in neutralizing the enemy."

Upon reaching its limit of advance, the platoon set up a defensive position. While settling in, Sgt. John G. Avak spotted what appeared to be a gun tube behind a wall. Quickly reacting, he shot several 40mm grenades from his M-203 grenade launcher and scored direct hits in and around the weapon. A detail cautiously moved forward and discovered an SPG-9, 73mm recoilless rifle. Dead crewmen lay in and around the gun. The detail found one live Iraqi, whom it took prisoner.

EYEWITNESS TO MAYHEM

Correspondent Philip Robertson made the dangerous trip to Najaf in a hired taxi. A few miles from the city, he could plainly see a thick cloud of black smoke rising from the western suburbs and drifting toward the Imam Ali shrine. He followed the main north-south highway until he reached the amusement park, where he turned west on a secondary road toward the Old City.

As Robertson's car approached the cemetery, several dust-covered militiamen, toting RPGs over their shoulders, slowly walked by. Their faces were expressionless—eyes distant and empty of emotion. Robertson was surprised by their apparent disinterest. Normally, the car would have been stopped, the passengers ordered out and harshly interrogated. Instead, his car was waved on, into the cemetery.

He quickly grasped the significance of the militiamen's lethargy when he saw the graveyard. It was a shambles from the fighting. Tombs, mausoleums, and crypts were blown up and destroyed. Rubble littered the ground. The acrid smell of cordite, mingled with the stench of death, filled his nostrils.

Later, Robertson crouched on the roof of a hotel in the dark, watching a two-hour gun battle. He saw lines of machine-gun tracers pierce the night sky and then float through the air until they burnt out. Flashes, followed by the heavy crump of detonations, thundered in the cemetery as each side sought out the other. Ominously, small-arms fire erupted throughout the city; Robertson later found out it was from anti-al-Sadr forces attacking Mahdi fighters in a deadly game of hide and seek. The deserted streets and alleyways became battlegrounds—sniper versus sniper. Iraqi versus Iraqi.

Robertson met the middle-aged Iraqi owner of a small bookstore. "Al Mahdi Army fighters have made a point of threatening his life," Robertson said.

"It happened all the time," the scared man told Robertson. A Muqtada gunman had told the storeowner, "We know you are a spy for the Americans. You are worth $10,000 if we kill you."

"That is their style," the merchant told Robertson. "The al-Mahdi fighters think everyone is a spy who is not part of their organization." He showed Robertson a photo of a man in Iraqi clothes who had been hung. A sign described the dead man as a collaborator. "They are proud of it. They published it themselves," he said in disgust, referring to the Mahdi Army. He then pointed to a building a few blocks away, where people were executed after an Islamic court found them guilty of spying. "Najaf is dying," he said mournfully.

Correspondent Nermeen al-Mufti made his way into the city in company with an escort of men affiliated with al-Sadr. They traveled off the beaten track because the highway was lined with checkpoints and frequently targeted. The road was heavily traveled by buses and small trucks "carrying pictures of al-Sadr and his martyred father, along with green and black flags." Al-Mufti claimed the vehicles were transporting food and medical supplies that had been donated by the residents of Baghdad to al-Sadr's supporters. His vehicle passed through Revolutionary Circle without incident, although he indicated, "One is acutely aware of the U.S. forces."

He was able to enter the shrine "after being questioned and searched." He made note of "hundreds of men inside . . . young and old men with machine guns, wearing green and black bandanas . . . ready to defend the holy place." He noted that many of the new arrivals were still dressed in civilian clothes; some were even barefoot. The defenders assured him that they never fired from inside the shrine as a mark of respect for its holy status. They claimed that photos of firing that emanated from the shrine were false and were computer generated by the Americans.

Al-Mufti observed a number of wounded militiamen lying in the courtyard. He was told it was hard to get them to the hospital, which had also been shelled, according to the militia. Al-Mufti saw only a single volunteer doctor. While al-Mufti was inside, a man was killed near one of the gates to the shrine. "A wave of grief washed over the shrine," he said.

The militia wanted to believe rumors. "One hears of the many miracles of the Mahdi Army and of divine intervention during the battle," he noted. One of the stories he heard told of a mortar that started firing on its own. Al-Mufti asked who was reloading it. His question was "disdainfully ignored."

Ghaith Abdul-Ahad of the *Guardian* filed a report from inside the city: "One of Najaf's oldest religious schools . . . a few yards away from the main Imam Ali mosque . . . had been converted into a makeshift hospital and morgue. Wounded fighters lay on the floor . . . [A] pile of used, bloodied bandages and stretchers were piled in the corner." He observed nine bodies wrapped in blankets. "The injuries of the dead said a lot about the precision of American snipers," he wrote.

Scott Baldauf, South Asia bureau chief of the *Christian Science Monitor*, reported on what he had seen. "When we left Najaf, the Friday prayers were just beginning. The message of the prayer was very tense. They were urging the fighters to stay, hold on, and fight to the end. 'God is on our side' was a phrase that was repeated again and again." From his location, he saw aircraft strafing militia positions and had just received confirmation that a helicopter (piloted by Steve Mount) had been shot down.

Baldauf indicated that many of the residents of the city had not been allowed to leave because there was no transportation in or out, and there were so many roadblocks, leaving would have been difficult even if transport had been available. "Ad hoc barriers—a street light post, lines of rocks, trashcans—have been left in the road." He reached a residential neighborhood in the center of the city and was flagged down by a man who warned him that there was heavy fighting just down the street.

Baldauf and two companions took refuge in a Good Samaritan's home. "The battle lines kept changing around us," he recalled. "At one point a team of Mahdi Army fighters drove into the neighborhood, set up a mortar, fired two rounds, and then put the mortar tube back in the car and took off—all in just under a minute." Baldauf and his companions held their breath, afraid of Marine counter mortar fire. Later that afternoon, the fighting stopped, and they took advantage of the lull to drive to the main hospital to get a feel for the intensity of the fighting. At the main hospital, civilian cars were bringing in the wounded. They watched as an injured man was wheeled in bleeding profusely. An injured policeman was led in. When he saw Baldauf, he became belligerent and shouted insults. A doctor interceded, but told the journalist, "Please leave now. I cannot protect you from the people inside."

Before leaving, Baldauf tried to determine how many casualties there had been. "We got different stories from the same hospital," he said. "One doctor told me there were about fifty dead. However, the official record counted only eleven." Many casualties were sent directly to the morgue, "[s]o the bookkeeping may not have been keeping up with the death toll."

After leaving the hospital, Baldauf's crew drove into the Old City, which he thought "was perfect for street fighting: narrow alleys, densely clustered concrete homes, plenty of nooks to provide cover from American helicopters or passing armored vehicles." He was surprised to see residents watching the fighting, despite the danger. As helicopters fired rockets into the cemetery, they ran to the street corners to see the explosions.

As Baldauf's and his two companions approached the shrine, they ran into small squads of Mahdi militiamen. "They brought their own weapons—mostly Kalashnikovs, but a few RPGs as well," he recounted, "and have been receiving food and water from local residents." Just outside the walls of the shrine, Baldauf "observed hundreds of fighters sitting on the ground in front of shuttered shops that normally would have been the busiest in the city. They looked exhausted, and surprised to see foreigners."

The three listened to a cleric exhort the fighters through a loudspeaker: "God bless you. You are the righteous citizens. Don't give up. May God give you the strength to win victory against your enemy. God is great!"

NBC Middle East bureau chief Richard Engel had an up-close and personal encounter with the Mahdi Militia while traveling through a poor Shiite district. "I saw the Mahdi Militia," he wrote. "A boy who looked about twelve years old was standing by two burning tires and blocks of wood piled in the center of the road. The boy was waving a pistol telling us to stop." His vehicle stopped, and one of the passengers got out—a serious mistake.

"Five or six gunmen gathered around the open door, suddenly curious about the vehicle," Engel wrote. Engel was forced to get out. His interpreter tried to fast-talk the men into letting them go. Suddenly, there were loud bursts of small-arms fire. "The gunfire scattered the militiamen," Engel said. "They were holding their rifles at their chests, ready to fire. They were hopelessly disorganized and haphazardly pointing their guns at one another, and at us. If one had fired, we would have all been shot."

The aftermath of the fight, as seen from a tank commander's hatch. Two Abrams main battle tanks can be seen on the left, advancing cautiously down the rubble-strewn roadway. *Capt. Mike Throckmorton, U.S. Army*

Engel broke free and jumped back in the armored Jeep Cherokee. "The boy watched me . . . and was now pointing his pistol at me through the glass. The bullet would not have penetrated, but if he'd fired, the shot would surely have excited the other gunmen and triggered what Iraqi soldiers call a 'death blossom,' a bubble of intense gunfire at everyone and everything in the street." The boy finally lowered his pistol and pulled the barrier aside, allowing Engel's car to speed from the area.

Kianne Sadeq, a CNN producer, traveled to Najaf along with ten other correspondents. They were unable to get to the mosque because of heavy sniper fire—from both sides. Sadeq recalled, "Because you don't know where these bullets are flying." A local resident told her that a dead body lay in the street for three days because the snipers were so active that it was impossible to recover it.

The correspondents group was finally able to work its way to the mosque. Sadeq recorded her observations: "The entire street, about 100 to 150 meters leading up to the Imam Ali mosque, is completely destroyed. All the shops—I mean it's completely destroyed. Windows are shattered, the pillars are broken, and stores are shuttered. It's just a ghost land." While inside, she heard constant firing—rocket-propelled grenades, mortar fire. "[A]ll different kinds of loud firing [is] constantly going on . . . [I]t keeps going on and on and on . . ." The mosque appeared to her to have "just minor damage . . . nothing serious."

CHAPTER 8

Painful Negotiations and Fateful Decisions

REPORTS OF THE HEAVY fighting quickly spread throughout Iraq, placing great pressure on Ayad Allawi's fragile government to end the attack. Allawi was said to want to bring al-Sadr into the political system rather than having to fight him. His position was supported by senior members of the government, who threatened to resign. However, there was another faction, including Governor al-Zurufi, that wanted al-Sadr's head and that told the Marines that it was OK to "level the place."

Apicella said, "When I was in the governor's compound, I can't tell you how many Iraqis came up to me and said, 'Why are you guys screwing around? Why don't you just go in and kill them all?' " The hardliners even wanted to demolish the shrine if it would eliminate al-Sadr and his army.

"We'll build another one," they insisted. "We're more worried about getting rid of al-Sadr and the militia than we are about the buildings and the shrine itself."

Brigadier General Dennis J. Hejlik, USMC, was not taken in by the specious talk of the bombing the mosque. "I told Zurufi that it wouldn't be his bombs that destroyed the shrine," he said.

Allawi was caught in the middle. Consequently, the interim government pursued a double-edged policy—negotiations coupled with attacks—in a carrot-and-stick philosophy. On August 11 and again on August 13, the interim government announced a cease-fire so that talks with al-Sadr could get underway. At the same time, MNF-I stopped all offensive operations in the city. Dr. Mowaffaq Rubai'e, the Iraqi national security advisor, arranged a meeting with al-Sadr to review a government-approved list of conditions to stop the fighting.

"Rubai'e stayed at the governor's compound throughout the battle," Hejlik said. "I would periodically brief him on our operations to keep him in the loop, but it was not in the nature of gaining his approval." The negotiations were conducted solely by the Iraqis. "I would get rumors about the negotiations," Hejlik recalled, "but I did not attend them." He was at one meeting in which Rubai'e met Grand Ayatollah al-Sistani. "I was about twenty feet away as the two talked softly," he said. Hejlik thought that al-Sadr may have been there in a group of several Iraqis. "The figure looked like him—a short little dumpy guy with a beard."

The struggle for Najaf was also a test between al-Sadr and Grand Ayatollah al-Sistani's ability to control the Shiite masses. In October 2003, pro–al-Sadr mobs besieged al-Sistani's home, demanding that he leave Iraq and return to Iran. (Al-Sistani was of Iranian descent.) Al-Sistani put out a call for protection, and 1,500 tribesmen responded, surrounding his home and those of other like-minded ayatollahs. One of the defenders had heard the call on the radio. "Suddenly I saw the villagers grabbing their guns and preparing to rush to Najaf. 'Sistani is under attack,' they told me. That was all they needed to know." Al-Sadr was forced to back down.

On the eve of the Marine attack on the city, al-Sistani, who rarely left his home, secretly left Najaf and showed up in London, seeking treatment for an unspecified heart aliment. His absence and subsequent delay in entering a hospital raised questions on the timing of the trip. Patrick Cockburn wrote, "Iraqis interpreted this as tacit permission for the United States to advance into the city."

Ali A. Allawi, a member of the Iraqi Governing Council, agreed: "Al-Sistani was unwilling to provide a layer of protection to al-Sadr by his presence in the city."

"A firm rendezvous point and time were agreed to," Ali Allawi explained. "Just before the mediation party set off for the meeting, the area came under intense bombardment by U.S. Marines, and U.S. Special Forces were seen heading in the direction of the rendezvous." Al-Sadr fled the scene, thinking the meeting was a trap to capture or kill him. The failed negotiations prompted charge and countercharge from the interim government and al-Sadr as to who was at fault. The two sides began a high-stakes confrontation that lasted until August 20, when the two sides met again. Al-Sadr was unwilling to concede, and the talks broke off for the third time.

FATEFUL DECISION

Meanwhile, by the evening of August 6, the battalion had reached a decision point. Iraqi special forces had infiltrated the city and reported there were thousands of militiamen in and around the cemetery and Old City. "We had made it to the edge of the hotels, but the amount of fire was just overwhelming," Mayer said. "We didn't have enough force to go against what we thought were between two and four thousand men."

Moran echoed Mayer's evaluation of the situation. "The enemy was in multistory buildings three hundred meters away, looking down on us," he pointed out. "They were well armed and more than capable of withstanding a company-sized attack. They were willing to die fighting us. We were wearing ourselves out just doing small, limited attacks." The battalion's situation reports flowed upward to the highest level of coalition forces, Multi-National Corps–Iraq.

"We requested reinforcements of at least two battalions," Lieutenant Colonel Johnston said. "I would assume the MEF went back [to U.S. Army general George W. Casey, Multi-National Forces–Iraq] and said, 'Hey, these guys have got a huge fight on their hands. Send in reinforcements.'"

Casey reacted quickly to the request and directed the 1st Cavalry Division (a.k.a., First Team) to send two battalion task forces to Najaf. The division, in turn, ordered its 2nd and 39th Brigades to each provide one of the battalions. Colonel Michael D. Formica, commanding officer, 2nd Brigade, said, "I

General George W. Casey (left), commander of Multi-National Forces–Iraq, authorized two U.S. Army mechanized battalions to reinforce the 11th MEU. The two battalions represented a good portion of his strategic reserve. *Defenseimagery.mil* DA-SD-05-03381

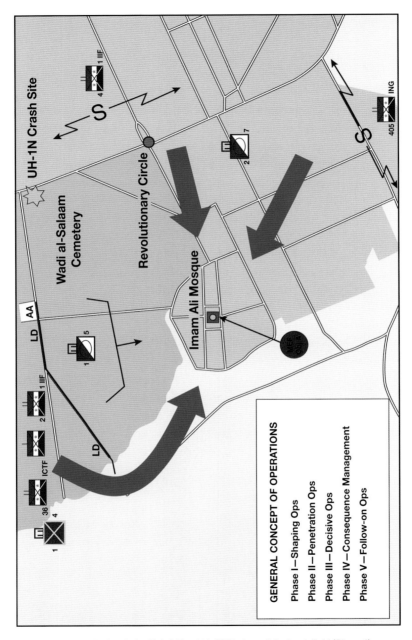

The five stages of the battle for Najaf. The 11th MEU shaped the battlefield (Phase I) to prepare it for the next phase, penetrating the militia defenses (Phase II) for the final attack (Phase III). Phase IV involved rebuilding and repairing damaged and destroyed infrastructure, while Phase V involved training Iraqi forces to take over security of the city. *Patricia Isaacs, from an 11th MEU operational slide*

received a call from the division chief of staff, who told me he needed a battalion task force in eight hours to move to Najaf. I knew who I was going to send. I picked my mech battalion [mechanized infantry], 1st Battalion, 5th Cavalry Regiment, 2nd Brigade Combat Team, 1st Cavalry Division."

The 39th Brigade tasked 2nd Battalion, 7th Cavalry (armor battalion) Regiment, 3rd Brigade Combat Team, 1st Cavalry Division, to support the 11th MEU. Johnston remembered the phone call. "[I'm told,] 'You're going to have 2-7, and they're going to be at your front door in two days.' I'm like, 2-7? What is 2-7? You mean 2nd Battalion, 7th Marines?"

"No," he was told, "Task Force 2-7 Cavalry."

The operation was designated Pacific Thrust, and a special command arrangement was established. The Najaf and Qadisiyah provinces were transferred from the Polish command and temporarily placed under I MEF (a.k.a., MEF Forward), commanded by Brigadier General Hejlik. "General Conway told me to get down there and do two things," Hejlik recalled. "Take the political pressure off Haslam and make sure Marines work for Marines. I drove down there with twenty-five men and set up a headquarters in the governor's compound within fifteen hours of the notification."

Mayer was pleased with the assignment. "Hejlik sat down with me and said, 'I'm not here to lead the tactical fight. I'm here really as a political-military guy to interface with the Iraqi national guard, the Iraqi Ministry of Defense, the governor, and higher headquarters. You and Colonel Haslam fight the fight!' "

On August 9, a high-level strategy meeting was held at the behest of Governor Zurufi at his compound. "We need to finish this quickly," he pleaded.

Historian Francis Kozlowski wrote that attendees included "Allawi, his defense minister, and key coalition military leaders, including General Casey, Lt. Gens. Thomas F. Metz [and] James T. Conway, and Brig. Gen. Dennis J. Hejlik." The conferees decided that the fight was too big for the Polish-led Multinational Division Central South (MND-CS). The Poles simply did not have the experience or the resources to control the fight.

"It resolved a huge issue," Johnston recalled, "because we would have been the only unit in Center South that had an offensive capacity. Based on the Poles rules of engagement, they were not going to go out and attack and quite frankly I couldn't even communicate with the MND-CS. We would have been on our own."

The decision was reached to shift operational control of the battle space to the I Marine Expeditionary Force, headquartered in Fallujah. "Initially,

Lieutenant General Thomas F. Metz, commander, Multi-National Corps–Iraq, whose area of operations included the province of Najaf. *Defenseimagery.mil DM-SD-07-22947*

MNF-I wanted to assign a U.S. Army brigadier general to be in charge of the battle space," Hejlik recounted. "However, Lieutenant General Conway made the case to General Casey, in the strongest terms, that I MEF should control all Marines, and Casey finally agreed." The meeting resulted in "the decision to take down Najaf," Hejlik recalled. There was also general agreement to ease the fire-support approval process and to reduce the restricted zones.

Haslam was quick to declare, "The assignment of Hejlik was great. The distractions he took off me—state department, all the VIPs, the Ministry of Defense—it was the right decision."

Johnston agreed. "The MEF Forward [Hejlik] basically rolled on top of us and provided top cover. They gave me a couple of majors for my '3 shop [operations section] to help me." The MEU was being inundated with requests for information, in addition to trying to control five battalions. "It was unbelievably painful to try and fight the fight and then try to answer all the mail at the same time," Johnston complained. "It was at the point where it was impossible to do all the things we were being asked to do. We were literally working twenty-four hours a day."

Despite Johnston's complaint, Hejlik thought Johnston was "very good at what he did, level headed and aggressive, with a lot of common sense."

The conference also included a large number of embedded media and the TV news channel Al Arabiya, which broadcast live. "It wasn't thirty minutes later when there were mortar rounds landing in the governor's compound, which cut short the discussion," Lieutenant Colonel Apicella exclaimed. Many of the reporters were using cell phones to report the event. Apicella was upset. He told the compound security, "The media can't come in here with cell phones . . . [T]hey can't file their stories as long as there are high value targets here."

The militia was also monitoring the police radios. "You'd sit in the JCC [joint coordination center], and you'd hear them," Apicella said. "They'd be screaming at the IPs [Iraqi police], and the IPs would scream back . . . just all kinds of things on the net . . . little kids laughing, men burping, farting . . . disrupting communications. It was just crazy."

A short time after Hejlik established his headquarters, Mowaffaq Rubai'e, Iraq's national security adviser and a former member of the Iraqi Governing Council, arrived at the compound with his security element. "They looked like thugs," Hejlik recalled. "I gave them a couple of tents, which they used as their headquarters until the final cease-fire."

Rubai'e conducted the interim government's mediation efforts with the "full knowledge of the prime minister, the U.S. embassy, and the MNF command," according to Ali Allawi.

"Rubai'e did all the negotiations," Hejlik noted, "and maintained communication with Allawi [the Iraqi prime minister] on a daily basis." Hejlik sensed that Rubai'e was not a fan of al-Sadr, but continued the dialog with

Brigadier General Dennis J. Hejlik was placed in charge of the forces in Najaf. He colocated with MEU headquarters, but did not get involved in the tactical fight. Instead, he dealt with higher headquarters and the Iraqi government, letting the MEU fight the fight.
Defenseimagery.mil 090617-M-1609K-004

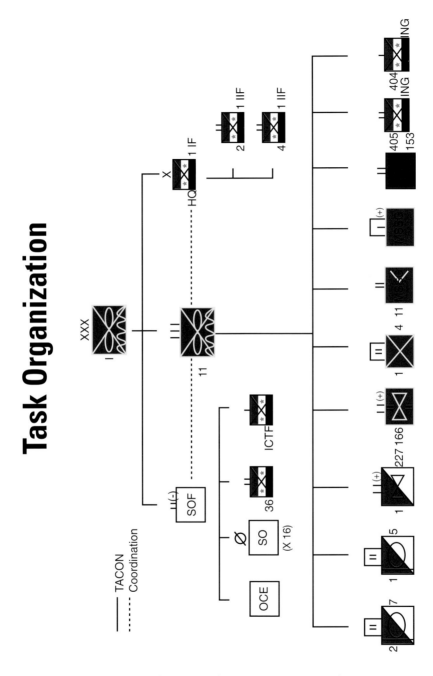

Task Organization

Brigadier General Hejlik's I MEF (MEF Forward) consisted of the 11th MEU (two mechanized cavalry battalions, a Marine infantry battalion, aviation and logistic support, Iraqi national guardsmen), a Special Operations force, and an Iraqi intervention force brigade. *USMC*

An Iraqi Intervention Force (IIF) solider prepares to flexi-cuff a Mahdi Militia suspect. The plastic restraints were an easy and cheap method of immobilizing a detainee's hands.
Defenseimagery.mil DA-SD-07-19831

the cleric in order to resolve the fighting. The Marine general found Rubai'e easy to work with. "I met with him daily to brief him on the situation," Heljik recalled. "Everything went through Rubai'e and then to Generals Conway, Metz, and Casey." Hejlik pointed out, however, that Rubai'e was not privy to some sensitive information and did not have approval authority over tactical decisions.

Hejlik's command consisted of army and Marine ground units, as well as the army's 1st Battalion, 227th Aviation Regiment (Task Force Attack), 4th Brigade Combat Team, 1st Cavalry Division, and several Iraqi units: the 1st Brigade, Iraqi Intervention Force (IIF); the Iraqi 36th Commando Battalion; the Iraqi Counter-Terrorism Force (ICTF); the 405th Iraqi National Guard Battalion; and three Iraqi National Guard companies.

However, the national guard units were not combat ready. Lieutenant Colonel Johnston recalled, [A]ll of a sudden, the Iraqi forces started rolling in. God bless them, but they came in with very little in the way of sustainment." The three national-guard companies had to be supplied with ammunition and equipment before they were ready to perform in an operational role. Because of security concerns in their own areas, they were ordered back to their bases before they could get into the fight. The 405th Battalion was the only one to remain for the entire battle. It performed well in clearing the city following the cease-fire.

Iraqi forces operated with the 11th MEU in a support role. Here, two Iraqi soldiers have detained five suspected Mahdi militiamen by flexi-cuffing them. The Iraqis proved invaluable in interrogating and ferreting out al-Sadr's fighters. *Defenseimagery.mil DA-SD-07-19828*

The BLT initially had a ninety-day plan to train the Iraqi national guard (ING). "Our plan," Mayer pointed out, "was to train them at the individual, platoon, and company level so that in the mid- to late October time frame, they could conduct a battalion-sized attack against the Mahdi Militia with 1/4 in support." He planned on using three ING battalions: the 402nd Battalion, based in Hillah; the 404th Battalion in Diwaniyah; and Najaf's 405th Battalion. Unfortunately, the BLT's training program was thrown into a cocked hat by the start of the fighting on August 5. Because of their lack of training, the ING units were used primarily to man vehicle and tactical-control checkpoints. For example, on August 5, Governor Zurufi ordered the ING and the police to seal off both Kufa and Najaf.

Additionally, small units were used in offensive operations. On August 7, an ING unit killed four militiamen and captured two while raiding al-Sadr's house in Najaf. Five days later, the 36th Commando Battalion and the Iraqi Counter-Terrorism Force (ICTF) conducted a direct-action mission on the Sahlah mosque in Kufa, which resulted in three militiamen killed in action and eight captured. However, the heavy lifting was still done by U.S. forces. "Our confidence in the ING was not the greatest," Johnston remarked, "because we just hadn't fought with them before."

Iraqi Resistance Report

In a report posted at 4:24 p.m. Mecca time, Mafkarat al-Islam reported that a battle was underway between U.S. aggressor forces and supporters of Shi'ite religious leader Muqtada as-Sadr. The U.S. invaders have recently sent reinforcements to the area where they insist they are intent upon arresting or killing as-Sadr.

The decision was made on the morning of August 7 to conduct a retrograde back to FOB Hotel. "We knew we were going to get two cavalry battalions," Haslam recalled, "and we had pretty much accomplished what we needed to do. So I told Mayer to pull out: 'We'll cover the ground you gained with aviation to keep them out of the cemetery.'"

Moran admitted, "We didn't have a well-defined overall objective, and we had pretty much accomplished in three days of fighting what we wanted to do. We pulled back to rest, refit, and redefine our objectives."

The word of the withdrawal made its way through the ranks. Lieutenant Sellars sent a runner to gather the platoon NCOs. Once notified that Sellars and the staff sergeant wanted to talk with him, Wallace worked his way over to the platoon headquarters. He remembered, "We sat down next to the lieutenant, and he's like, 'We're pulling out at 0800.' We're looking like, 'You're kidding us, right?' [Sellars said,] 'No, we're really pulling out.'" The first thing that went through Wallace's mind was a shower. "If you've ever been in 120-degree heat wearing a flak jacket, you develop prickly heat on your back, and it's just the nastiest rash you could ever imagine . . . [E]verybody had it . . . and the only thing that will cure it is a shower."

Sellars was just as ecstatic. "The chance to clean up was a godsend. A shower was nice after being in the midst of people's graves. I fell into a grave up to my armpits. That was kind of nasty, . . . but the whole place was like that. It just smelled like dead people everywhere you went. We wanted to wash that smell off—get it out of your nose."

The battalion withdrew from the cemetery under cover of the tank platoon and Weapons Company. "I didn't see any reason for sitting in the cemetery just continuing to lose people to enemy fire," Mayer said. "We knew by this time that two cav units were coming down, and so we pulled back and staged along Route Miami."

"Alpha Company went first," Moran pointed out, "81's [the 81mm Mortar Platoon] followed and then Charlie, with LAR Platoon covering

The eight-wheeled light armored reconnaissance (LAR) vehicle can travel at more than sixty miles per hour and accelerate from zero to twenty miles per hour in ten seconds. It is armed with a 25mm chain gun, TOW missile system, and two 7.62mm machine guns.
Defenseimagery.mil DM-SD-07-17433

the withdrawal. Weapons Company secured the route and protected the police station."

"We left the cemetery with five men killed in action and sixty men wounded in action," Mayer recalled sadly. For the first time, Sellars's platoon had a moment to think about what they had experienced. "We'd lost Lance Corporal Wells, and it hit a lot of the guys pretty hard . . . [W]e were the only platoon in the company to lose a guy, . . . but the men held each other together."

Morrissey reflected, "You spend eight years training for days like these, and it seems like your entire goal is to get in an environment. But when you get into it, the reality of it smacks you in the face."

1ST BATTALION, 5TH CAVALRY REGIMENT (BLACK KNIGHTS)

Lieutenant Colonel Myles Miyamasu, commanding officer of the army's 1st Battalion, 5th Cavalry Regiment (1-5 Calvalry, mechanized infantry), had just returned from a meeting with a local tribal leader when, as he said, "I get a phone call [from] the brigade commander [Colonel Michael Formica], who said, 'All right, you have something to write on?'"

"Why, sure,'" Miyamasu replied. "Stand by." Miyamasu grabbed the nearest scrap of paper, an *Army Times* subscription blank, thinking that his boss wanted to pass some innocuous information. He acknowledged that he was ready to copy.

"All right," Colonel Formica said, "here's the deal. You're going to deploy as Task Force Najaf within the next twelve to twenty-four hours. You are to take your battalion and report to the 11th MEU." The colonel indicated that a helicopter would land at Miyamasu's position in an hour to fly him to visit his new commander. "We will start sending you combat multipliers as soon as we hang up. What are your questions?"

Miyamasu still not having caught up, stammered, "Sir, am I coming back?"

"Don't know," Formica answered abruptly and hung up.

"That was the warning order—my phone call of approximately one minute," Miyamasu told an army historian. So much for detailed orders.

Slate correspondent Alex Bereson, one of the few reporters embedded with American forces in Najaf, described Miyamasu as "a lean lieutenant colonel, who never seemed to lose his cool or even raise his voice. His sole vice was smoking, so far as I could tell." Bereson was given full access to the tactical operations center (TOC), "a room where a dozen officers sat at computers plotting artillery strikes and mapping suspected enemy locations on a giant flat-panel TV screen." The TOC was manned by representatives of

The insignia of the 1st Cavalry Division was originally approved in 1921 and authorized for wear in 1934. Yellow is the traditional cavalry color, and the horse's head refers to the division's original mounts. Black is symbolic of iron and alludes to the transition from horses to tanks and armor. The black diagonal stripe represents a sword, a mark of military honor. The one diagonal bend, as well as the horse's head, alludes to the division's numerical designation. *U.S. Army Institute of Heraldry*

the battalion's staff sections—personnel, operations, intelligence, logistics, and fire-support coordination—who maintained up-to-the-minute operational status.

The 1st Battalion, 5th Cavalry Regiment, was part of the 2nd Brigade Combat Team of the 1st Cavalry Division. The battalion had been in Iraq for approximately seven months and had four to five months remaining on its deployment. Prior to receiving the one-minute phone call from Formica, the 1-5 Cav had been conducting stability and security operations from Camp Bonzai (named for the 1-5 Cav's battle cry) in the Kadhimyah District of northwest Baghdad. Units of the battalion were kept busy with patrols, cordon and searches of surrounding neighborhoods, and route security for main thoroughfares running through its area of responsibility. Miyamasu

Lt. Col. Myles Miyamasu

The U.S. Army's Lieutenant Colonel Myles Miyamasu assumed command of 1/5 Cavalry at Fort Hood, Texas, in June 2002. He took the battalion through a two-year training cycle before deploying to Iraq. "Predeployment was quite interesting," Miyamasu said, "because the division thought it would be part of the initial offensive." But the division did not receive orders to deploy until December 2003. At that point, Miyamasu had over twenty months as commanding officer. The 11th MEU considered him an extremely competent officer, who knew how to effectively direct his battalion in a fight.

expected to remain in Baghdad for the duration of his time in Iraq, so "the deployment notification caught all of us off guard," he related. "We had no idea that Najaf was in that much of a dire straight."

First Lieutenant Steven D. Stauch echoed his commander's comment: "We had been watching CNN a little bit earlier that day and knew there was some fighting going on, that some Marines had some problems. But, the actual specifics were very unclear."

Despite the surprise, Miyamasu never missed a beat. "I gave a verbal warning order to the staff and talked to the company commanders," he recounted.

Captain Benjamin P. McFall III, Charlie Company commander, remembered, "I was coming in to talk with my battalion commander . . . and all of a sudden I'm told, 'Hey, stop what you're doing. Pack your bags, we're going to Najaf.' My first question was, 'Where is Najaf?'"

Miyamasu learned that two Blackhawk helicopters were on the way to take him for a liaison visit to the 11th MEU headquarters. "I grabbed my S-3 [operations officer], the S-2 [intelligence officer], my FSO [fire support officer], four company executive officers, and ran to the helipad," he said. Within a little more than an hour, he was in Najaf.

Miyamasu and his staff swept into the MEU headquarters, and after the usual introductions, he was suddenly asked by Haslam, "When are you going to be here?"

Somewhat taken back, Miyamasu replied, "Sir, I think I'm supposed to be here in less than twenty-four hours," which seemed to elicit some relief from the Marine staff.

"My Marines had been fighting for three straight days," Lieutenant Colonel Mayer emphasized. "Our mission was to destroy the enemy, and we weren't doing that. We, in turn, were taking casualties ourselves, and I didn't see any good sitting in the cemetery, which was dominated by the Old City and just continuing to lose people to mortar, machine gun, and sniper fire." Mayer requested to pull out of the confines of the cemetery, rearm, refit, rest up, and join the army in a coordinated attack with overwhelming force.

Miyamasu spent about two and a half hours on the ground, trying to get up to speed on the tactical situation. "We had no intelligence prior to our departure from Camp Bonzai," he said. "All we knew was that a helicopter had been shot down and that Muqtada al-Sadr was assembling forces in the Najaf area. We had no idea how many people were down there, nor did we know that the shrine had been taken over by al-Sadr's forces." All he knew for sure was that Haslam wanted him quickly.

"As soon as you get here," the MEU commander said, "you're going into the cemetery."

Miyamasu mentally noted, "It seemed to me like they were in a situation they [the MEU] was struggling to either understand or control." However, "It was made very clear to me that our job was to destroy the militia."

Lieutenant Colonel Johnston conducted a brief for the soldiers using an imagery map of the area. "I rolled it out," he explained, "and with the 1-5 Cav ops officer, I put in boundaries with the usual tactical symbols and told them 'Here's your boundary with 1/4, here's where I need you to go, and here's your limit of advance . . . a kind of frag [fragmentary, vice-detailed plan] order." Johnston pointed out that the "bad guys were fighting from the exclusion zone, with the mosque right in the middle of it." He made the mosque an objective because, "If we could take it back, that would pretty much eliminate the Mahdi Militia's reason for being in Najaf." This initial brief served as the outline for 1-5 Cav's entire nineteen-day fight. "We got some good, mission-type orders," Miyamasu recalled, "but that's about it."

With time rapidly running out, Miyamasu had to leave the meeting to get his battalion on the road. "I left my S-3, S-2, a liaison officer, and the company XOs behind. I directed them to find us a place to stay and to park our vehicles." Upon his arrival back at Camp Bonzai, he found "multipliers coming in from all over . . . five-thousand-gallon fuel trucks, bulldozers, engineers, combat camera, PAO [public affairs officer], and EOD [explosive ordinance disposal] personnel. We didn't have any idea who was supposed to come; they just drove through the gate."

Captain Kevin Badger remembered, "Everybody in the Corps sent assets to Bonzai, which is only one grid square. We had serials on the two or three different roads, trying to organize this gargantuan mass . . . and they're

The 1-5 Cav loaded its Abrams tanks and Bradley fighting vehicles on heavy-equipment transporters (HETs) after receiving the word to deploy to Najaf. HETs are used to transport, deploy, and evacuate tanks, armored personnel carriers, self-propelled artillery, and other heavy vehicles. HETs save wear and tear on the smaller vehicles and using them is more cost-effective than driving the vehicles themselves from place to place. 1-5's move from Camp Bonzai, north of Baghdad, was made without incident. *Defenseimagery.mil 060525-M-3988H-006*

coming in piecemeal, like people showing up saying, 'Hey, I'm Sergeant Smith, and I'm here to join you guys in Najaf.' 'OK,' we'd say and try to put them in a serial."

The battalion was organized into three serials under the control of the company commanders for the long drive to Najaf. They were hard pressed to get ready. "We packed up everything and loaded mission-essential equipment, prepped all of our vehicles, loaded the HETs [heavy-equipment transports], and marshaled together a convoy," Captain McFall said.

At one point, Miyamasu told his lead company, "You have to go out the door, otherwise we're not going to have enough space . . . You just have to go." There was not enough time for a route reconnaissance, so the convoys had to rely on maps. "The only map we had was one single 1/100,000 series map," Miyamasu complained. "The first serial departed with one, the second serial did not have a map, but the third deployed with ten, which we were able to scrounge." He left in the first serial at 0230, with Captain McFall's Bravo Company. He arrived at FOB Duke sixteen hours later without incident.

Abrams M1A2 (SEP) Main Battle Tank

The Abrams M1A2 main battle tank is named for Gen. Creighton W. Abrams, former army chief of staff and commander of the 37th Armored Battalion, which served in Europe during World War II. The Abrams is the backbone of the armored forces. The sixty-three-ton M1A2 is powered by a 1,500-horsepower gas-turbine engine, which enables it to reach a top speed of over forty miles per hour. Its main armament is a 120mm XM256 smoothbore cannon that fires an armor-piercing, fin-stabilized, discarding-sabot round featuring a depleted uranium penetrator. The gun has an engagement range approaching four thousand meters. Its target-acquisition system includes a thermal imaging that is based on heat differences radiated by objects in the field of vision. The gunner's sight can fire a range measurement to within ten meters of accuracy. The Abrams also has an onboard digital computer that automatically computes the fire-control solution. The Abrams has a four-man crew—commander, driver, loader, and gunner—who control its three machine guns: a .50-caliber Browning M2 "Ma Duce," located in the commander's station, and two 7.62mm M240 machine guns.

The 1/5 Cav deployed with an advanced system-enhancement package (SEP) upgrade on its tanks. The kit enhanced the armor, provided for compartmentalized fuel and ammunition storage, and enabled the engines to be a multifuel system. The tank was also fitted with a second-generation thermal system that enabled the tank to fire in daylight or darkness.

During their predeployment training at the National Training Center at Fort Irwin, California, in July 2003, the 1/5 Cav prepared for high-intensity conventional warfare, security and stability operations, and military operations in urban terrain. Near the end of its training, the battalion was reorganized into a combined-arms task force. The battalion switched its Alpha Company for Alpha Company, 2nd Battalion, 12th Cavalry, which gave it an armor capability. Alpha Company 2/12, in turn, traded one of its tank platoons for a Bradley platoon, which gave it infantry dismounts.

Captain Badger's Alpha Company was next. "We left on the sixth at 0530," he recalled. "That was a real fun day!" Badger had the largest convoy: fifty-one vehicles and over one hundred soldiers. His convoy was immediately delayed. "We weren't even out of Baghdad when we hit an IED stuffed into a box in the road," he recalled. "We stopped." Badger remembered thinking, "I got fuelers and stuff; it's daylight, so let's take our time and call in EOD. I'm not going to drive my soldiers by something that could kill them!" They sat in the road for two hours waiting for the EOD team, which never showed up.

Badger's Iraqi interpreter grew impatient and with a "Let me go see," he low-crawled out to the box. "Yes, yes, yes," he exclaimed, "It's a bomb, it's a bomb!" The interpreter quickly retreated to a safe distance. About five minutes later, the box exploded, much to Badger's relief. He immediately ordered the convoy forward. It arrived at FOB Duke seventeen hours later, completely exhausted.

Captain Darren Keahtigh's Bravo Company was next on the step. "We kept getting delayed because our HETs were slow," he recalled with exasperation. "We had a lot of tanks with us, and those HETs just don't move that fast . . . [W]e had one accident along the way, which took a long time to pull out of the ditch."

By 0400, August 7, the entire battalion had assembled at FOB Duke, twenty-eight hours after being notified of the mission. Miyamasu was quite pleased. "We had very little time to prepare," he said. "We didn't know the route very well, and most of the soldiers had been going for better than twenty-four hours without sleep."

Army historian Mark D. Sherry wrote in *Tip of the Spear*, "The men unloaded tanks and infantry fighting vehicles from [the] heavy equipment transporters [HETs], performed maintenance checks on each vehicle, and arranged for more ammunition. Their efforts were slowed by the bare-bones facilities . . . and the lack of adequate staging areas."

Miyamasu met for the second time with the MEU staff to review the mission: "Colonel Haslam confirmed that we were to attack into the cemetery."

Mark Sherry noted, "Haslam's verbal guidance was [for the 1-5 Cav] to move to the northern edge of the cemetery, designated Phase Line Harlem, and prepare to enter the fight as soon as possible, attacking from north to south in coordination with BLT 1/4, which would be in the city on the cavalry's east, or left, flank." Miyamasu planned an initial entry with two companies on line: Bravo (Bushmaster), 1-5 Cav, and Charlie (Commando), 1-5 Cav. Alpha Company (Mad Dog), 2-12 Cav, was to move to an attack position "in a lightly populated, semi-agricultural area on the eastern border of the cemetery at a point where the burial ground expanded to its maximum width," according to Sherry. When Bravo and Charlie came abreast of Alpha (at Phase Line Bronx), they would then attack south, with all three companies on line.

The battalion spent all of August 7 refitting, drawing additional supplies of ammunition, and planning the attack. Miyamasu's order of battle placed Alpha Company, 2-12 Cav (which included six M1A2 Abrams tanks with

Bradley M2A3 Armored Fighting Vehicle

The Bradley armored fighting vehicle comes in two variants: the M2, which transports infantry on the battlefield, and the M3 cavalry reconnaissance vehicle. The M2 carries a three-man crew—commander, driver, and gunner—plus six fully equipped infantrymen. The M3 has a three-man crew plus two scouts. The Bradley's main armament is a 25mm Bushmaster chain gun that fires at a rate of two hundred rounds per minute and can be converted to five hundred rounds per minute. The Bushmaster has a range of two thousand meters. A 7.62mm machine gun is mounted coaxially.

The M2 is also equipped with a TOW BGM-71 antitank missile system. This twin-tube launcher is mounted on the left side of the turret. The target-acquisition system uses an optical sight, which detects the infrared signal from the back of the in-flight missile. A double-wire command link between the missile and the gunner is dispensed from two spools at the back of the missile.

The Bradley has two smoke-grenade dischargers, each loaded with four smoke grenades. It is also fitted with an engine smoke-generating system. Its hull is made of welded aluminum and spaced laminate armor. In addition, it has appliquéd steel armor with provisions for additional passive armor or explosive reactor armor. Its 600-horsepower engine gives it a maximum speed of sixty-six miles per hour.

The Bradley armored fighting vehicle's main armament is a 25mm Bushmaster chain gun that can fire five hundred rounds a minute up to a range of two thousand meters. It also carries a 7.62mm machine gun and a TOW missile launcher. The 1-5 Cav had thirteen Bradleys. *Defenseimagery.mil DF-SD-07-04080*

systems-enhancement package [SEP], four M2A3 Bradleys, and four M114 armored fighting vehicles), on the eastern flank; Bravo Company, 1-5 Cav (including two M2A3 Bradleys and ten M114 armored fighting vehicles), in the center; and Charlie Company, 1-5 Cav (which included seven M2A3 Bradleys and eight M114s), on the western flank. Two M121 vehicles mounting 120mm mortars and Miyamasu's own command vehicle were located behind the assault elements. Battalion scouts screened the rear areas, searching for militia units trying to move in behind them. Captain Badger recalled, "The intent of the order was to let Charlie and Bravo clear the cemetery to Phase Line Bronx, and then we [Alpha Company] would join in the attack." Miyamasu established the time for attack at 0500, August 9.

Alpha Company redeployed to FOB Hotel on August 8 in preparation for the next morning's attack. FOB Hotel was located seven to eight kilometers north of the cemetery, which would put the company in a good attack position. "At this point, we conducted all of our supply pickup," First Lieutenant Stauch pointed out. "We didn't have a complete load of ammunition, so all of our tanks and Bradleys received a full load of ammunition. We also loaded TOW missiles, hand grenades, and AT4s [one-shot antitank weapons]." Alpha Company was the strongest unit in the battalion. Its 1st Platoon (commanded by 2nd Lt. Douglas J. Schaffer) was mounted in four Bradleys; 2nd Platoon (commanded by 2nd Lt. James M. Goins) had four Abrams; and the 3rd Platoon consisted of two Abrams and four armored fighting vehicles. In addition, Badger's headquarters fielded three Humvees and a Bradley fire-support team (FIST) vehicle.

2ND BATTALION, 7TH CAVALRY REGIMENT (GHOST BATTALION)

We did some pretty robust destruction for the Marines in Najaf.
    —Major Tim Karcher, 2nd Battalion, 7th Cavalry Regiment

The 2nd Battalion, 7th Cavalry Regiment, was cross-attached to the 39th Enhanced Separate Brigade of the Arkansas National Guard. "We were the first active duty battalion to be directly attached to a national-guard brigade," 1st Lt. Michael S. Erwin recalled, "although organically we were part of the 3rd Brigade, 1st Cavalry Division." The battalion was located approximately twenty-five miles north of Baghdad at Camp Taji, which had been the main base of the former Medina Division, part of Saddam Hussein's Republican Guard.

Lieutenant Colonel James E. Rainey

Lieutenant Colonel James E. Rainey started out as a light infantryman in the 82nd Airborne Division and the 3rd Battalion, 75th Ranger Regiment. As a captain, he commanded a company in the 1st Cavalry Division and the 3rd Infantry Regiment, the Old Guard, the army's ceremonial unit in Washington, D.C. As a major, he attended the Command and General Staff College, and the School of Advanced Military Studies (SAMS). Graduates of the latter are known as "Jedi Knights." Following SAMS, he was assigned as a division planner and chief of plans for the 2nd Infantry Division. Upon completing that tour, he became the operations officer 1st Battalion, 9th Cavalry Regiment, and subsequently the executive officer for the III Corps commander and executive officer for the 3rd Brigade, 1st Cavalry. In May 2004, he took command of the 2nd Battalion, 7th Cavalry.

Major Michael S. Erwin said the Rainey took over 2-7 Cav after its commander and command sergeant major were relieved early in the deployment because of a "bad command climate."

"The battalion's morale was in the toilet," Erwin claimed. "Camp Taji was taking mortars and rockets all the time. For example, on May 24th, we took an eighteen-minute, twenty-two-round barrage from four different positions. The insurgents walked the rounds in on all sides of the camp." Erwin explained that the base was surrounded by former members of Hussein's Republican Guard, which had been disbanded by Ambassador Bremer's short-sighted policy, implying that those well-trained Iraqi soldiers were the cause of the indirect-fire and IED attacks.

Erwin indicated that within a short period of time, Rainey turned the battalion around. He characterized the officer as "everything you'd look for, hope for, in a military leader . . . a motivator. He had warrior ethos out the ass!"

Rainey also impressed the Marines. Lieutenant General Dennis J. Hejlik described him as "a big, rough Nebraska farm boy—a type of guy who would push the limits on everything. But he wasn't reckless. He was definitely a rock 'em, sock 'em soldier."

Erwin thought that Rainey's attitude had a great deal to do with how the Marines accepted the 2-7 Cav joining the battle in Najaf. "We told them they had a tough fight going on," he said, "and we were there to support them however we could. This helped with the Marines' perception of us as fighters."

Lieutenant Colonel James E. Rainey (right), commander of the 2-7 Cavalry; Col. Anthony M. Haslam (center), commander of the 11th MEU; and a personal security detachment soldier.
Defenseimagery.mil DF-SD-07-09676

The battalion's primary mission there, according to Lt. Col. James E. Rainey (call sign Ghost Six), 2-7's battalion commander, was to "protect Taji, which is where all of our aviation assets were based, as well as the Division Support Command."

Rainey's mechanized infantry battalion was responsible for a largely rural area of some 685 square kilometers. "It was 90 percent Sunni and 10 percent Wahhabist/Salafist kinds of guys," Rainey explained. "There was a lot of former regime—Baathists, Iraqi Intelligence Service guys, and Fedayeen—who went to ground there. It was not someplace where we could win the hearts and minds of the people. We were out fighting every day because of the IED threat and indirect fire attacks, where the insurgents tried to inflict casualties and destroy aircraft."

In addition to protecting Taji, the battalion also "served as the theater response force or the theater quick reaction force, or something like that," Capt. Edward Twaddell III, the Alpha Company commander, recalled.

The 1st Cavalry Division reached out to the 39th Brigade and tasked them with providing a battalion to support the Marines. "About 1030 on the eighth [August 8], we received notification that we would reposition to Najaf," Capt. Chris Brooke, the 2-7 Cav's plans officer recalled.

Rainey explained, "It was a tactical decision based on the fact that the other three [mechanized infantry] battalions [in the division] were more decisively engaged and more critical to the overall division fight then us." The other battalions were in Baghdad and would have been much harder to pull out of that embattled hot spot.

Twaddell thought, "It was easier to pull 2-7 out of that area rather than, say, a committed battalion in central Baghdad and move them across the theater to whatever the contingency operation had arisen." He was rather blasé about the orders, "All right," he thought, "that's kind of cool."

First Lieutenant Michael Throckmorton was more circumspect. "This could be a terrible fight," he recalls thinking. "I'm not looking forward to this."

Rainey sent an advance party to meet with the MEU. It consisted of Major Tim Karcher, the operations officer, two assistants, a logistics representative, and Mike Erwin, the young intelligence officer. "It [the advance-party meeting] was a surprise because it was so sudden," Erwin said. "I was partially prepared because I started doing my homework when we were assigned as the theater reserve after 1-5 Cav was committed to Najaf. I pulled up a map of Najaf and started marking down where the insurgent attacks were occurring." Erwin was "blown away" by the frequency and the number of attacks. There were reports that twenty to thirty ill-trained

Mahdi militiamen were routinely killed. The reports said that the Iraqis were untrained, ages fifteen to eighteen, and hopped up on drugs. Suddenly, he received word that the battalion was going to be committed. "Lieutenant Colonel Rainey came up to me and said, 'Erwin, you're going down to Najaf. Don't fuck it up!' It was really funny," Erwin recalled, tongue in cheek. "Here I was, just a twenty-four-year old lieutenant . . . and now I'm the senior intelligence officer." (Erwin had been the assistant until his boss had gone home on leave.)

The group boarded an army CH-47 Chinook helicopter and flew from Taji to Baghdad to FOB Duke, arriving about 0400. After a couple of hours sleep, they were escorted to the MEU combat operations center (COC) to meet their counterparts. Erwin remembered walking into the COC at about 0600 and grabbing coffee to help him clear the cobwebs from his brain. Getting only two hours sleep and making a long helicopter ride were disorienting. As he sipped the coffee, he had a chance to observe the Marine command center. Even at this early hour, it was a hub of focused activity. He noted several subdued conversations going on around the large, gridded aerial photographs of Najaf that were pinned to walls. Staff officers and enlisted radio operators manned banks of radios and computers linking the MEU with its scattered units and to higher headquarters. The scene was not unlike his own unit's tactical operations center (TOC), except that he was surprised to see the intelligence officer, Maj. Michael J. Lindemann, dozing in his chair. "I never saw a guy so tired in my life," he exclaimed. Erwin learned that the officer rarely left the building, preferring to sleep at his desk.

After the introductions—handshakes all around—the officers got down to business. Johnston wanted to know what the 2-7 Cav's capabilities were. "I had no idea what they would bring to the fight," Johnston admitted, "and I didn't have a chance to look it up." He quickly learned that the mechanized battalion was a highly potent fighting force comprising fourteen M1A2 SEP main battle tanks, thirty M2A3 armored fighting vehicles, and twelve lightly armored Humvees organized into three maneuver elements, plus two organic mechanized companies, Alpha and Charlie, and an attached tank-heavy company, Charlie 3-8. The battalion's heavy firepower made up for its small number of dismounted infantry: about 250 men.

"We quickly gained a pretty close relationship with the Marines, especially Major Karcher," Erwin said. "He came down there as the voice of our battalion commander, saying we would do whatever needed to be done. I think that really played a big role in establishing the relationship."

After being briefed on 2-7 Cav's capabilities, the group split into functional areas—operations, logistics, and intelligence—to continue the brief.

"Right off the bat, we got a good situational awareness brief," Erwin recalled of the intelligence discussion. "It was a basic, bare-bones look at the overall situation, but that's all we needed because we had been following events for some time at Camp Taji."

During the brief, he learned that militia reinforcements were coming into Najaf from Sadr City via Kufa. Erwin remembered that several of these armed men were picked up in the fighting. The detainees said they were simply pilgrims visiting the mosque—a claim that stretched their credibility to the limit. In one case, a badly wounded "visitor" was brought in after throwing a hand grenade at U.S. forces. The attempt backfired, leaving him pocked with shrapnel.

Operationally, Johnston wanted the 2-7 Cav to "come in from the south of the city and push north," so the militia would be squeezed from three different directions—by 1/4 from the west, the 1-5 Cav from the north, and the 2-7 Cav from the south and east. There was no time to issue a "long, drawn-out order," so Johnston gave Karcher a brief, mission-type order—an operational concept without specifying how the mission is to be accomplished. "It was task, purpose, and graphics," Johnston said. "They [2-7 Cav] looked at them and knew what they needed to do. They just said, 'Point us in the right direction, and we're good to go.'"

Erwin was not fazed at all with the brevity of the tasking: "We understood that we were to develop a flexible plan to support the overall scheme of maneuver as it related to the southern part of the city." Before the meeting broke up, the MEU supplied the advance party with "tons of maps and graphics," which the advance party studied in preparation for briefing Rainey as soon as he arrived.

Back at Taji, the battalion rushed to get ready for the long road march to Najaf. Enough clothing and comfort items to last two weeks were stuffed into duffle bags and crammed into every available space in and on the vehicles, along with ammunition, extra radio batteries, and critical spare parts. Staff Sergeant Heath J. Demuth didn't get the word: "I remember being told to pack for three to five days; for me, that meant extra cigarettes, water, and a toothbrush. Eight days later, I returned with prickly heat and a smile on my face."

The battalion's armored vehicles were carefully loaded on HETs because, according to Twaddell, the rubber pads on the tracks were melting off in the oppressive summer heat. "It would have been a long bumpy ride," he explained, "like having your running shoes melt on a long run." One crewman from each Abram and Bradley rode with his vehicle on the HETs in case of an attack. The remainder of the men flew by helicopter to FOB Duke.

Within hours, the battalion was packed up and ready to go. "To this day, I still don't know how they did it while continuing to conduct maintenance on the vehicle fleet," Brooke said. "There are so many moving pieces to a mechanized task force, particularly its maintenance package, that are absolutely essential to its mission accomplishment." Much of the credit for the effort went to Capt. Jake Brown, the Support Company commander, who was referred to as the "logamagican." "It was a great example of how noncommissioned officers and junior leaders truly can make incredible things happen," Brooke explained. "I remember being absolutely amazed at the speed and efficiency [with which] our companies transitioned out of their sectors and prepared for movement and repositioned halfway across the theater."

First Lieutenant Jimmy Campbell, the scout-platoon commander, was assigned to escort the first of three serials. "I remember the route called for us to take the convoys down Route Senators [Highway 1] south through Baghdad's Green Zone, which I thought was absurd," he said. "There was no way the HETs would be able to negotiate the city's traffic-congested highways." In addition to having heavy traffic, Baghdad was the scene of intense fighting between al-Sadr's militia and coalition forces, including one of the 2-7 Cav's sister battalions. Campbell knew the road network well, having led many patrols through the city. He suggested instead taking Route Force, which was "an excellent interstate highway around the western side of the city." Captain Peter Glass, the convoy commander, and the experienced HET drivers agreed and accepted Campbell's recommendation.

The convoy made good time until it reached Route Irish, just below the city. "The HETs kept having flat tires," Campbell grumbled. "It was awful. I remember being stopped on Irish, right in the heat of the day, for two hours while the drivers struggled to change the flat. We had no sooner gotten started when another HET had a flat! It was quite frustrating."

The convoy continued south through the open desert, which seemed empty, except for the occasional checkpoint manned by a single rifle squad.

"It was kind of weird," Twaddell marveled, "because there was nothing else around—an outpost in the middle of nowhere."

Late in the afternoon, the convoy finally reached Convoy Support Center Scania (CSC Scania), about 100 kilometers south of Baghdad, where it laagered for the night.

"The trip from Taji to Scania shouldn't have taken more than three hours," Campbell lamented. "Instead it took us more than eight hours." The other serials experienced the same difficulties.

Lieutenant Throckmorton recalled, "We left Taji at 1300 and broke down five minutes later. In all, we broke down five times and didn't get into Scandia until 2300."

Twaddell described the austere outpost as a "truck stop for convoys." CSC Scania was designed to provide a safe way station for convoys. It consisted of a large parking area, a small mess hall, and a post exchange (PX) where the drivers could relax in relative security.

With the battalion safely on the road, Rainey flew to FOB Duke to meet with his advance party. "He got on the ground, and we briefed him for two hours on what we had learned before his meeting with the MEU commander," Erwin recalled. Haslam was immediately impressed with the 2-7 Cav's enthusiastic battalion commander. He projected a positive, can-do attitude. "We're here to help," Rainey emphasized. "Tell us what you want us to do, and we'll do it."

The MEU staff briefed Rainey on the overall situation and gave him a frag order outlining the mission. "I told Rainey . . . 'I need you at Revolutionary Circle,' " Haslam said.

"It was a different way of doing business," Erwin recalled. "We were given the commander's intent without specifics. It was rather open ended—block the enemy from the south and east, and go make it happen."

Rainey was very comfortable with the sketchy mission outline. He told his staff, "Here's how I want to do it. Work out the details." Karcher, Brooke, and Erwin conducted a mission analysis and went to work developing a detailed plan. The intent was to have the plan ready by the time the battalion arrived.

The serials continued to have breakdowns, but finally reached the outskirts of Najaf about two hours after leaving CSC Scania. "We heard explosions and small-arms fire coming from the city," Lieutenant Throckmorton said, "and we saw two Marine Cobras firing into the city."

Late in the afternoon of August 10, the battalion wheeled into FOB Duke's huge dirt parking area, raising a large dust cloud that settled on men and vehicles. One soldier described the talcum-powderlike sand as "moon dust." The soldiers quickly learned that the austere FOB Duke was a far cry from the relative comfort of Camp Taji. "This place [Duke] is as desolate as it gets," Lieutenant Throckmorton said. "No nothing for miles." The area was devoid of any shade, and the afternoon sun beat down unmercifully. Heat waves reflected off the vehicles, making them almost too hot to touch and greatly increasing the discomfort of the men as they struggled to unload the HETs and make the Abrams and Bradleys ready for immediate combat.

As the junior officers and NCOs brought order to the chaos, the company commanders were called to a briefing at the battalion headquarters, where Rainey gave his commander's intent. Erwin recalled him saying, "I want you guys to get in there and develop the situation and take some of the pressure off 1/4 and 1-5 Cav." Erwin gave the intelligence brief, laying out the enemy situation, which he had ascertained from studying contact reports and the MEU briefings. Major Karcher followed with the operations plan and the scheme of maneuver. "Our plan was aimed at seizing areas from which we could dominate portions of the city," he said.

"We were given detailed instructions," Captain Twaddell remembered. "It pretty much looked like a pincer movement. The Marines were in the west, 1-5 Cav in the north, and we were coming in from the south." Erwin remarked, "The MEU gave us one of the tougher missions."

Major Karcher assigned the battalion's three companies routes of attack toward the Old City. Twaddell explained, "Charlie Company 3-8 [Team Cougar] was to push up the escarpment from the southwest. Charlie Company 2-7 [Team Comanche] with Alpha Company 2-7 [Team Apache] in trace were to attack from the south. We were going to squeeze the militia."

Erwin reiterated the main points of his intelligence brief. "I laid it all out," he said, "the enemy situation, their TTPs [tactics, techniques, and

Soldiers lay out machine-gun ammunition (.50-caliber and 7.62mm) to load in their Abrams main battle tank. *Capt. Michael Throckmorton, U.S. Army*

procedures], and that the enemy would fight hard." Despite the brief, he felt that many of the soldiers were surprised by the level of fighting. "Until you actually experience combat yourself, it didn't really resonate," he said. "Most of the battalion spent the rest of the day and part of the eleventh [August 11] preparing for the attack—cleaning and bore-sighting weapons, performing final vehicle maintenance, and stockpiling ammunition.

While the battalion prepared its vehicles, Campbell's twenty-three-man scout platoon, manning six up-armored Humvees that mounted one heavy and one light machine gun, were assigned to check the roads. "Rainey told me to recon the routes that we were going to use for the attack," he said, "and to see if there were any routes between the two avenues of approach that he could use to facilitate command and control." Rainey was an up-front type of commander, an officer who dropped in on his units when they were in contact—not to micromanage, but to keep his fingers on the pulse of his battalion. He was constantly on the move.

Major Christopher Conley said, "Rainey and Karcher traveled in two separate Bradleys with just a couple of soldiers as their personal security detachment."

Campbell was told to get as close to the city as possible, but cautioned not to get decisively engaged. The platoon drove around for over three hours on the outskirts of the city without a shot being fired. "We didn't uncover anything particularly significant, other than the fact that the main route from the west called for an uphill attack into the town," he recalled. "I discussed it with my NCOs, and we all felt that Charlie 3-8 would probably receive their first contact as soon as they crested the incline, which is exactly what happened." He reported the results of the route reconnaissance to Karcher, emphasizing that the dirt and gravel roads were highly trafficable.

On the evening of August 11, Rainey ordered the battalion headquarters to displace so it would be in a better position to support the attack. "We left Duke at 2100," Conley said, "and by the time we organized the new location, it was nearly daylight." Having been up all night, Conley was dog tired and turned in for a few hours of sleep. "Within a few minutes, Chris Brooke shook me awake. 'Hey man,' I remember him saying, 'we've got to jump the TOC to Camp David, and I'm leaving right now.' I was still half asleep, and I couldn't figure out why we were going to the presidential retreat!" Conley was left with organizing the move. As the last vehicle left, it suddenly dawned on him that he didn't have a ride. He had to beg Campbell for a lift, which cost him much face.

The convoy reached Camp David, the headquarters of the 5th Special Forces Group. Erwin recalled, "The SF soldiers bent over backward to help us, despite the fact that our tracked vehicles tore up the place. They loaned us a couple of buildings where we set up our command post." Conley established the operations office in a small room just big enough for six or seven men. He maintained contact with the widely separated units by having a communications vehicle park next to the building and run its antenna cables through the window.

CHAPTER 9

Raids and Feints

We're coming after them.

—Capt. Robert Sotire

1ST BATTALION, 4TH MARINES

THE BATTALION WAS TASKED with executing quick-reaction raids designed to target specific enemy assembly areas in central Najaf and the city of Kufa. The latter city, according to Moran was "the political epicenter of the Mahdi Militia uprising. That's where Muqtada al-Sadr started as an imam and a rabble rouser, where he had first done his preaching against the coalition, and where he had a lot of financial and political backing, as well as a lot of heavily armed fighters."

Mayer consolidated the battalion at FOBs Hotel and Baker. The latter was very close to Kufa's Saleh mosque, a known enemy strongpoint. "The enemy had building defenses in Kufa for over a year," Mayer said. "No American unit had been there since April, so it was unknown to us. The battalion was tasked with doing a series of raids, spoiling attacks to cut the rat lines [militia infiltration routes] between Kufa and the Imam Ali shrine, . . . and to clean up pockets of resistance."

In all, six company-size or battalion-minus raids were conducted—at a large school, the Kufa Technical College, a hospital complex, a schoolyard assembly area, the Saleh mosque, and finally, al-Sadr's personal residence. Moran stated that the purpose of the raids was, "to keep the enemy off balance and bleed away his strength to make sure he wasn't able to focus his main effort on Najaf and the shrine."

In addition to conducting the raids, all three battalions were also keeping the pressure on the militia by probing their defenses in the Old City. Lieutenant Colonel Mayer recalled one especially trying night:

> I wanted to see what the militia's strength was in the Old City. I took my forward command element and tried to sneak in from the desert along a vehicle trail we spotted on an aerial photograph. Our four vehicles got about halfway up the road when 82mm mortar rounds began raining down on our column. We immediately went into our battle drill. Captain Lowe jumped out of the vehicle to guide our vehicles as we tried to turn around. His action was an amazing display of courage in the face of the deadly barrage. Fortunately, we only suffered one slightly wounded man when he was struck in the foot by a small piece of shrapnel.

Sotire remembered, "There was a media frenzy, as the reporters tried to figure out what was going on." The MEU public affairs officer, Capt. Carrie C. Batson, established regularly scheduled press briefings and published a series of informational press releases. Reporters clamored to go out on operations with the rifle companies. Sotire's Alpha Company was assigned two of them. "They didn't know what to expect," Sotire said. "I gave them my guidance. Stay with the vehicle, always have someone around for protection, and don't go anywhere alone. I needed to have accountability."

On one night operation, his company was assigned to clear two school buildings. "Not a lot happened at the schools," he recalled, "but on the way

Lieutenant Colonel John Mayer briefs his commanders and staff before launching a raid. Note the unique pointer. *1st Lt. William Birdzell, USMC*

out, we got hit with a complex ambush that was initiated by an RPG. It missed, but some shrapnel hit the vehicles. I looked in the back and saw the *New York Times* reporter flat on his back, holding his camera above the window taking photos without looking." Sotire said that the reporters gained a new respect for what the Marines were doing, but many of them quickly disappeared.

Lieutenant Zjawin remembered the incident: "My platoon was jammed in two trucks that we had fitted with Hillbilly armor [improvised steel plates] for protection. It was darker than pitch, so I was using my optics to see the road as we pulled off the objective. Suddenly the sky turned red with tracers, and someone shouted over the radio, 'Contact right!'" Zjawin initially thought it was friendly fire, but then saw ghostlike figures running across an open field. "My men opened up with a vengeance and waxed a couple. The militia fired several RPGs, one of which skipped underneath a truck and exploded. My squad leader shouted, 'The second truck is gone!'" Zjawin felt a surge of adrenalin course through his bloodstream. "I grabbed the radio and tried to contact the squad leader on the truck. After what seemed like hours, he responded, 'We're OK, except for minor peppering.'" The trucks continued through the ambush site and made it back to the FOB without additional trouble. Looking back at the incident, Zjawin did not believe his men had "exhibited good fire discipline because they just wanted to kill something." He had a heart to heart with them, and "they got much better."

Embedded reporters photograph Alpha Company boarding Marine amphibious assault vehicles (AAV) to conduct a raid. During one raid, the reporters encountered more than they wanted when the convoy was ambushed and had to fight its way out. They learned to respect the men who had to do the fighting. *Defenseimagery.mil DM-SD-05-14324*

AL-SADR'S HOUSE (AUGUST 12)

On August 12, the battalion supported a raid on al-Sadr's house and the surrounding buildings. Intelligence had identified the area as a major militia strongpoint and logistics base. The raid force consisted of Charlie Company, the Reconnaissance Platoon, CAAT-Alpha, three Iraqi national guard platoons from the 405th Battalion, and the Iraqis' Special Forces advisers, Operational Detachment Alpha-512 (ODA-512). "We were told that we were going to go with our ING counterparts," Sellars said, "who had lost about 60 to 70 percent of their numbers from when we were training them a few weeks before the fight broke out."

The objective of the operation was to seize four buildings—al-Sadr's house and an adjoining building, a school, and the Al Amer maternity hospital, which were adjacent to a junkyard and 800 meters of open ground. The open space was the same location of Borneo's shootout on August 5. "The maternity hospital, right next door to al-Sadr's house, was believed to have over a one hundred fighters holed up in it," Mayer said. "The doctors also said that the militia had been using it as their headquarters."

Mayer and his command group accompanied the force to provide command and control of the operation. "The raid was designed [as] a two-company attack and conducted during daylight, because the ING was not prepared for night operations," he said. "I looked at it as the first step in prepping the ING for the final attack on the Imam Ali shrine." Mayer's plan called for CAAT-Alpha—one section north and the other south—to cordon off the objective. Charlie Company's 1st and 3rd Platoons were to take the hospital, while the 2nd Platoon was positioned to provide support by fire. The ING was tasked to move adjacent to Charlie Company and to protect its flank. "Intelligence led me to believe that the Iraqi zone was free of enemy," Mayer said, "but the enemy, of course, has a say, and they ended up facing the ING." The Reconnaissance Platoon was attached to Charlie Company and assigned to protect the company's right flank.

Captain Jason "Frenchy" Grogan (call sign Rocky 07) led a mixed section of one Cobra and one Huey in support of the raid. "The ODO [operations duty officer] handed me a sheaf of PowerPoint slides," Grogan recalled. "There wasn't much to them—a bunch of lines and arrows and a couple of radio frequencies. After I studied them for a few minutes, it dawned on me that we were going after al-Sadr himself—at his house!" The operation commenced about 0800 with Charlie Company's move to the ING compound to organize the Iraqi force for the operation.

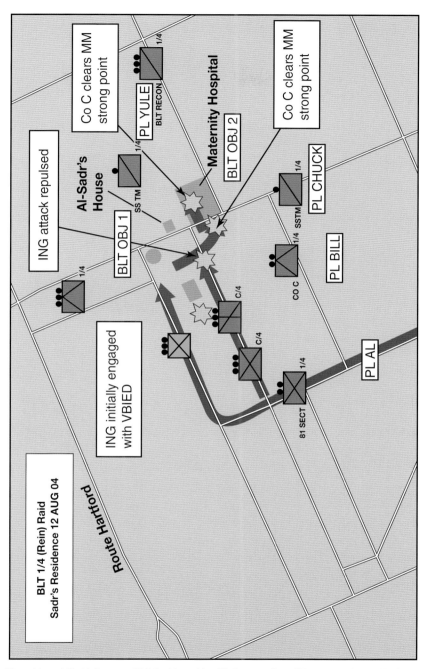

The raid on al-Sadr's house, which had been identified as a major militia strongpoint and logistic base. The force consisted of Charlie Company, Reconnaissance Platoon, and three Iraqi national guard platoons. *Patricia Isaacs, from an 11th MEU operational slide*

A Cobra gunship makes a firing run on Mahdi Militia positions in the Wadi al-Salaam cemetery. The photo was taken from the second helicopter in the section, a Huey gunship piloted by Maj. Glen Butler. *Lt. Col. Glen G. Butler, USMC*

As the column moved along the road, Grogan's section flew overhead. "We set up an orbit and essentially flew top cover by scouting ahead and around them looking for threats," he said. "A few RPGs were shot at us, and some small-arms fire, but nothing really intensive. Up ahead of the column, there were a couple of civilian fuel trucks burning and that created a lot of smoke. But there really wasn't too much going on." By the time Charlie Company resumed its march from the compound, Grogan's Cobra had run low on fuel. "We thought we were done because there wasn't much of anything going on," he explained. "We went back to FOB Duke and were hot refueling [taking on fuel with the engines still turning] when we got the call to get back out there. Things had gone bad!"

As Borneo's first section moved into position, it came under small-arms fire. Four armed men ran from a building toward the hospital. Two stopped to fire at Borneo's vehicle—a deadly mistake, because the gunner let loose a burst from his MK-19, bringing the men down in the street. The other two men stupidly took cover under a fuel truck, which was set on fire by the MK-19. This initial firefight brought on a general engagement with militiamen in the area.

In the meantime, the main column of the ING and Charlie Company arrived in the vicinity of the objective.

"We pulled up and stopped about eight hundred meters away across a big field," Sellars said. "We dismounted and pushed across into a building complex."

Corporal Wallace recalled, "We started clearing houses, Corporal Jenkins's squad on the left. We cleared the first house, came around a corner, and started taking fire from an apartment complex."

Sellars's platoon pushed into the complex. "It was chaotic because the people had built walls between two apartments, so you would have to run up an independent flight stairs to get to each apartment," he said. "The guys would have to run up the stairs, clear the apartment, turn around and go to the next set of stairs, and do the same thing." The heat and physical effort exhausted his men. "I had two guys go tits up [collapse], and I had to send them back with heat exhaustion," he recalled.

Sellars's platoon finally reached a building in front of the hospital. "We hoofed it to this open area, where I had to give my Marines ten minutes before we could move again. It had to be 120 degrees that day, and everybody was about to die!" After recovering, the 1st and 3rd Platoons continued the assault. "We set up a SMAW [a MK-153 shoulder-launched multipurpose assault weapon—organic to the Weapons Platoon and used by the 0351 assaultman] [and] shot to breach the wall of the hospital," Sellars explained. "However, it went right through the wall, leaving a hole the size of the rocket, and exploded somewhere inside the hospital grounds."

The two lieutenants were somewhat perplexed. "We're like, 'Shit, that didn't work. Reload!' This time the rocketman umphs it, and the

The canopy of Capt. Jason "Frenchy" Grogan's Cobra, struck by shrapnel. The metal also pierced his flight helmet almost in the same location as Captain Mount's had been hit, but did not cause injury. *Lt. Col. Glen G. Butler, USMC*

A SMAW (shoulder-launched multipurpose assault weapon), described by Lt. Sellers as a small shot. The launcher was designed to be an antiarmor weapon, but performed admirably against Najaf's cement buildings. *Defenseimagery.mil DM-SD-07-23099*

thing hits the dirt in front of the wall, which just kind of pushed it over. 'Yay!,' and we all run inside."

Wallace's squad was the first one in. "They've got a big glass door there. It's locked, so we ended up breaking the glass," he said.

Unfortunately, the door was a split-level door, and only the bottom panel broke. So the men were forced to crawl through. "I've got a guy who cuts his wrist, and he's bleeding like a stuck pig," Sellars recalled, "so we pulled him out to get the doc to look at him."

Sellars remembered that as he entered the hospital, "there's people sticking their heads out of the rooms. He said, "[W]e're thinking, 'All right, it's the Mahdi Militia.' My men shouted out orders to them. 'Get down, get down!' 'Come here, come here!' 'Go, go!' So they came walking down the hall—all its doctors and nurses."

Wallace remembered it was "kind of weird because we expected to be shooting, and instead a bunch of civilians step out in the hallway with their arms up. We're like, 'What's going on? There are supposed to be bad guys in here.'" One of the doctors said there had been a couple of militiamen, but they fled when the shooting first started. After the initial encounter, about forty people were gathered and placed in a single room while the platoon finished clearing the facility.

"We started kicking in doors, which were all steel and locked," Sellars explained. "After twenty minutes, a janitor finally appeared with the keys, just as people started coming out of one room. I'm like, 'Where are you coming from?'

"'The babies,' one replied.

"I said, 'What do you mean babies?'"

It turned out the room was filled with newborns. Sellars was shocked and remembered thinking, "Thank God no one took a shot at us because we would have fragged the room before entering it!"

After finding the hospital was clear of the enemy, both platoons exited upon hearing that the ING and ODA-512 were in trouble. The ING had encountered heavy resistance at the school, a four-story building held by a platoon-sized enemy force. As the ING moved toward the building, the enemy opened fire, killing and wounding over a dozen ING soldiers in the initial burst of fire. Staff Sergeant Frederick Allen moved his vehicle into the line of fire to cover the evacuation of casualties.

"Once the heavy machine-gun fire began, I moved to see what the situation was," Mayer said. "I arrived to join the back of the ING stack just in time to see Captain Tarlavsky die." Captain Michael Yury Tarlavsky and one of his men had stormed into the building. As they had run up the stairs to the second floor, T-arlavsky was killed by small-arms fire, and the senior noncommissioned officer was seriously wounded. After Tarlavsky fell, the leaderless ING retreated back to their base, said Mayer.

United States forces developed detailed plans for the swift evacuation of casualties. Most often the wounded were loaded on whatever vehicle was handy and taken to a forward medical aid station. After initial treatment, they were evacuated via helicopter to the rear for more extensive treatment. *Defenseimagery.mil 041119-M-2583M-065*

Silver Star Citations

Captain Michael Yury Tarlavsky
The President of the United States takes pride in presenting the Silver Star Medal (Posthumously) to Michael Yury Tarlavsky, Captain (Infantry), U.S. Army, for conspicuous gallantry and intrepidity in action against the enemy while serving with the 1st Battalion, 5th Special Forces (Airborne), during combat operations in support of Operation Iraqi Freedom, on 12 August 2004, in Iraq. Captain Tarlavsky distinguished himself when his unit came under small arms fire and grenade attack in Najaf, Iraq.

Sergeant First Class Frederick Allen
The President of the United States takes pleasure in presenting the Silver Star Medal to Frederick Allen, Sergeant First Class (the Staff Sergeant), U.S. Army, for conspicuous gallantry and intrepidity in action while serving with Operational Detachment Alpha 512 (ODA-512), 5th Special Forces Group (Airborne), during combat operations in support of Operation Iraqi Freedom, at An Najaf, Iraq, on 12 August 2004. Sergeant First Class Allen, the other members of Operational Detachment–Alpha 512, along with 51 Iraqi National Guardsmen, engaged approximately 15–20 Mahdi Militiamen embedded inside a school. The detachment, with the Iraqi National Guard in the lead, advanced toward their objective and came under immediate and intense enemy fire from inside the school. Sergeant First Class Allen, the gunner in the detachment's 2d vehicle, ordered his GMV forward, placing himself in the direct line of fire to allow the Iraqi National Guard elements to regroup and reorganize after sustaining several casualties. Multiple times in the fight, Sergeant First Class Allen selflessly stayed in the line of fire battling the enemy, so that others could make it back to cover. Sergeant First Allen's actions are in keeping with the finest traditions of military heroism and reflect distinct credit upon himself, this command, and the United States Army.

"There was a lot of chatter on the net," Grogan recalled. "The army Special Forces guys had gotten ambushed in a four-story building. They'd charged in, and their captain—a great guy, who I had met—was shot and killed." The two casualties were quickly evacuated. "We were assigned to escort the Humvees that were taking them out. The Iraqis had already fled. It was now an all-Marine show."

As Charlie Company's 3rd Platoon and the Reconnaissance Platoon ran to assist the Special Forces, they came under heavy small-arms and machine-gun fire. Despite the fire, 3rd Platoon reached the building and rushed inside. The enemy was on the second floor, where, according to

Sellars, "They pretty much just rolled grenades down the stairs, then popped around the corner, without even showing themselves, and fired at random." One Marine was severely wounded when a grenade landed underneath him, sending shrapnel into his intestines. Enemy fire was intense, hindering the evacuation of the wounded man. First Sergeant Justin LeHew purposely exposed himself to draw enemy fire, allowing Mayer's personal security detachment to enter the building and evacuate the Marine to the FOB.

While the 3rd Platoon fought in the school, Sellars's platoon got in position to assault another hospital directly across the street from al-Sadr's house. "There was a bunch of buses just across from the hospital," Wallace recalled, "and we're using them as cover because we're taking fire from 3rd Platoon's building." There was a fifty-meter gap between the buses and the next covered position. A brick and masonry wall stood in their way.

"Chimp Gibbons [Capt. Randy "Chimp" Gibbons] and his guys were pinned down and couldn't get around the wall," Captain Grogan recalled. "Gibbons wanted us to blow a hole in it. We were carrying Hellfires, TOWs, and 2.75-inch rockets. None of them are particularly good for blowing huge holes in things, but we decided to give the rockets a try." After warning Gibbons to get his men back, Grogan dropped the Cobra as low as he could. "We hung there for a second, almost stationary," he said. "The geometry of the setup was such that we just didn't have much tracking time." He rippled seven rockets and instantly pulled the helicopter into a hard left turn to get away from enemy fire.

The rockets smashed into the wall and brought down a section. One of Wallace's men started through the hole. "I see an RPG come right over his

A heavily armed Marine squad forcibly enters a courtyard. Not knowing what might lay beyond the wall—an IED, militiaman, innocent civilian—made the clearing a tough, nerve-racking job. *Defenseimagery.mil DM-SD-06-01245*

head and explode in a wall down the road," Wallace exclaimed, "and I'm the next one to go!" Wallace made it across and had an engineer set to blow open a door when Sellars arrived.

Sellars recalled, "I look down the way and see another entranceway." He asked if they had tried that one, and no one had. So he told them to just kick it. "So one of my Marines kicks it, and the door opens." They went inside and discovered another door that needed to be blown. "The engineers prepare a charge . . . 'Run!' one shouted. The charge is so big that it blew out every window in the building. There's so much dust we couldn't see, so we sat outside waiting for the dust to clear." Later, the platoon was able to search the school building, but didn't find anything except AK-47 shell casings all over the floor.

After suffering several casualties, Mayer ordered the 3rd Platoon to withdraw from the school. "I figured it wasn't worth losing any more men charging up fortified concrete stairways," Mayer explained, "so we surrounded the building and called in air support."

Grogan was overhead working out a plan to use two Marine AV-8B Harriers. He illuminated the target with his laser designator.

"The airplane comes over, and you see the five-hundred-pound bomb drop and nothing happens," Sellars recalled. "'Damn it, that's a dud. All right, we'll just hit it again!' This time, instead of a bomb, they're going to launch a Maverick missile. This thing comes screaming in from the northeast, hits the school, and takes down the whole front entrance. There was not much left of the school at all."

"We were kind of bummed out that we didn't get Sadr's house, but we got the school," Wallace rationalized. "It was just as good, I guess."

Sadr's house was still up for grabs. "All of a sudden," Sellars recalled, "I see 2nd Platoon come running across the street. They bowl over the door—they're big guys—knock the door in and go into the house."

"Sadr is pretty famous to us," Jenkins said, "so we're like, 'Wow, let's go! Let's get him!'" The 2nd platoon didn't find anything but a few AK-47s

Iraqi Resistance Report

International news networks showed footage of the U.S. Marine aggressors attacking the area around the empty home of Muqtada as-Sadr in the eastern part of an-Najaf, breaking down a door and storming inside the empty structure.

and a couple of hand grenades underneath the kitchen sink. "No Sadr, no militia, no dog, no cat, nothing," Jenkins recalled with disappointment. But they did get bragging rights as the first ones in al-Sadr's house.

Mayer remembered, "The biggest thing about Sadr's house was he had pictures of all the American icons in his bedroom: Clint Eastwood, Indiana Jones, and Bruce Willis in *Die Hard*." Mayer was amused by the dichotomy of an anti-American fanatic having photos of Hollywood's finest on his dresser.

With all objectives cleared, Mayer gave the order to withdraw. The raid had cost the U.S. forces dearly: Captain Tarlavsky and one Iraqi national guardsman killed, and four Marines, a soldier, and sixteen Iraqis wounded. The enemy lost three confirmed dead and eighteen wounded. Haslam estimated forty enemy casualties in the demolished school building.

Early the next morning, the MEU supported a raid by Iraqi commandos on the Imam Salah mosque, located directly north of the Kufa mosque, which intelligence reported was occupied by a number of militia. The force consisted of the MEU's Maritime Special Purpose Force (MSPF, a specially trained infantry platoon), an LAR platoon, CAAT-Bravo, and the Iraqi 36th Commando Battalion, with its Special Forces advisors. The commando unit was made up of Iraqi-Kurdish troops and an Iraqi counter-terrorist force.

The LAR platoon covered the movement to the objective and established a support-by-fire position about fifty meters from the mosque, while the MSPF and CAAT-Bravo set up a cordon around the area. Unfortunately,

Iraqi 36th Commando Battalion

The Iraqi 36th Commando Battalion was originally known as the Political Battalion because it was formed from militias of the five major political groups in Iraq: Ayad Allawi's Iraq National Accord (INA), Ahmed Chalabi's Iraqi National Congress (INC), the Supreme Council for Islamic Revolution in Iraq (SCIRI), and the two main Kurdish groups, the Patriotic Union of Kurdistan (PUK) and the Kurdish Democratic Party (KDP). About 110 soldiers were taken from each group so that the unit represented the Iraqi nation and not just one political party. It was trained by U.S. Special Forces advisors in two separate locations near Baghdad. Upon completion of training, the battalion was considered combat ready. Despite the training, there was a high desertion rate—40 to 50 percent among the Sunnis and Shiites, but only 5 percent among the Kurds—in early combat operations. The 36th Commando Battalion's uniform patch is in the shape of Iraq and uses the colors of the Iraqi flag as a backdrop. The number 36 is centered in green.

Iraqi Resistance Report

Adnan as-Zarafi, the puppet governor of an-Najaf announced that the Jaysh al-Mahdi had taken full control of the al-Ghurri puppet police station. According to the Middle East News Agency as-Zarafi said that the puppet police were preparing in a big way to drive the Jaysh al-Mahdi out of the station, but he made no mention as to whether he was referring to armed action or negotiation.

---

the commandos took a wrong turn, and the assault on the mosque was delayed for over half an hour, which allowed many of the enemy fighters to flee. The LAR platoon observed approximately thirty armed men fleeing the area. They held their fire to avoid compromising the raid. After arriving, the commandos stormed the mosque, killing four militiamen and capturing nine. The MSPF Marines killed two more that were firing at them from the rooftops. The raid force withdrew without any friendly casualties.

At one point, Sellars was told that a Kurdish unit was going to enter the fight. "The 50th Special Forces Brigade came down with a whole bunch of ODAs and Special Forces guys with nametags that just read Bob and Ron or Smith, and patches on their sleeves like 'Have a nice day someplace else,' with a picture of a smiley face and a bullet hole through it." Rumor had it that the Kurds were going to handle the Mahdi Militia. Ever the skeptic, Sellars remembered thinking, "Great, we'll just drive around the perimeter, drop off the Kurds, and they will kill all the bad guys in the city." It turned out these Kurds were not used except to gather intelligence. "They would dress up like regular Iraqis, go inside the mosque, and send back video of what they'd seen," he said.

IRAQI POLICE STATION (AUGUST 19)

Intelligence reports indicated that a significant number of militiamen were occupying a police station in Kufa. Mayer directed Sotire's Alpha Company to launch a mechanized raid to eliminate the enemy.

"The raid was the highlight of all the raids we pulled," Sotire said proudly. "The company was tight from sharing the hardships of training. The men were highly motivated, aggressive, and proud of their motto, 'Alpha Raiders.'"

They had never rehearsed a mechanized operation, however. "Lieutenant Colonel Mayer told me we were going to mech up [ride in Amtracs],"

Sotire recalled, "and it wasn't a suggestion." Sotire immediately started the planning process by reviewing intelligence reports, identifying possible course of action, ascertaining the enemy situation, and working up a fire-support plan. He turned the load plan over to the first sergeant, who then had to assign men to the vehicles while maintaining tactical integrity. "The scheme of maneuver dictated the load plan," Sotire explained, "and I hadn't worked one up yet. The first sergeant had to revise the plan several times to take into account the last-minute assignment of attachments and my plan changes. At one point, I thought he might have a meltdown. He was not a happy man."

The mechanized raid force consisted of a reinforced Alpha Company aboard twelve amphibious assault vehicles (AAV), the attached tank platoon, and Mayer's command element. The raid force began the attack at 2200. on August 21. Lieutenant Thomas's tank platoon, Team Tiger, was the lead element. Thomas explained, "We were about 200 to 300 meters ahead of the AAVs. Our job was basically to take fire, and if we felt it was too intense, we would pull back and let the AC-130 gunship come in and neutralize them." Thomas pushed forward—two tanks forward and two back, as a covering force—almost to the Kufa shrine. The area was extremely restricted. "The buildings were three to four stories high with only fifteen feet clearance on either side," he recalled. "There

Marines debark from an amphibious assault vehicle (AAV). Alpha Company used the AAVs for its raid on the Kufa Technical College, even though they had not used them before. Tanks led the raid, as the AAVs were not heavily armored.
Defenseimagery.mil 06903-F-1644L-058

was a small cemetery near the mosque." As the tanks reached the graveyard, the insurgents opened fire with a volley of RPGs.

First Lieutenant Richard Zjawin, 1st Platoon, Alpha Company, remembered, "We weren't even out of FOB Baker before we heard the tank platoon engaging multiple targets. I heard them say over the radio, 'Maintain ground, maintain ground,' as if they were going to be overrun."

Moran empathized with the embattled tankers: "From all around, poor Tiger was the center of enemy attention!"

Lieutenant Thomas radioed Sotire urgently requesting infantry support because he feared the militia might overrun his tanks. Sotire was monitoring the battalion tactical net and was eager to help Thomas. "I called the battalion commander and begged permission to leave the holding area," Sotire said, "but he said that the tanks were OK. RPGs couldn't penetrate their armor. He told me to wait until he gave the word to go." Basher was on station. The gunners could pick up hot spots through its optics.

"The AC-130 radioed in that they had insurgents with hot RPG tubes within twenty-five meters of us," Thomas recalled. "I wasn't sure their weapons system was that accurate, but they assured me it was, so I told them to fire away."

The battalion after-action report noted, "The enemy fire came with such intensity that Lieutenant Thomas thought his unit might be overrun." One of his tanks fired its main gun into a building, against orders that authorized only machine-gun fire because of the closeness of the mosque. It was thought that the action may have saved his crew.

Moran was more sanguine: "Nothing the enemy had could really destroy one of his [Thomas's] tanks or even really hurt it, so everyone that shot at

Alpha Company's August 21 night attack into the city, as viewed through night-vision goggles.
Maj. R. Bruce Sotire, USMC

him just kind of made him mad." Mayer's tactic to hold the company was extremely effective. The tanks were bait to get the enemy to expose themselves to the AC-130. It was the perfect softening technique to use before launching the raid force.

The fight was close enough that Sotire could hear the explosions and see Basher's cannon fire streaming toward the ground. He was straining to go. Then suddenly Mayer called and unleashed Alpha's pent up infantrymen with a simple order: "Go!" The Amtracs lurched forward, their open hatches bristling with rifles and machine guns. Lieutenant Christopher Smith's 1st Platoon rode in the lead tracs to provide security and isolate the objective. Sotire's command trac was next in the column, followed by the assault element, Zjawin's 2nd Platoon, the company's weapons platoon, battalion headquarters, and rear security. The column roared toward the objective. "We had practiced this raid technique so much that it was automatic," Sotire said.

The lead trac reached its dismount point 500 meters from the objective. Smith's men quickly took position to provide security around the police station. Sotire's headquarters element established a location that allowed him to have direct observation of the target. The weapons platoon's 60mm mortars and machine guns were located close by. Zjawin's assault element rolled up adjacent to the police station and off-loaded. His Marines stormed into the building.

"I tasked my first squad to clear the first deck," Zjawin explained. "As soon as they cleared the floor, my second squad and the machine-gun squad were to go to the roof to provide a base of fire. My third squad stood by to pick up the clearing mission."

Clearing a house, as seen through night-vision goggles. *Defenseimgery.mil DM-SD-06-01247*

Sotire was confident of his men. "We had done quite a bit of close-quarters training," he explained, "but it's still a high-risk procedure going room to room with direct-fire weapons in unfamiliar surroundings using NVGs [night-vision goggles]."

Zjawin's first squad entered the building through a side entrance without encountering resistance and started clearing the first floor. The second squad entered and formed a stack behind them. "My platoon sergeant heard noises in the basement," Zjawin recalled. "I told him to take the third squad and investigate."

They warily climbed down a stairway and discovered twenty-seven Iraqi men, two AK-47s, and burning documents in a large room at the base of the stairs. The platoon sergeant, taking in the scene, ordered the Iraqis to be flexi-cuffed and taken to a holding area for evacuation. As they were brought out, one of Zjawin's men recognized two employees that worked at the FOB for the construction firm of Kellogg, Brown, and Root. The two tried to convince the skeptical Marines that they had been captured by the militia and forced into the basement. Later, a Marine identified one of the men on a website teaching insurgents how to fire a mortar. The other was released after interrogation. He was found dead a few days later in the Old City.

The first squad continued working its way through the first floor. "I now have control of the floor, or at least I thought I did," Zjawin explained. "I saw Lance Corporal Brennen pointing down the hallway, orienting on a door. I'm looking at him, and I said, 'Brennen, what are you doing?' Just as

Iraqi detainees taken by Alpha Company during its raid on the Iraqi police station on August 19. The detainees were turned over to human exploitation teams for interrogation. Two of the men were identified as working at the FOB for a civilian contract firm. *Capt. Richard Zjawin, USMC*

I said that, three or four insurgents opened up on me!" The deafening roar of gunfire narrowly missed Zjawin and tore up the walls around him. "At that moment, everything went real slow as I brought up my rifle," he said. "Rounds snapped past my head. I remember shooting and diving out of the hallway."

Brennen and another Marine were also shooting, trying to suppress the enemy fire. Zjawin pulled up his ballistic glasses, just as the window over his head blew out, spraying him with glass fragments. "I have this dirt and glass fragments in my face, and I can't see. I sat there thinking, 'God, I'm screwed! I'm out of the fight.' Everything is going on around me—shooting, my radio operator shoving a handset in my face, yelling that the captain wants me—just like a scene out of the movie *Saving Private Ryan*, when everybody wants him, and he freezes for a few seconds."

Suddenly, Brennen screamed that he had been hit in the hand, snapping Zjawin out of the shock. He yelled, "Somebody give me a grenade." He pulled the pin while thinking, "I wasn't going to do it right because I hadn't thrown one of the things for so long." He threw it as hard as he could at a low angle into the room "so the bad guys couldn't throw it back." Zjawin scrambled for cover behind a cinder-block wall and waited for the explosion. "The five seconds were the longest in my life," he exclaimed. There was a huge blast. "The concussion picked me up off the floor and knocked me around," he said. "I heard screaming from the room. My men were trained to assault immediately after a grenade, but they hesitated, and the survivors began firing again." Zjawin and another man threw in two more grenades, "and the room went up like a torch." Flames quickly engulfed the entire police station.

Sotire could see the conflagration and told Zjawin to get his men out of the building. "There was nothing there worth exploiting and getting men hurt," Sotire said.

By this time, it was getting light outside, and the militiamen started shooting from the cemetery and buildings on three sides of the police station. Militia snipers were firing from one particularly dominant building and caught Sotire in the middle of the street. "Sixty Marines opened up shooting directly over me," he exclaimed. Hundreds of bullets impacted inside and outside the sniper lair, silencing whoever was there.

Next, the militia started walking mortar fire toward the company. It was time to leave. Sotire ordered a withdrawal. "I realized I hadn't checked in with the battalion commander," he recalled. "Tracers arched over my head as I ran back to the radio operator." In the confusion, he didn't notice that

Mayer had come forward and was standing literally a few feet from him. Sotire was startled when Mayer spoke. "At that point," Sotire said, "a tracer round skimmed right past my knees. 'Bruce,' Mayer said matter-of-factly, 'I think we better move.'" They both smiled at the moment of shared danger. Sotire remembered admiring Mayer's combat leadership: "It is rare when you encounter a senior officer who is so comfortable with his subordinate to allow him to fight without micromanaging the situation. He taught me a lot of things I will use throughout my career in the Corps."

As the company started to pull out, Sotire received a radio call from Basher, asking him to confirm the location of his men, which he did. The gunship then passed the word that an RPG team was sneaking toward their location. After receiving clearance to fire, Basher shot several 40mm rounds. "It was so close that my men thought the aircraft was firing at them," Sotire recalled, "so I had them check the area. They found the bodies of the RPG team."

Basher continued to pummel several enemy groups closing in on the company. "The withdrawal was now well underway," Sotire said. "The load plan was screwed up because of the additional detainees, but we had to evacuate. In addition, one of the tracs broke down, which left us short of vehicles." Sotire was very concerned about personnel accountability and pressed his unit leaders to double-check their counts. Finally convinced that every man was accounted for, he stepped aboard the last Amtrac. Upon reaching the FOB, he got one more count; all hands were present and accounted for.

Team Tiger was the last element to withdraw. "We pulled out," Thomas said, "but my tank backed into a wall and crushed its exhaust, which put engine fumes back into the tank." The fumes threatened to overcome the crew. They made it halfway back to FOB Baker before the engine quit. "It was daylight," Thomas recalled, "And the enemy started walking mortars in toward us." The tankers' only option was to tow the disabled vehicle. Thomas and his loader hurriedly dismounted and hauled out the tow cables. "We hooked up to another tank, but we had to do it several times because the cables came unhooked. Luckily, we weren't injured!"

The MEU estimated that forty-five militiamen were killed in the raid on the Iraqi police station.

KUFA TECHNICAL COLLEGE (AUGUST 21)

The Kufa Technical College, on the western bank of the Euphrates River, was adjacent to the Kufa mosque, where Imam Ali had been mortally

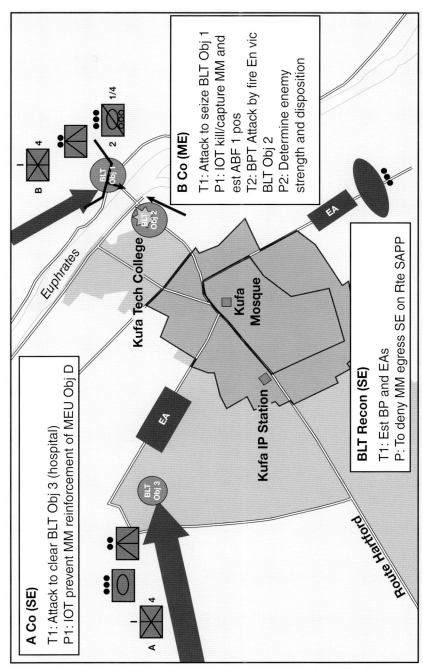

The Kufa Tech College raid consisted of two platoons from Bravo Company, reinforced by the LAV Platoon, CAAT-Alpha, and a six-tube section from the 81mm Mortar Platoon. Alpha Company and the Battalion Reconnaissance Platoon provided support. *Patricia Isaacs, from an 11th MEU operations slide*

wounded in AD 661. The college overlooked a key bridge where Route Hartford crossed the main road to Diwaniyah and FOB Echo. The bridge was controlled by the militia, who was reported to have rigged it with explosives. The college itself was a fairly large complex of ten multi-story buildings; the enemy used it as a rest and recuperation center and to control access to the bridge. Its significance, according to Capt. Sam Carrasco, lay in the fact that "the location provided the fighters with a direct route to support the cemetery and al-Sadr's fighters in the Imam Ali shrine."

"The Mahdi Militia bused raw recruits from the Baghdad slums to Najaf, where they laagered in the college for a few days," he said. After the recruits were fed and heard some preaching, they would infiltrate the Old City. "The fighters would then run a live fire exercise or two against soft targets," Carrasco continued. "Finally, they would be fed into the meat grinder in the cemetery or the defensive perimeter in the Old City."

Captain Carrasco briefed battalion command on the idea of a raid on the technical college. "It didn't take long to convince Major Moran of its importance," he said. "Moran liked the idea because it made sense at the tactical level to eliminate the militia's base of operations." It still took more than a week for the raid to be approved. "It was probably because the MEU wanted to keep the fight localized in and around the Old City," Carrasco said.

The operation was finally approved on August 18. It was planned as a destruction raid and designated battalion objective two, an "attack by fire" objective. Carrasco was overjoyed. "I wanted the mission because the men were upset and tired of the constant mortar and sniper fire that we had taken in the cemetery," he explained. "They needed to see the Mahdi Militia for what they were, an unprofessional, and mostly disorganized rabble—not an eight-hundred-pound gorilla."

Major Moran described the overall plan for the raid: "We would set up on the east side of the river, fire at the enemy, bring in air support—the AC-130 and Cobra attack helicopters—shoot at whatever enemy exposed themselves, and kill them." The battalion commander noted, "It was an ideal target because the fifty-meter wide river would provide ideal fields of fire. There was no need for ground troops to enter the campus." The destruction raid was scheduled for the early morning hours of August 21.

Captain Carrasco mulled over the details of the plan for several days. "I opted to take a circuitous southern route and envelop the objective from east to west, along the MSR [main supply route]," he explained. "The route would take us out of my area of operations, but I believed it would mask our movement until we reached the assault position." Carrasco designated 1st Lt. Edward "Hoot" Stahl's 3rd Platoon as the main effort and 1st Lt. Michael Cap's 2nd Platoon as the secondary effort. He decided to keep the Weapons Platoon together, rather than attach it out. The plan called for the 3rd Platoon, with the assault section, to infiltrate the campus via a palm grove to reach its attack-by-fire position, while the 2nd Platoon cleared three small buildings before taking its assault-by-fire position. The machine-gun section was tasked with providing support from the top of an abandoned police station. The plan gave the force great fields of fire. The technical college and its courtyard were completely exposed—no more than eight hundred meters away—at point-blank range.

The raid force was designated Task Force Blackhorse, the company call sign. It consisted of two heavily reinforced platoons from Bravo Company (2nd and 3rd Platoons), Borneo's CAAT-Alpha, the LAV Platoon, a six-tube section from Breshears's 81mm Mortar Platoon, and a battalion sniper team. In addition, the army provided a psychological-operations detachment and a tactical human-intelligence team. A two-tube battery of Marine 155mm artillery was assigned in direct support. Air support—a section of skids and Basher on-station—for the raid was coordinated by Captain Lowe, Bravo Company's FAC. Task Force Blackhorse was an extremely potent force.

Bravo Company crossed the line of departure on schedule. Ten minutes from the objective, the convoy came upon an unexpected Iraqi police checkpoint. "Fortunately, my men held their fire," Captain Carrasco said, "and the Iraqis moved back. You could see they were not happy, and to this day I believe they tipped the militia off to our presence." The assault force reached the release point. Borneo's CAAT-Alpha pushed out to cover the southern flank, while the LAR platoon covered the northern approach. The AAVs with the 2nd Platoon roared up and disgorged their passengers. "I moved with them and saw they were getting ready to assault the wrong objective," Carrasco said. The darkness, combined with the strange surroundings and the adrenaline rush, disoriented them. He grabbed the platoon commander and quickly pointed out the correct building. Meanwhile, the 3rd Platoon moved rapidly to its attack-by-fire position.

By this time, CAAT-Alpha's four-vehicle section had moved into a position only 150 meters from the college. "We pulled up and waited to see what would happen," Borneo recalled. "We sat there for maybe five minutes when some guy with an itchy trigger finger decided to take a shot at us.

First Lieutenant David N. Cedarleaf, leader of Bravo Company's Weapons Platoon and fire-support team (FIST). He led the platoon during the Kufa Technical College raid on August 21. *USMC History Division*

It was the wrong call for him, because we engaged him with MK-19, .50-caliber, and the LAV's 25mm cannon fire."

The battalion after-action report noted, "Corporal Aguayo Sierras had his gunner fire two TOW missiles at a window that the platoon was receiving RPG fire from. LAR's 25mm cannon, combined with the MK-19s, were producing devastating effects on the enemy and destroyed three separate machine gun positions." The militia machine guns also opened fire on the Marines who were moving into position.

"At that moment," Captain Carrasco recalled, "I saw my radio operator crouch down and cover his ears. There was a sudden explosion about five meters from me. I hit the ground and shouted, 'Incoming!'" His grinning radio operator patted him on the shoulder, explaining that it was only a hand grenade that one of the men had thrown. "It scared me to death," Carrasco exclaimed.

First Lieutenant David N. Cedarleaf was Bravo Company's Weapons Platoon commander and FIST (fire-support team) leader. "The lead element rolled up on the objective, a one-story building facing the river across from the college," he explained. "The 2nd Platoon was supposed to lead, but they came under machine-gun fire and took cover. My FIST team was supposed to follow them, but ended up in the lead for a few minutes."

Iraqi Resistance Report

Iraqi puppet government officials acknowledged that violent battles were raging between U.S. aggressors and the Jay al-Mahdi militia in the city of Kufa. Loud explosions shook the industrial section of the city as U.S. aggressor troops attempted to enter the as-Sahlah area but were repulsed by intense gunfire.

The platoon returned the fire, which allowed the team to gain the protection of the building. In the meantime, the 3rd Platoon and the assault section had worked their way along the river bank adjacent to the college. Cedarleaf's fire-support representatives made their way to the top floor of the police station and, together with Captain Lowe, worked up several targets for the supporting AC-130 and helicopter gunships. The 2nd platoon and the machine-gun section joined them.

"The machine guns on the roof suppressed the militia's positions south of the college and killed those fighters who were attempting to reinforce the college," Captain Carrasco reported. However, the militia machine guns continued to fire, and militiamen were able to launch a few RPGs, which exploded in the treetops. The 81mm Mortar Platoon and the company 60mm mortar section hurled high-explosive shells into the campus in an effort to knock out the enemy's guns.

Lowe cleared targets for the helicopter gunships. "They came in over the Marines along the river," Cedarleaf said. "Brass from expended cartridges fell on them. They were close enough to see the impact of bullets on the buildings, which was a great morale boost." The ROEs stated that everything west of the river was fair game, so the Marines poured it on. "It was simply amazing," Cedarleaf exclaimed. "Everything was working—the AC-130, gunships, mortars, infantry weapons. It was the most intense rain of fire I had ever seen. The whole place was just an impact area!"

The MEU became concerned that too much fire was being unleashed and told Captain Carrasco to stop using the mortars. "Apparently the MEU was watching our raid via the Predator feed and became very concerned about the overwhelming firepower," Cedarleaf said. "I was very much against this, as it was the only thing that we had to reach the defilade on the far side of the courtyard." But Carrasco complied and gave the order to pull out.

The men quickly boarded the AAVs, leaving Carrasco, the FIST, and the machine-gun section to cover the withdrawal. "We shot fire missions to cover it," Cedarleaf recalled. "My FIST team remained on the roof, calling in missions, until the final 60mm mortar target, and then we pulled out."

Carrasco said, "I kept running from position to position, checking on the few guys that were still with me." He gave the signal for CAAT-Alpha and the LAR platoon to pull out. They drove along the return route to provide security for the withdrawal.

Finally, it was Carrasco's turn. "I was getting antsy," he recalled. The remainder of the company pulled off the rooftop, boarded their vehicles, and started back.

"Suddenly, I heard AK-47s, followed by the sharp report of M-16s. An overloaded minivan with eight Mahdi Militia had careened around a corner toward one of our checkpoints and opened fire. First Sergeant Joe Morales, Sgt. Conner Gwynn, and Lance Cpl. Bryan Bengle killed the occupants with small-arms fire."

Task Force Blackhorse made it back to FOB Hotel without incident. "The Marines were sky high," Captain Carrasco remembered. "Apparently, we hit the college just as thirty foreign fighters showed up."

Cedarleaf reported, "The results were simply staggering. An initial intelligence report indicated that 100 to 150 of the enemy were killed. A few days later, the figure was revised upward to over 300, including the thirty Wahhabis." Whatever the final results, the destruction was so great that the militia did not use the college again. "We killed whatever was there," Cedarleaf emphasized.

CHAPTER 10

Tomb Job

It was like New Orleans meets Baghdad.
—U.S. Army officer describing the Wadi al-Salaam cemetery

1ST BATTALION, 5TH CAVALRY REGIMENT
(BLACK KNIGHTS)

ALPHA COMPANY JUMPED OFF early in the morning of August 8. "We cleared the little carnival area with negative contact," Alpha Company's commander, Capt. Kevin Badger, said. "We didn't find anything." The company held up until about 1400, when, Badger said, "Colonel Miyamasu called and told me to initiate operations in AO Mad Dog [Alpha Company's area of operations]."

First Lieutenant Steven D. Stauch added, "We were basically on station as a kind of reserve for about two hours at that point. We waited for Bravo and Charlie to clear down to Phase Line Bronx, and once they got to that point, then we were brought in to start clearing our sector." Each company was given about a one-thousand-meter frontage.

"We knew front was due south," said Lt. Col. Myles Miyamasu, the 1-5 Cav's commanding officer. "But because of the construct of the cemetery— the lack of roads, lack of trails—it became very difficult to establish a line that you would say . . . is the front. So the front really became an area."

At 0500, on August 9, Bravo and Charlie Companies attacked, using narrow dirt pathways to wend their way through the cemetery's maze.

"There were eight to ten lanes about a tank or Bradley wide," Badger said. "They were straight, about fifty to one hundred meters apart." While the pathways provided some ease of movement, they severely restricted maneuvering and provided the militia with well-defined lines of fire. Militia mortar teams did not have to worry about deflection, just range. In addition, the pathways pointed out the battalion's axis of advance, making it easier for militia RPG teams to set up ambushes. Badger anticipated this tactic. "I just gave one lane per team [an Abrams and a Bradley] for mutual support," he recalled. "I also had dismounted infantry in close support. The tank-Bradley combination and the infantry formed my killer-hunter team."

The narrow lanes created another problem for the tanks. "The gun tube kept hitting the tombs when we tried to traverse it," Beam said, "and we had to worry about maneuvering."

Up to this point, the battalion had not seen the labyrinth of crypts and mausoleums. "When we pulled into the cemetery, I called Bushmaster [Bravo Company] and told him to stop where he was," Miyamasu said. "It was the first time we had seen it, and it was just amazing. The complexity of the place didn't really strike us until then. I remember thinking, 'Well, this isn't your momma's cemetery!'"

Captain Keahtigh, Bravo Company, remembered, "The attack was something very moving. We've all seen large cemeteries, but this one was enormous. It stretched for miles. There were times when we couldn't even see each other 100 meters apart. It was a very unique environment—an urban environment."

Private First Class Thomas F. Cosby, a tank gunner, was more succinct:

1-5 Cavalry Attack Formation

The article "Armor in Urban Terrain: The Critical Enabler" (published in the March/April 2005 issue of the journal *Armor*) described the Black Knights' attack formation: "A combined arms section became the preferred maneuver element. The section normally included a tank and Bradley attacking abreast, trailed by an M1114. The tanks often advanced slightly ahead of the Bradley to absorb the initial energy of enemy ambushes. The Bradleys would protect the flank and elevated shots against the tank, and the M1114 provided local and rear security for the lead vehicles using its M240 machine gun. Dismounted soldiers would disperse to the flanks of the section to eliminate enemy attempting to get into the blind spots of the armor."

"Shoot, it had a million tombs, easily!"

Bravo Company led the attack. "It wasn't easy," Keahtigh recalled. "We were briefed that we would be starting at a shanty village, but when we got there, it was the beginning of the cemetery."

Miyamasu let him off easy. "Darren, bless his heart, got us into the cemetery at the wrong point," he recalled. "I said, 'Don't worry about it. Let's clear back of us and then we'll move further south.'"

Bravo reoriented itself and started clearing the mausoleums, which in some cases were actually three- and four-story buildings. Initially, the soldiers had reservations about clearing the tombs. "It's a sacred place," Keahtigh said. "You know all the boys are religious in some way . . . and they didn't want to do it . . . [B]ut they [militia] forced us to do it." Bravo developed a clearing SOP. "If they looked like they had been tampered with, had new locks, we cleared them," Keahtigh said.

Sergeant Hector Guzman felt badly. "It doesn't feel right that we're desecrating graves," he said. "But that's what we had to do."

Charlie Company took position on Bravo's right flank, and the two pushed south toward Phase Line Bronx, a terrain feature in the cemetery that the 1-5 Cav used as a tactical-control measure. "This whole process took about five hours," Miyamasu recalled. "By this time, the men started to get a feel for the underground crypts, the height of the mausoleums, the

An aerial photo of the Wadi al-Salaam cemetery. The cemetery covered several square miles in a jumble of crypts, mausoleums, and brick tombs. The 1-5 Cav was directed to fight through it because of its armor protection.
Lt. Col. Glen G. Butler, USMC

narrowness of the walkways, and the fact that a lot of the older tombs were brittle." Charlie Company came upon several excavations. "We were like, 'What are those holes?' We threw some grenades in them to be safe."

The men in the battalion were not used to the heat—Badger estimated that the temperatures ranged from 115 to 125 degrees Fahrenheit—so the physical effort quickly tired them. "We were thinking, where's the enemy?" Capt. Benjamin McFall, commander of Charlie Company, recounted. "This is hard; this is hot work."

"The weather was ridiculously hot," Sgt. Joshua W. Beams complained. "You're pretty much sitting in the desert with no air conditioning. We had a lot of heat casualties. We were drinking a lot of hot water, because the tank's exhaust blows right back on the turret where we had our water sitting."

The heat also affected their equipment. "Sometimes your fire-control system wouldn't work," Cosby related. "If the computer is overheating, it will malfunction and wouldn't calculate distances correctly. The tank might shoot high, wide, or low." Then there was the heat from the electronics in the tank itself. "Those systems make the tank even hotter," Cosby said, "and our A/C was broken." He stuffed the blower for the tank's nuclear, biological, and chemical (NBC) protection system down his shirt, which helped him cool off.

Keahtigh remembered one man who became a heat casualty: "He went down instantly. He just sat down, drinking water, and the next thing you know, he bowled over."

Miyamasu recalled that as the 1-5 Cav crossed Phase Line Bronx, "We

A dismounted soldier working his way through the debris of the cemetery. A Bradley cautiously advances alongside. *Defenseimagery.mil DM-SC-07-14986*

started making our first contact, which I believe were mortar rounds—not effective, but definitely the right range." It was the first time many of the soldiers had been under fire.

"It was an eye opener," Badger commented. "The men were getting an idea of what they were up against—mortars hitting within a few meters of you, helicopters shooting, aimed sniper fire. It was full-up combat." The battalion took fire all along its front, and as it advanced, the volume of RPG and mortar fire started to pick up.

"We had mortars falling like raindrops for the first few days," Beams recalled.

They quickly discovered there was a positive side to the cemetery. "The graves and mausoleums were made with a very sandy, soft material," Badger explained, "so when a mortar round exploded, the predominance of the shrapnel was sucked up by the sandy soil, and there was just a plume of smoke."

Keahtigh agreed: "If the round didn't land within twenty meters of you, it didn't have much effect."

Badger looked at the first day of the cemetery battle as a baptism of fire. "As long as I'm in uniform, I'll never forget this," he said. "There's a difference between shooting targets and shooting people." He also learned what it sounds like to be shot at by small-arms fire. "You just hear a snap or a crack when a bullet passes by."

In one instance, his inexperience almost cost him his life. "I found myself on the main thoroughfare through the cemetery," he said. "I had lost communications with the tank commander, so my driver and I got out and walked over toward it. The soldier turned around and saw us. He opened his hatch and started waving his arms, shouting 'Get out of here!'" Badger didn't realize he was the target for militia small-arms fire. "Once we realized the danger, we jumped over a wall and took cover," he said. He was lucky. "A round went through my legs and clipped my pant leg as I was running. I remember thinking, 'This shit's real!'" As he and his driver reached the safety of his vehicle, Badger turned to the soldier and said excitedly, "OK. We're not going to do that anymore."

Badger's combat experience in Baghdad had been relatively mild. It had been a "hold-fire type situation, unless actually engaged," he said. The rules of engagement (ROE) in Najaf were completely different. "The colonel [Miyamasu] told everyone to fire a hundred-round burst of coax [a machine gun] down our lane in the cemetery," Badger recalled. This firing order served two purposes: it allowed the soldiers to test-fire their weapons and told them they shouldn't be afraid to shoot. "It was a great psychological tactic to get us ready for the fight," Badger said. The coax machine gun, zeroed at about two hundred meters, would often flush the militiamen out of cover, setting them up for disaster. Heavy machine-gun fire also helped to prevent coordinated attacks from multistory buildings.

In many ways, Najaf represented a conventional battle. "We had tanks, Brads [Bradleys], Humvees, and a designated enemy in a designated battleground," Badger explained. "My mission was simple: clear the sector and destroy enemy forces." He remembered briefing his men, saying, "If you see a person with an RPG, that's a target. He doesn't have to wear a uniform or point a weapon at you. They're bad guys."

Early in the attack, he received a call from one of his tank commanders saying, "I've got an RPG."

"Shoot it!" Badger replied without hesitation. "I thought at that point everybody understood that we're in an environment where we're going to shoot a lot."

First Lieutenant Christopher S. Dunn remembered, "The main military [militia] wore all black or had black armbands. They were to be engaged whenever we saw them."

At one point early in the fighting, Badger said, "I'll never forget kind of looking around and thinking, 'I can't believe Kevin Badger from Dallas, Texas, a boy who grew up playing soccer, is standing in a cemetery in Iraq in a

Dismounts from the 1-5 Cavalry clear a portion of the Wadi al-Salaam cemetery while a Humvee mounting a .50-caliber machine gun provides overwatch protection. *Maj. Michael Irwin, U.S. Army*

major combat fight.' It was surreal."

The advance slowed down. Heat, enemy fire, and the need to search the crypts limited the speed of the attack. "We were probably moving a hundred meters every hour to an hour and a half—two hours," Badger estimated. "We didn't have enough dismounts. You're talking about maybe twenty guys at the most clearing nine hundred meters of cemetery. Clearance is not what we did . . . [I]t was more limited than that."

Reports of enemy contact filled the radio nets. "My first platoon called over the radio—'I've got contact,'" McFall recalled. "I remember thinking, 'Well, where is the contact? I don't hear it.' All of a sudden, another platoon called over the net, 'Contact,' and then the third. My whole company was reporting contact." There were so many rockets that he compared it to the "the rockets' red glare" described in the "Star-Spangled Banner."

His radio came alive with excited chatter: "RPGs!" "Small arms!" "Holy cow, a mortar landed five meters from me!" "I had an RPG go between me and my gunner!" "I just got hit by an IED!" "Holy shit, I just got ambushed!"

Charlie Company was unable to maneuver laterally because of the narrow lanes; it had to keep going forward. "There were RPGs and mortars everywhere," McFall recalled. "Everything was going; all the weapons were kicking in."

Sergeant Lyle Pete spotted three men armed with RPGs entering a building on the edge of the cemetery. "They'd jump out and fire them [the RPGs] and jump back inside," he said. "That was the second time [that day we'd] taken fire from that location." Small-arms fire crackled all around him as he scrambled to find a firing position. A nearby Bradley started pumping 25mm-cannon rounds into the building.

Sergeant First Class Mike Dewilde led a three-man team up the steps of a mausoleum, whose square, walled-in concrete roof provided protection. They set up an M-240 machine gun along the wall and started shooting at the elusive militiamen dodging through the tombs.

"The problem with these guys," Spc. Joel Klootwyk explained, "is they can hide behind anything out there. You gotta wait for them to shoot before you know where they're at."

Bravo Company was also taking heavy fire. "My second platoon was the first in heavy combat," Keahtigh explained. "The lieutenant had a heavy Puerto Rican accent, so when he got excited on the radio, it was tough to understand him. I told him to calm down. 'It's all right,' I said, 'I'm only two hundred meters behind, and I know where you're at.'" The cemetery was so restricted that Keahtigh couldn't get a Bradley in to help out, so he walked the lieutenant through an attack plan: "I told him to get his AT-4s out and initiate the attack with them. Then launch your M-203s and suppress with one squad and assault with the other one." At one point, the militia pushed forward, attacking in three- to five-man groups. "I've never been counterattacked," Keahtigh exclaimed. "We started firing 25mm from the Bradleys, 120mm tank-man gun, and we brought in AH-1 Cobras on them."

The Cobras were cleared hot for multiple attacks by an air force joint tactical air controller (JTAC), call sign Toxin 21. "We got off three thousand rounds from the GAU [a gun] and fourteen rockets," Maj. Glen Butler said. On one of his runs, he fired a Hellfire missile about seventy-five meters in front of Keahtigh's vehicle.

The young officer radioed Miyamasu, "Sir, that's a little close!"

Miyamasu replied, "Hey, Darren, did it scare you?"

"Yeah, that scared the shit out of me. That thing's big and loud!"

"Think about the enemy," Miyamasu replied solemnly.

Butler recalled, "We took small-arms fire and saw puffs of smoke from RPGs in the air as we made our passes." His run in took him parallel to Keahtigh's Abrams. "It was pretty cool to see them shooting their main guns."

The tanks were firing because the militia was closing in. "They were really bold," Beams recalled. "They had no problem running up fifty meters in front of a tank with an RPG and trying to shoot us. But they were finding out real quick that the RPG-7s were just blowing up; they didn't hurt us."

Second Lieutenant Douglas J. Schaffer was very concerned with the cemetery's jumbled maze because "there were a lot of places to hide . . . It was a nasty place to fight."

The battalion's dismounts (infantry) started to find supply caches hidden in the tombs. "We found lots of weapons," Beams recalled, "RPGs, mortars, and beds where people had been sleeping. We figured they would sleep there, wait for somebody to come by, and shoot at them."

Stauch thought that the enemy was using small caches—"a couple of RPGs here, a couple there, a couple of hand grenades here and there, never more than five, eight, ten at the most in any one spot. They seemed to be arrayed in fallback positions, working their way back toward the mosque." The captured weapons and ammunition were photographed and taken to the rear to prove that the militia was using the cemetery as a battlefield.

As the battalion continued advancing south through the cemetery, political restrictions not only hindered operations, but also posed a direct

A Cobra gunship over the dry lake west of Najaf. The Imam Ali shrine is located on the left. Black smoke marks the location of an airstrike on Mahdi Militia cemetery positions. *Lt. Col. Glen G. Butler, USMC*

threat to the soldiers. "The exclusionary zones were effectively preventing us from engaging the enemy," Miyamasu emphasized. "The artillery and mortars could not fire for us without the release authority by higher headquarters." In some instances, approval took an inordinate time.

Dunn described watching a militia mortar team. "We couldn't engage because they were sitting next to the shrine," he recalled. "But because your bullet might ricochet off a car, or the ground, or a building, you just sat there and pretty much took it." When they requested permission to fire, "The battalion had to call the MEU, who would have to call the next higher level," Dunn said. "So then twenty-five minutes later you'd get a reply. Unfortunately, by this time, the guy who just shot six mortar rounds at you had packed his stuff in the back of his truck and waved goodbye. That was a little frustrating for some of the guys," he said, tongue in cheek.

By late afternoon, the battalion had advanced 500 meters into the cemetery. As dusk approached, Miyamasu radioed Haslam and requested permission to pull back and rearm. The request was granted, and the battalion pulled back to Phase Line Bronx, where "[we] set out our security element by establishing observation posts and set in our sniper for the night," Keahtigh recalled. "We rotated everybody back to FOB Hotel to rearm and refuel. We got some water, ammo, and more grenades."

Miyamasu called a unit leaders' meeting to plan the next day's attack. It was the first time the company commanders had an opportunity to meet face-to-face with him since the start of the attack. "We're all wide-eyed," Keahtigh recalled. "Man, what did we walk into? These Mahdi Army guys aren't playing. They were shooting final protective fire at us and had the entire cemetery zeroed in with indirect fires to support their extensive defensive plans. We're like, 'Wow!'"

Tactical Logistics

Marine Service Support Group-11 (MSSG-11) provided logistics support for the 11th MEU in the form of supply maintenance, deliberate engineering, medical and dental, automated information processing, utilities, landing support, disbursing, legal and postal service, and transportation. Captain Joseph M. Garaux was in charge of the sixty-seven Marines of the Transportation Support Detachment.

"During the battle of Najaf, we provided ground transportation for troops, ammunition, and a wide variety of other much-needed supplies," Garaux said. His detachment was split into two sections: "They were all over the place. They would go from the battlefield to wherever they had to go on short notice."

The MEU was augmented by the army's 364th Supply Company (Direct Support), Logistics Task Force Victory, and the 264th Corps Support Battalion (Airborne). The 364th Supply Company was headquartered at FOB Echo, near Diwaniyah, with a detachment at FOB Duke.

The company performed tactical fuel distribution; wholesale line-haul of fuel; and fuel storage and issue. It also provided Class II (general supplies), Class III (petroleum, oils, and lubricants), Class IV (construction and barrier material), Class V (ammunition), Class IX (repair parts) support; transportation support; heavy-equipment transporter (HET) support: direct support maintenance; field services (shower, laundry, and light clothing repair); and potable water production.

At the height of the battle in Najaf, the logistic units had to support the equivalent of six battalions of Marine, army, coalition, Iraqi, and aviation assets. Their biggest challenges were the variety of support, time, and distance factors, primarily fuel, ammunition, and water factors. For example, within the MEU battle space, fifty-seven miles of bad road separated FOB Echo from FOB Duke, while bulk JP8 [fuel] had to be transported over 160 miles. A single round trip, according to logistician Captain John H. Chaffin, "required soldiers to drive 320 miles in 130-degree heat. Three hours was the best response time we could achieve for an emergency resupply from FOB Echo to FOB Duke."

> ## Iraqi Resistance Report
>
> Iraqi sources told [the] Qatari News Agency Qana that occupation forces responded to the Jaysh al-Mahdi attack using helicopter gunships to rocket and shell the city, from which columns of smoke can be seen rising.

Miyamasu let the three officers blow off steam and then calmly took charge. "I don't mean to give them [the militiamen] too much, but they're good," he told them. "These guys really make us work to kill them, but in the end, they're dead!"

The planning session broke up in the early hours of the morning. "Everybody was tired," McFall remembered. "I mean we were just exhausted. We had been in contact for nine hours straight." The entire battalion was in the same shape. Three days of little sleep, coupled with the heat, humidity, and the adrenalin-induced alertness had pushed their bodies almost to the limit.

Badger was told that his company would have four hours off before going back to the cemetery. "The only place we [Badger and his first sergeant] could find to lay down was in the helicopter that got shot down. It was my bed the first night in Najaf. I picked the right side, because my first sergeant picked the other side of the aircraft. His side was covered with oil. When we got up, he was hot under the collar. 'Ah, shit, that sucked,' he exclaimed, as he tried to clean himself up."

The battalion spent a fairly calm night. "All of a sudden the insurgents stopped shooting," Keahtigh said. "They don't fight at night; they just pull back."

Not all the insurgents had stopped, however. Several were waiting for an Alpha Company convoy that was headed back to FOB Hotel for resupply. "When it was our turn to go back," Stauch explained, "we were ambushed. It was a very significant volume of fire from small arms and RPGs . . . machine guns from multiple locations and at least five RPGs that were volley fired." It appeared that the militia used the illumination of those streetlights that were still working to pinpoint Stauch's vehicles. "As soon as we got out of the dark and into the light, the enemy started shooting at us," he noted. "I think the thing that saved our lives that night was that we had no lights on our vehicles, so they didn't know we were there until we burst into the light. They were reacting to us, as opposed to being able to track us."

ONCE MORE INTO THE BREACH

These guys really make us work to kill them, but in the end, they're dead.

—Lt. Col. Myles Miyamasu

At 0600, the Black Knights kicked off their attack with three companies on line. "Bravo [was] in the center," Keahtigh explained, "with Mad Dog [Alpha Company] in the east and Commando [Charlie Company] in the west." Initially, there was little enemy contact.

"Around 1000 that morning, the battle really started for us," Private First Class Cosby pointed out.

Bravo Company's second platoon had the first contact.

"The platoon led with Bradleys," Keahtigh recalled. "I told them to push forward and just be careful." As the lead fighting vehicle pulled around the corner, it opened fire with its 25mm cannon. Keahtigh heard the distinctive boom of the weapon. "I'm kind of cringing," he said, because he did not know what it was shooting at. "Suddenly, the Bradley takes an RPG round, but he keeps pushing through!" The fight is on. "I got the company on line," he said, "and we start engaging the militia to the south. They are firing back at us. Sniper rounds are going off. RPGs are being launched at us . . . and we're digging in and we're fighting!" An after-action report noted, "There was a very high dud rate on our tanks and many of the near misses were duds as well."

Keahtigh had his Bradleys lay down suppression fire with their 25mm cannon, as his dismounts cleared the area to keep the militia at bay. "I got my ops [observation post] up, my sniper up," he said. "We're having a sniper war between theirs and ours . . . and the whole time I'm commander-in-control." The battalion had had only two trained sniper teams when they went into the cemetery, but on the second day, army Special Operations snipers appeared.

"I asked them, 'Who sent you down here?' " Miyamasu recalled, "They said, 'Oh, we heard you guys needed some sniper teams.' I go, 'Yeah, I'll take you.' "

The militia snipers realized they couldn't hurt the armor crewmen—although they did hit one of Schaffer's men in the leg—so they tried a new tactic. "They would shoot out tank and Bradley sights," Keahtigh explained. "That does more damage than an RPG hitting them and bouncing off." The battalion quickly learned that in an urban environment with heavy sniper fire, the tankers needed to "keep the ballistic doors closed and scan with the auxiliary sights."

Badger said, "Once they [the tankers] identified a target, [they] would open them [the ballistic doors] up, shoot, and close them again." He thought this method of firing would save the sight system.

Miyamasu ordered Bravo Company to hold in place. "That's when we bring up the other companies in kind of a semicircle," Keahtigh said, "and we're all tied in, shooting up smoke so that we can all see our left and right limits." The battalion put out a tremendous amount of firepower—120mm and 25mm cannon shells, 7.62-caliber machine guns, rifles, small arms, hand grenades, AT-4 antitank missiles, and the occasional TOW missile. "It was a full spectrum battle right there!" Keahtigh exclaimed. The 120mm main-gun round proved to be a great equalizer. "As soon as we began destroying enemy forces with the main guns, they broke and ran," Keahtigh added. "The engagements were often at short range, where the concussive effect of the cannon was lethal, even if the enemy was not directly hit by the round." A report later confirmed Keahtigh's assessment.

On the extreme right flank, Captain McFall's Charlie Company established contact as it crossed the phase line. "[There were] RPGs, mortars, snipers in the west . . . shrapnel and bullets everywhere," he said. He remembered thinking, "'Oh, my God, everybody's everywhere; they're going to get us!' I never experienced anything like it in my life." McFall was too busy to worry. "I had a company to command," he emphasized. "As a leader, you understand what is really important, what you need to pay attention to. I learned what I need to do and what I might have done differently. I think the biggest thing the experience taught me was about myself."

McFall ordered his dismounts into the cemetery. "When they were searching the tombs, they found a lot of hypodermic needles," he said. "So my assumption was that the militia[men] were using drugs. They also found caches of fifty-pound bags of rice [and] beans, and lots of clothes. It was enough to supply fifty guys for a month."

Badger's Alpha Company came up on Bravo's left flank. "Not exactly on line," Badger said, "but we were about as close as you could get in that type of environment." He maneuvered his company forward, using the east-west roads as phase lines to control movement. "I could look down the crossroad that was a phase line and see the front noses of my vehicles. I'd say, 'OK, we're all in line, go, keep moving.'" At one point, he "snuck an Abrams up, probably a little bit forward of where I was supposed to be, and as it turned the corner, the tank commander called me frantically. 'Hey, I

got at least ten people that just ran into the first floor of this building!'"
Badger requested permission to allow the tank to shoot, which was granted
because the building was on an azimuth, away from the shrine. "The tank
fired two HEAT [high-explosive antitank] rounds into the building and
collapsed it!" he said.

In another instance, Badger's men reported eight armed gunmen holed
up in a building, and they requested permission to fire. The request was
denied. "So eight people survived because of the exclusionary zone," he
said. "It's very frustrating."

Tank gunner Cosby saw a sniper on a roof through his optic sight. "I
engaged him," he said. "He was like a thousand yards away, out of range
of the coax [machine gun] . . . so we called a Bradley in on him. They shot
some 25mm, and I think they got him."

Sometime later, Cosby spotted three militiamen firing from a storefront
about seven hundred meters away. "They thought I couldn't see them," he
said. "At that point, the enemy underestimated the optics on our sights . . .
but I saw them clearly. I had my sights on ten power, and they looked like
they were only a hundred meters away." The three militiamen played hide
and seek, ducking in and out of the doorway. "I decided to try to draw them
out by making them believe I didn't see them," Cosby said. Finally, all of
them stood in the doorway. "And that's when I used the coax," he said. "I
think I got all three."

Lieutenant Dunn's 3rd Platoon ran into more and more of the militiamen the farther south it went. "There were more guys running around
the cemetery, because they could get in and out easier," he recalled.

Schaffer's 1st Platoon was oriented on the main north-south road. "We
sent the tanks down there, all the way to the boundary road of the old city,"
Schaffer recalled, "with the Bradleys on the access road to support them. We
took a lot of intense RPG fire from a building. That ended with my platoon
sergeant, who put two main-gun rounds into the building. After that, it
got real quiet. You know, they kind of took their ball and went home . . .
[T]hey didn't want to play anymore that day." Schaffer's men told him that
the second day's fight "was just as heavy as anything the battalion saw in
2003 crossing the berm."

By the end of the second day, Miyamasu was concerned about continuing
to attack through the cemetery. "If I want them [the militiamen] to fight
me all the time, then I have to be prepared to fight them all the time," he
reasoned. "And if I don't know how long I have to fight them, then I am
not prepared to do that." He knew from an operational perspective that the

overall objective of the fight was to "get the shrine back into the hands of the school or the imams," but the when and the how had not been decided. "I'm not sure when we're going to eject people out of the shrine, given that we have certain constraints," he recalled thinking. "But in the meantime, I'm not going to let people come through."

Haslam agreed with Miyamasu's interdiction strategy and authorized him to go to company-level operations. Miyamasu said, "We ended up establishing a rotation where one company would be in the cemetery and two companies would be out of contact. We initially started with a twelve-hour cycle. Every company would get twelve on, twenty-four off. Since we didn't know what our ultimate objective was, we had to conserve combat power." The rotation allowed the battalion to perform maintenance on its vehicles and give the men much-needed rest and food. Miyamasu also secured the use of an air-conditioned building at FOB Baker so that one company at a time could get out of the heat for at least one night out of three.

Lieutenant Dunn recalled, "We started setting up a screen line on an east-west running road on the north end of the cemetery, one company at a time."

"I gave free range to the company commanders on where they wanted to go," Miyamasu said. "I told them, 'Hey, I need you to focus here or here or here.'"

The companies conducted limited attacks to attrite the enemy and keep it off balance. "Some days we'd go deep, some days we'd go shallow," Badger said. "It turned into a daily movement to contact."

Stauch recalled, "We'd send a tank here or a tank there down toward the Old City and conduct limited attacks with Bradleys and dismounts, trying to weed out as many of the enemy snipers and RPG positions as we could. We got pretty significant enemy kills pretty much each day."

August 15 was a very bad day for Badger's Alpha Company. Second Lieutenant James M. "Mike" Goins, a tank commander, and Spc. Mark A. Zupata, a loader, were killed in action.

"Mike [Goins] was on the far western side of the cemetery as part of a hunter-killer [Abrams-Bradley] team," Badger explained. "He identified an enemy mortar team with his optics and called for permission to shoot because it was close to the exclusionary zone." The request was routed to higher headquarters. The Abrams' hatches were open, which was standard operating procedure in Alpha Company at the time. "A militia fighter ran up the front of the tank when Goins turned his attention back down into his gunsight and the loader [Zapata] was facing in another direction," Badger

Medics from the 1-5 Cavalry desperately try to save one of the company's two tankers wounded on August 15. They were unsuccessful, and the men died of their wounds. *Defenseimagery.mil DF-SD-07-08082*

explained. The gunman fired his AK-47 into the loader at point-blank range. "Mark [Zapata] took a round or two in the head," Badger said emotionally, "and the guy shot into the tank and hit Mike between the plates of his flak jacket and clipped his heart."

The tank driver, alarmed by the gunfire, backed up and drove over a mausoleum, which collapsed, trapping the tank in the debris. "A huge, fifteen-foot roof section landed on top of the turret," Beams recalled, "so he was stuck there with two badly wounded men who were bleeding on him." The driver sent out a plaintive call for help: "We've been hit! We've got casualties!"

The distress call galvanized the command group. Lieutenant Stauch and the company first sergeant were among the first to arrive. "We weren't clear as to whether the two crewmen were dead or not [Badger thought the lieutenant had a faint pulse], so [we] threw the two men in the medic trac and escorted it back to FOB Hotel," Stauch said.

While the wounded men were being evacuated, Badger was trying to coordinate recovery of the trapped vehicle in the face of heavy mortar fire. "We were fighting the hordes off, because now, the bad guys have a demobilized tank and they've got us cornered," Badger said.

Badger surrounded the area with several armored vehicles and dismounted infantry. "We were receiving mortars all over us," he explained, "and how we didn't get any [men] wounded, I have no idea. One [mortar]

On August 15, Lt. Michael Goins and Spc. Mark Zupata died when a Mahdi militiaman raced from cover, sprang onto their tank, and shot them. In the chaotic moments that followed, the tank driver backed the Abrams into a tomb, which collapsed. *U.S. Army's 49th Military History Detachment*

blew up right next to my driver, who was standing outside the door, firing his rifle." Badger tried bringing in close air support, but because they were near the exclusionary zone, his request was denied. "We took mortars the entire time we were there," he recalled.

A recovery vehicle and a maintenance team finally reached the trapped tank and extricated it from the collapsed mausoleum. "It was a two-hour recovery process," Badger said. "We got it out just before it got dark. It had significant damage to the top of the turret, but . . . once we pulled it out, it was drivable."

After the tank reached the assembly area, Beams helped clean it up. "We had to get the survivors out, clean the blood out, and get all the personal gear off," he recalled. "That was a real tough night for everybody."

The company soon learned that both tank crewmen had died. Their deaths were taken hard. "It sucked," Beams said angrily. "We're soldiers, and somebody may get killed in combat . . . but these guys were pretty much executed."

His gunner remarked, "Up to that point, we felt pretty much invincible. The deaths let us know that there were people really out there trying to kill us."

Badger was particularly affected. "He [Goins] was my favorite," he said sorrowfully, "my star lieutenant."

Dunn wanted revenge. "You want to go out and find the guy who did it," he said angrily. "You have no idea where he is . . . but you want to try."

The company held a memorial service during its next cycle off the line. The ceremony was attended by the division commander, sergeant major, and brigade commander, as well as by the battalion staff. "That was tough," Dunn admitted. "It helped a little bit, but even then it was difficult. There was definitely a change in the company after the service."

Keahtigh's Bravo Company was resting at FOB Baker after just coming off the line when the call came in saying that Alpha Company was in heavy contact and had taken casualties. "The radio watch woke me up," Keahtigh recalled. "I briefed the company to get ready to assume the line." Soon after, Miyamasu called him to find out how long before he could take over Alpha's mission.

"I told him five minutes," Keahtigh said.

"Assume the line," Miyamasu replied.

During the relief, Keahtigh met Badger, who didn't want to give up the fight. Keahtigh remembered, "I said to him, 'Hey brother, I got this fight for you. I can take care of this piece; do what you have to do.'" Alpha Company pulled back but the next night went back on the screen line.

As a result of the incident, Badger included another element in his hunter-killer teams. "I turned them into a Bradley, Abrams, and Humvee team," he explained. "The Humvee team was to follow about a hundred to two hundred meters behind the tank to make sure nobody's sneaking up on them."

Badger was convinced the time delay in approving Goins's request to fire near the exclusionary zone was to blame for his tankers' deaths. "Battalion called FOB Duke, FOB Duke called General Casey in Baghdad or whoever was in charge," Badger said, exasperated with the delayed approval system.

"At times, it was ten to fifteen minutes for the line commander to receive approval," Miyamasu complained. "When it was imposed, every headquarters that was above us kept expanding the zone. It was kind of hard to control the effects of fires when you're basically at a no-fire line, no penetration line, and one kilometer from the place where the enemy was holding out." He badgered Haslam to allow him to employ all the available firepower: "I said, 'Sir, if you want to destroy the militia, we need to be able to shoot artillery and get attack aviation to attack specific targets.' We had the firepower advantage. The enemy could not withstand it, if we were allowed to employ it."

Haslam, on his part, fought with I MEF and MNF-I to loosen the restrictions. "We tried to work it to where we could go inside the ring road and drop ordnance." He was eventually able to reduce the zone from a thousand meters from the shrine to three hundred—and at the end of the fight, down to one hundred meters.

1ST BATTALION, 4TH MARINE REGIMENT, BRAVO COMPANY

After losing Goins and Zupata, Lieutenant Colonel Miyamasu requested additional infantry support. "Bravo Company was tasked to provide a reinforced rifle platoon to provide local security for each cavalry troop because the cemetery was so treacherous," Captain Carrasco said. "We had two close calls the very first night." A machine-gun team spotted three men coming toward them through the cemetery. "I looked through my NVGs and saw them," Carrasco said. "The first two men were not wearing helmets, but the third one was. I passed the word to hold fire, while one of my men shouted to them to come in." The three men were soldiers from one of the Bradleys on a security patrol; they had not gotten the word to keep their helmets on and stay close to their vehicles. Captain Carrasco "chewed them out" and sent them on their way.

Another soldier was not so lucky. Two of Carrasco's men spotted a man on top of a mausoleum with a rifle, scoping them out. The men fired, knocking the figure off the structure. A team went forward and discovered a cavalry trooper lying on the ground with minor shrapnel wounds. It turned out that the soldier had removed his blouse and helmet to "look around." His dark complexion and lack of identifying equipment almost cost him his life. Carrasco talked with him at the aid station. "He was very apologetic," the officer said. "He claimed he wanted to get in on the action." And he did, but not the way he imagined.

Captain Carrasco said that after the two incidents "the cav troop commander and I developed an SOP, which precluded further incidents."

For more than a week, Bravo Company's two platoons worked alongside the cavalry troops, slogging through the 120-plus-degree heat among the fetid graves and tombstones of the Wadi al-Salaam. The men developed rashes under their arms and in their crotches; walking was sometimes agony. Uniforms were stiff with grime, covered with a mixture of clay and body fluids that coated the fabric, making it even more impervious to air. The men were beyond tired—they were exhausted. The heat, physical demands, and adrenalin rushes triggered by the sudden crack of a sniper's bullet or mortar blast were wearing them down.

Captain Carrasco remembered they were initially subject to a considerable amount of indirect fire. "I went out the first two days and discovered that every intersection in the cemetery was zeroed in by the militia's 82mm or 120mm mortars," he said. He quickly learned that the militia fighters were quite capable mortarmen. "They were able to place effective fires on us if we didn't maintain noise and light discipline," Carrasco recalled. "Every time we didn't, we would come under some form of indirect fire. Fortunately, the militia weren't able to make major adjustments off the road intersections."

At one point, Captain Carrasco and his command group were caught in the middle of a road that led directly to the Imam Ali mosque. "We were on the long axis of a machine gun. As we ran out of the impact area, we began taking 82mm-mortar fire, interspersed with two to three rounds of 120mm. The 82s were bracketing our position," he remembered. Under cover of the mortar barrage, several militia fighters started maneuvering toward them. "We were taking small-arms fire and mortars, and it was getting heavier," he said. "There is no worse feeling than to watch your men's positions get hit. I ran to them, fearing the worst. Instead I found them covered with dust from the explosions, but no worse for wear."

Carrasco's men unleashed a heavy return fire, stopping the exposed militiamen in their tracks. The attack showed a degree of tactical sophistication that had not been seen before—using indirect fire to cover a ground assault, or "fire and maneuver" in military parlance.

Navy Lt. W. Douglas Moorehead, SEAL team commander, commented, "The closer we got to the mosque, the better the militia got. Early on in the fighting, the Iraqis were foolhardy; desperate charges against armor with nothing but AK-47s and RPGs. As they were killed off, better-trained militia took their place."

Carrasco received word to pull his men out of the impact area. The men quickly boarded a detachment of AAVs. Carrasco's small command group and the 2nd Platoon commander, Lt. "Hoot" Stahl, were still in the street, waiting until every man had been accounted for. "Suddenly, a mortar round landed about three meters to Stahl's left and about five meters ahead of me," Carrasco said. "All I saw was a flash. The explosion knocked me on my butt! My ears were ringing. I jumped to my feet and ran toward the cloud of smoke and dirt. The first thing I saw was Stahl's helmet on the ground. A lump grew in my throat [because I was] thinking he had been killed. Unbelievably, Stahl staggered out of the cloud, moaning unintelligibly, and fell down. I checked him out. There was no sign of a wound; he had been knocked silly. He finally got unsteadily to his feet and climbed aboard one of the AAVs."

As Carrasco ran to his own vehicle, he paused to look at the mortar. "It didn't explode like it should have," he recalled, "The shrapnel went in one direction and the concussive effect in our direction." As one Marine wag said, "It's often better to be lucky than good."

Two nights later, Bravo's 2nd Platoon was not so fortunate. The platoon was hit by a barrage of very accurate 120mm mortar fire that severely wounded Lance Corporal Myrick and cost Sgt. Harvey E. Perkerson his life. "I ran to the BAS [battalion aid station] as they were brought in," Carrasco recalled sadly. "I held Myrick and tried to calm him as they pulled ruler-sized metal shards out of his body." He looked over at Sergeant Perkerson's body. "I had never seen a dead Marine before . . . and it cut me deeply. I used to speak to him on the boat ride. He was a great Marine and a better dad. He loved his family." Sergeant Perkerson was officially pronounced dead by one of the doctors. "I saw my first sergeant lean over and hug him—tears streaming down his face—and kiss him on the forehead," said Carrasco. "I put my hands on his and recited a prayer my father had whispered to me as a child: 'May the Lord bless you and keep you, and may the Lord make his face to shine upon you, may the Lord give you peace.'"

Just as Carrasco left the BAS, Lieutenant Colonel Mayer arrived. "He put his arms on my shoulders and told me how sorry he was," Carrasco recalled. "He then asked, 'Was the security mission worth it?' I told him it was because of our success." Carrasco tried to reconcile the loss. "It was only a matter of time before one or more of us get hit," he said. "We are Marines. It's our job to be where the steel is flying."

Bravo Company proved to be indispensable to the cavalry battalion. During the sweeps of the cemetery, militia RPG teams would try to get close to Miyamasu's armored vehicles. "We would take them under small-arms and machine-gun fire," Captain Carrasco explained. "As we beat them back, they became vulnerable to the Bradley's 25mm cannon and the tankers' 7.62mm coax. We enjoyed considerable success and killed quite a few of the militia fighters."

CHAPTER 11

Ghost Attack

We were breathing bone meal.
—Spc. John Willingham, Oregon National Guard

2ND BATTALION, 7TH CAVALRY REGIMENT (GHOST BATTALION)

CAPTAIN CHRISTOPHER CONLEY RECALLED attending a meeting at the MEU headquarters in which all three commanders—Mayer, Miyamasu, and Rainey, along with one captain from their battalion—met to discuss the takedown of the city. With three extremely powerful maneuver battalions backed up by air and artillery support, it was absolutely critical to divide the city into sectors of responsibility to avoid blue-on-blue (friendly fire) mishaps.

"They gathered around a map of Najaf and figured out how they were going to organize the fight," Conley said. "I felt privileged watching the men in action—no egos, no service rivalry—just three military professionals calmly working out a plan to defeat al-Sadr's Mahdi Militia." However, he noted that even among professionals, there was some good-natured interservice ribbing. "The two army commanders asked Mayer how he was going to explain a bunch of soldiers making Marine Corps history," Conley remembered. He also recalled that Mayer gave as good as he got. The banter solidified the rapport among them.

Mayer said, "Myles, Jim, and I became good friends during the course of the three-week battle. They were great combat leaders who I thoroughly enjoyed working with. The three of us spent a lot of time together planning, coordinating, and synchronizing our actions." When the meeting broke up, the three commanders shook hands, wished each other well, and rejoined their commands.

When Rainey returned to his headquarters at Camp David, he gave a final briefing to his commanders. The attack was scheduled to kick off on August 13 at 0300, while the enemy slept.

TEAM COUGAR

Team Cougar consisted of 1st and 2nd Platoons (Red and White), Charlie Company, 3rd Battalion, 8th Cavalry (eight M1A2 SEPs); 1st Platoon, Alpha Company, 2nd Battalion, 162nd Infantry Oregon National Guard (six Humvees); 2nd Platoon, Alpha Company, 153rd Engineer Battalion, South Dakota National Guard (three M113s); and a headquarters section (two M1A2 SEPs, two M113s)—a total of eighty to ninety soldiers.

First Lieutenant Michael Throckmorton, Team Cougar's executive officer, looked through the optics of his Abrams, scanning the darkness trying to identify possible threats. His tank and the four others of Lt. Omari Thompson's 1st Platoon (Red) had rolled out of FOB Duke at 2200, August 12, to establish a blocking position on the paved road south of the city.

"The plan called for called for Red Platoon to hold in position so that I could send White Platoon [2nd Platoon] up the escarpment first," Capt. Peter Glass, the commander of Team Cougar, explained. "They would use suppressive fire to ensure my company's unhindered movement up the escarpment." Team Cougar was to link up with Lieutenant Jimmy Campbell's scout platoon, who would lead guide it to the avenue of approach. The battalion staged fuel trucks along the route to top off Glass's mechanized vehicles prior to the attack. As the main effort, Team Cougar was given priority for fire support until it reached its first objective, named Lauren, after Glass's first daughter.

First Lieutenant Michael Throckmorton remembered, "We [Red Platoon] waited until 0500 before joining the rest of Team Cougar to secure a foothold in Najaf. It was supposed to be a night attack, but we got held up waiting for a scheduled artillery preparation to hit a thick grove of palm trees that paralleled the road at the base of the escarpment. The prepatory fires never happened because there were civilians in the area."

Captain Glass said, "Upon passing through Red Platoon, I received a spot report saying there were local nationals on the escarpment that could not be identified as hostile. I relayed the report on the battalion command

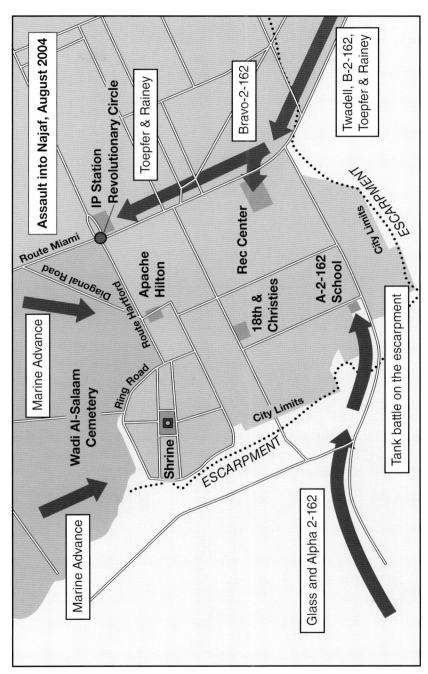

Assault into Najaf, August 2004

IP Station

Revolutionary Circle

Toepfer & Rainey

Bravo-2-162

Twadell, B-2-162, Toepfer & Rainey

Route Miami

Diagonal Road

Route Hartford

Apache Hilton

Rec Center

City Limits

ESCARPMENT

Marine Advance

Wadi Al-Salaam Cemetery

Ring Road

18th & Christies

A-2-162 School

Tank battle on the escarpment

Shrine

City Limits

ESCARPMENT

Marine Advance

Glass and Alpha 2-162

Captain Glass (Team Cougar) advances from west to east up the escarpment into Najaf, while Captain Twaddell (Team Apache) and Captain Toepfer (Team Comanche) attack from the southeast. *Patricia Isaacs, based on a map from Capt. Michael Throckmorton, U.S. Army*

Team Cougar Tank Tactics

The article "Armor in Urban Terrain: The Critical Enabler," published in the March/April 2005 edition of the journal *Armor*, described Team Cougar's method of attack in Najaf's confined terrain. "To maximize the capabilities of its armor [Team Cougar] developed the 'lane attack.' Vehicles would move to 'points of domination' (an intersection for example) to maximize the ability to traverse the turret and use the CITV (Commanders Independent Thermal Viewer). The first tank would orient low, forward, and to an unprotected flank. The second tank would be two blocks behind, clearing forward and high over the lead tank. The CITV would cover an unprotected flank and rear. One block over, on a parallel street, would be a second section direction of attack that would be occupied by a wing tank section. Up to two platoons would be put on line, along four lanes, with infantry (in M1114s) in a reserve role behind the center echelon tank sections."

net." Based on this information, Lieutenant Colonel Rainey made the decision to cancel the artillery support. By now it was daylight, and the company was strung out along the road, fully exposed to the view of the militia on the escarpment, which lost no time in preparing a hot reception. Dozens of RPG teams swarmed into position.

Glass requested permission to move out without the artillery support. After receiving the go ahead, Team Cougar slowly advanced along the hard surface road past the palm grove and toward a bend in the road that led up the hill to the plateau. First Lieutenant John Baker's White Platoon led the way. As his lead Abrams crested the grade, "it was hit by an IED," Throckmorton exclaimed. "The militia also fired five or six RPGs that barely missed it. The tank immediately opened fire with its coax, .50-caliber, and 120mm main gun." The fight was on!

Staff Sergeant Santiago Larriva was in the lead tank: "We crested the top of the hill. It looked like a ghost town up there. There was nothing on the street except donkey carts. No people running around, no cars, no civilian traffic at all. That's when the RPGs started flying."

Lieutenant Baker was in the second tank, which was hit by two RPGs. "One glanced off the left-side skirt," Lieutenant Throckmorton recalled, "but the other penetrated the right number-one skirt and penetrated the left fuel cell." (Three months later, during the battle for Fallujah, Lieutenant Baker's tank would be hit in the opposite skirt.) The tank fought on even as the enemy poured an increasing amount of fire against the armored vehicles.

"There was a lot of cat and mouse up there," Staff Sergeant Larriva said. "They'd run up an alley eight hundred meters out; they'd stop in the middle and fire an RPG and keep going. You didn't know when it was coming, but you knew it was coming at some point. A lot of times it was when you least expected it." Second Platoon slowly moved up the escarpment despite the heavy fire.

An engineer farther back in the column observed the tanks rolling up the hill. "All of a sudden, explosions started going off all over the place," he said. "There were probably fifteen to twenty IEDs that exploded . . . and then the mortars came in."

Another engineer was baffled by the explosions. "I heard the blast and saw the puff of smoke," he said. "At first I thought it was odd . . . 'What a weird place for an IED.' And it didn't seem very big." After several more explosions, someone came over the radio net and said they were taking mortars.

The engineers staged at the bottom of the hill as Charlie Company battled its way into the city. They waited until there was enough room on the top escarpment to go to work. This was not the first time they had been shot at, but it was certainly the most intense fire they'd received. "When bullets start flying by and mortars go off within twenty to thirty feet from your track, it makes reality set in," Staff Sgt. Jeremy Kuccera emphasized. "I thought this is the real deal—an offensive into a contained city."

Captain Glass followed 2nd Platoon. "An RPG struck his tank in the doghouse [gunner's sight], knocked out communications, and screwed up his turret," Throckmorton remembered. "My tank had taken up a position facing west, along a high-speed avenue of approach, when the enemy got a lucky shot that hit in the doghouse and effectively disabled my tank's communications."

Without being able to talk with his commanders, Captain Glass decided to pull his tank back for repairs. "Enroute I saw my Lieutenant Throckmorton coming up the escarpment," Glass said. "I gave him a hand-and-arm signal to stop, and after [I explained] the situation, we exchanged tanks." Glass returned to the fray and continued to direct the attack.

The militia launched a furious attack against the Americans using automatic weapons, mortars, and RPGs. The armored vehicles were like magnets, attracting scores of the missiles, which were often launched at close range. Several of the fighters ducked behind a brick wall, thinking they were safe. One of the sixty-ton behemoths crashed through it, crushing them. Dozens of enemy fighters were cut down by the concentrated fire of the Abrams machine guns and 120mm cannon.

The business end of a buttoned-up M1A2 Abrams. Team Cougar attacked up the escarpment against intense RPG and automatic-weapons fire. Despite the fire, Cougar seized its objective without any personnel casualties. However, two of its Abrams were damaged, and one had to be sent to the rear for repair. *Defenseimagery.mil 040812-M-7719F-094*

"After the main gun fired the first few times, it changed the momentum of the fight," Throckmorton explained. "The militia fire slacked off." At one point, a section of AH-64 Apache helicopters joined the fight, launching Hellfire missiles against the militia positions. Gradually the concentrated firepower overwhelmed the enemy. Lieutenant Throckmorton estimated that upwards of seventy Mahdi militiamen were killed.

Team Cougar moved deeper into the city until it reached the initial company foothold, a three-story schoolhouse. Captain Glass ordered his attached dismounts, 1st Platoon, Bravo Company, 2nd Battalion, 162nd Infantry Oregon National Guard, to clear the building so it could be used for a command post. The guardsmen quickly secured it without incident. Inside, they found a cache of small-arms ammunition, rockets, RPG launchers, and, more ominously, sniper ammunition. Glass decided to use the school and the building immediately to the east as his head-quarters. The school was an excellent location. From its rooftop, observers could see all the way to the Imam Ali shrine three kilometers away and almost the entire southwest section of the city. The Oregonians were soon joined by a sniper team from the Marine Corps Special Operations Command Detachment One (MCSOCOM Det One—or just Det One), who quickly took advantage of the building's height to bring fire down on the militia.

The ubiquitous RPG launcher that the Mahdi Militia fired by the dozens, but which were unsuccessful in stopping the army's two mechanized battalions. The second launcher from the right has a photo of al-Sadr on the tube. *Defenseimagery.mil DM-SD-07-17326* The second photo shows the RPG itself, along with its booster charge. *Defenseimagery.mil DM-SD-07-17350*

Once the school was cleared, the guardsmen moved across the street to another building, much to their regret. John Bruning wrote in *The Devil's Sandbox: With the 2nd Battalion, 162nd Infantry at War in Iraq*, "Part of the platoon, led by SSgt Harold Cunningham, broke into the slaughterhouse. Blood and organic debris littered the building. The men couldn't tell if what had died here was animal or human. The scene was ultra-macabre, like something straight from a Stephen King novel."

Captain Glass emphasized, "In the 100-plus degree heat, the smell was disgusting!"

Glass pushed his armor out another block to outpost the area and called up the engineers. "They were a godsend," Throckmorton said. The South Dakota guardsmen quickly strung concertina barriers across the streets to prevent the enemy from infiltrating close to the foothold. After establishing his command post, Captain Glass sent two tanks at a time back to Camp David to refuel and rearm. "Every time we went back down the hill, we got ambushed at the palm grove," Lieutenant Throckmorton recalled. "We would just get hammered by RPGs and small-arms fire." The grove provided excellent cover for the enemy. It was over two hundred meters long, with trees forty feet high and quite a bit of foliage for concealment. One of the tanks was hit by an RPG in the tank commander's periscope. Shrapnel from the blast went into the loader's machine gun and sprayed all the crewmen; they had to be evacuated for treatment, but later returned to duty.

Rainey's battalion had accomplished its first objective by seizing a toehold in the southwest sector of the city. "The enemy fighters seemed to be caught off guard," Major Karcher said. "We ruptured their defenses. We had traumatized the enemy by hitting them so quickly and hard." It was now up to Team Apache and Team Comanche to complete the second phase of Rainey's plan.

TEAM COMANCHE: 2ND BATTALION, 7TH CAVALRY REGIMENT

Team Comanche was organized into two mechanized platoons: a tank platoon and a headquarters element. Each mechanized platoon consisted of four Bradleys, each with a three-man crew. The tank platoon had four M1A2 SEP Abrams main battle tanks. The company was commanded by Capt. Jason Toepfer.

As Team Cougar fought its way into the city, Team Comanche started its assault toward the first objective, an Iraqi police station at the intersection of Routes Miami and New York. The objective was located several hundred meters southeast of the Imam Ali mosque, close to Revolutionary Circle. Captain Jason Toepfer directed his tank platoon to lead the way, closely followed by the Bradley fighting vehicles. Toepfer wanted the heavy armor

Soldiers from the 2-7 Cavalry cautiously move through the buildings of the Old City. Note the Bradley providing fire support for them. *Defenseimagery.mil 070215-F-7234P-198*

An M1A2 (SEP) Abrams main battle tank speeding down one of the main streets in Najaf. The Abrams could take a hit from an RPG and keep on fighting. Neither of the two U.S. Army mechanized battalions suffered a tank-mobility kill during the fight. *Capt. Michael Throckmorton, U.S. Army*

up front to defeat the militia's RPG teams. The Bradleys followed, covering the Abrams with their 25mm cannons.

Staff Sergeant Gregory Van Horn commanded one of the Bradleys: "We got the good news that we were going to attack, toward the inner ring. That was our first taste of the real all-out gunfight in the city." As the tanks pushed up Route Miami and reached the edge of the city, the militia opened fire. "There was a mass of small-arms fire, RPGs coming from both sides of the road and straight ahead," Van Horn recalled. "We pushed down, directly behind two tanks. Once we got down there, the tanks peeled left, and we continued straight toward the objective."

Despite the furious resistance, Team Comanche reached the police station without taking casualties. The company had secured Rainey's second objective, a foothold in the rear of the militia's outer defenses. From this position, Team Comanche could cut off the Medina complex from nearby Kufa, which was believed to be the main supply route for militia forces. The company soon turned the police station into a fortress, from which it launched a series of limited attacks into the Old City in order to attrite the militia and keep it off balance.

On August 16, eight Polish GROM (Polish Special Forces: *Grupa Operacyjno-manewrowego*, "operational mobile reaction group") snipers joined the company and established their first observation post on the roof.

The police station's location also made it perfect for Lieutenant Colonel Rainey's forward command post. From here, he could easily move around via the road network and far enough forward to influence the action with his personal presence. Captain Conley said, "Rainey was constantly on the go from one company position to another."

TEAM APACHE: 2ND BATTALION, 7TH CAVALRY REGIMENT

Team Apache consisted of thirty-nine soldiers organized into two platoons: a mechanized platoon consisting of four Bradleys, each with a three-man crew, and five M1114 armored Humvees manned by 2nd Platoon, Bravo Company, 2nd Battalion, 162nd Infantry, Oregon National Guard.

Team Apache pushed out early in the morning, following in trace of its sister company, Team Comanche. "I led out with my Bradleys until I secured the objective and then brought up my light platoon," Twaddell said. The Marines had warned him that the militia was prone to using RPGs, and the partially armored Humvees "would not have had a good day."

The route Twaddell followed was relatively easy. The main road (Route Miami) was wide enough for two Bradleys to travel abreast, but got narrower in the residential areas. A rat's nest of low-hanging power lines ran throughout the old section of town. The local residents tapped into the main lines, leaving dangling wires that posed a danger to the mounted soldiers. "The Bradley silhouette was high enough that the radio antennas ran into them," Twaddell recalled. "One man in Comanche received a jolt and had to be evacuated."

Staff Sergeant David Specking said, "In the daytime you can see, but nighttime is rough on us. Even if you see it with night vision goggles, you can't judge the distance."

As the company reached the city limits, it started taking scattered small-arms fire. "I got the feeling the fighters hadn't faced mechanized units before and were trying to figure us out," Twaddell said. The company reached its position, an empty school building, by 1300. The school was in a good location because it was next to the road and, thus, easily identified. It had an open rooftop high enough that it was not overlooked by other buildings in the area. Twaddell dismounted the Oregon National Guard, who quickly searched and cleared the building. In the process, the guardsmen found the owners of the building, "who were not hostile and stayed out of the way," Twaddell said.

Once his men were established in the building, Twaddell dispatched two reconnaissance patrols, one mounted and the other on foot, to check out the immediate area. "I had the Bradleys stay even with the dismounts to provide overwatch," he said. "If the guys on the ground took fire, the vehicles could support by fire and evacuate any casualties. My initial limit of advance was Phase Line Christy." They discovered several abandoned RPGs and AK-47s, but for the most part, the patrols were uneventful. Alpha Company maintained the position for two days. "It was pretty boring," Twaddell complained. "I was disappointed that my company was not in the lead. I just kicked rocks, waiting for something to happen."

During the time he was in the school, Twaddell learned of the ongoing negotiations between al-Sadr and Allawi. "The battle seemed to be driven by politics," he said. "It would go back and forth until al-Sadr rejected the settlement offer. 'Go pound sand,' I characterized al-Sadr's rebuff. Then Allawi would retort, 'Sadr doesn't want to play, so let the Americans break some more stuff,' and the fight was back on."

During the first negotiations, Twaddell thought the battalion would pack up and go back to Taji, but when the talks broke down, he realized they would be there for some time. "The troops were frustrated," he remarked. "They asked, 'What are we doing?' Are we going to attack or what?'" At one point, dozens of Iraqis showed up to demonstrate. "They were yelling and screaming," he recalled, "but I told my men not to do anything. Keep calm. I was really impressed with their amount of restraint." Twaddell was convinced the militia used the demonstrations as a distraction so they could resupply their men in the city.

Captain Demian San Miguel and Sgt. 1st Class Ken Jackola of 2nd Platoon, 2nd Battalion, 162nd Infantry, Oregon National Guard. Note the insignia of the unit on their left shoulders. *Maj. Edward Twaddell, U.S. Army*

HEADQUARTERS: 2ND BATTALION, 7TH CAVALRY REGIMENT

Rainey decided to relocate the command post when the battalion moved farther into the city. "We jumped the TOC to a police station on the northeast corner of the Old City near Revolutionary Circle," Captain Conley said, "where we ran the battle and established our logistic base." The battalion's 120mm mortar platoon also relocated to the station's large courtyard, where it could more fully support the three companies. Conley said that the built-up nature of the city, with its three- or four-story buildings, limited the mortars' effectiveness because the rounds could not penetrate the roofs.

Nevertheless, Twaddell tried to use the heavy mortars on several militia fighters that were in a nearby alleyway. He raised eyebrows when he called for a five-meter adjustment, because mortars are normally an area-fire weapon. To the surprise of everyone, the last round of five landed right where he wanted it.

Unexpected reinforcements continued to show up. "People started coming out of the woodwork," Captain Conley recalled, "SEALs, Det One, and Special Forces snipers." The newcomers jested, "We want to play."

Marine Gunnery Sergeant John A. Dailey led an eight-man team of Det One snipers. "We got the word to go to Najaf and support [the] 2-7 Cavalry," he said. "I met Colonel Rainey and told him, 'I have a

Lieutenant Colonel James Rainey directing the attack of his battalion. A well-respected officer, Rainey was also well liked by his officers and men. He was a straight, off-the-shoulder type of commander that supported them in the fight. *Defenseimagery.mil DF-SD-07-09678*

bunch of snipers here looking for work.' Rainey replied, 'Great, I've got work for you to do.' He rustled up transportation, which took us to an old schoolhouse."

Navy Lt. W. Douglas Moorehead, SEAL Team Two, brought five snipers and a communicator from Baghdad. "A Black Hawk helicopter flew us from the Green Zone to Camp David, where Lieutenant Colonel Rainey briefed us," he recalled. "Rainey was concerned about the vulnerability of his vehicles in the city and wanted us to provide overwatch security." Moorehead's team was transported to a hotel on the northeast corner of Revolutionary Circle, where they established a sniper observation post on the fifth floor. He remarked, "With only a set of coordinates in my GPS and a point of contact scratched on a Post-it note stuffed in my cargo pocket,

Special Operations Force Snipers, Najaf

The Special Operations Force (SOF) sniper teams in Najaf consisted of Special Forces (army), Naval Special Warfare (SEAL), GROM (Polish), and Marine Corps Special Operations Command Detachment One (MCSOCOM Det One). Their mission was to (1) kill Mahdi Militia fighters, (2) deny the enemy the ability to place effective fire on friendly forces, and (3) attrite enemy forces. To accomplish these tasks, "SOF snipers were employed in conjunction with conventional infantry operations (2-7 Cavalry and 1-5 Cavalry) in direct support of their mission." Command and control of the sniper teams was exercised through ODA-510 located at Camp David. Navy Lieutenant W. Douglas Moorehead's six-man detachment from SEAL Team Two was the first SOF sniper team into the city. Moorehead's detachment was quickly followed by the Marine and Polish teams until, at the end of the battle, there was over fifty highly trained snipers employed against the Mahdi Militia.

The teams were assigned to both U.S. Army battalions and remained with them until the end of the fighting. The Seals were assigned to Team Apache, the GROM to Team Comanche, and Det One to Team Cougar, while Special Forces snipers were tasked to support 1-5 Cavalry. The teams were extremely effective, accounting for 109 confirmed enemy killed in action, or 10 percent of the total enemy KIA. At one point in the fighting, it was reported that "the greatest fear of the Mahdi Militia in and around the Imam Ali mosque was the American snipers." Moorehead remarked, "At the onset of the battle, our snipers observed the militia walking along the rooftops and down alleys. After out teams got into position and started shooting, the militia were only seen running from one point of cover to another. They were no longer observed on rooftops or in the side streets."

my element and I stepped off on what would be one of the most influential experiences of our lives to date."

A coalition team of snipers also appeared out of the blue. Captain Conley was amazed when a classmate from West Point showed up. "He was Polish and served as an interpreter for the GROM," Conley said. "They [the Polish snipers] looked like dudes out of the Middle Ages—hair down to midback, big bushy beards. We got a big kick out their appearance, but they could shoot!" The six-man GROM team was tasked with supporting Team Comanche, while the SEALs supported Team Apache, and Det One stayed with Team Cougar.

By the evening of August 18, a total of thirty-one snipers (nine SEALs, ten Marines, and twelve GROM) were in position and actively supporting the 2-7 Cavalry. Lieutenant Moorehead remarked, "The integration with 2-7 Cav has been seamless. It has truly been a pleasure to serve as their leader."

Lieutenant Campbell's scout platoon was employed on a variety of missions. "We performed supply escort, personal security, and assisting with the TOC movement," he recalled. "It was nonstop, but we weren't heavily involved in the fight. Lieutenant Colonel Rainey's philosophy was 'Kill them with fires instead of BDUs [battle dress uniforms—infantry].' Since the tanks and Bradleys had all the firepower and armor protection, he kept us out of the fight in the city. We weren't asked to blast into town, thankfully." The scout platoon was assigned to a position where it could provide support. "We cleared an abandoned hotel along one of the main routes through the city," Campbell said. "Our snipers set up in an elevator shaft at the top of the building, where they had clear fields of fire. They quickly eliminated some guys with cell phones and binoculars on the rooftops."

Marine Staff Sergeant Kevin Neal, a Det One sniper, recalled, "The bad guys started out on top of the roofs . . . and by the time the day ended, you never saw anyone on top of the buildings again! We dominated the rooftops." One of the Marine snipers recorded a kill at 1,200 meters.

Campbell also dismounted the long-range advanced scout surveillance system (LRASS) and hauled it up to the roof. "We had great eyes on the city," Staff Sergeant Roberts recalled. "We were able to spot propane bottles on light poles that were rigged as IEDs. They were designed to hit the turrets of tanks and Bradleys. We passed the information back to battalion."

The scout platoon's three-day stay at the hotel was memorable. "There was some mortar fire," Campbell remembered, "but the real excitement occurred when an RPG came through the door on the bottom floor. Fortunately, we were pretty well protected, and no one was injured."

Staff Sergeant Roberts and another soldier were on the stairs when the missile exploded. "Neither one of us were hurt, but it scared the living shit out of us," Roberts exclaimed. The scouts left the hotel and followed the battalion's "line" companies as they moved farther into the city.

TEAM COUGAR: 3RD BATTALION, 8TH CAVALRY REGIMENT

On August 13, Team Cougar was ordered to stand down while the Iraqis began a second negotiation session. After al-Sadr and the government failed to come to an agreement, the company received the green light to commence operations. For the next several days, Captain Glass used a hotel

Long-Range Advanced Scout Surveillance System (LRASS)

The LRASS is a forward-looking infrared (FLIR) system with long-range optics, an eye-safe laser rangefinder, a low-light television camera, and global positioning system (GPS) with altitude determination. The system is capable of providing ten-digit grid target readouts beyond ten kilometers with a sixty-meter circular error probability. It operates line-of-sight and provides real-time acquisition, target detection, recognition, and location information in adverse weather.

With its ten-digit grid target readouts, the LRASS system enabled Lt. Jimmy Campbell's scout platoon to locate and identify Mahdi Militia positions and bring fire to bear on them.
Department of Defense

242 BATTLE FOR THE CITY OF THE DEAD

as a base of operations to launch attacks further into the city. "The tanks and dismounts would move forward a few blocks and set up an observation post in a good location," Throckmorton said. "The dismounts would clear the building, and then we'd attrite the bad guys with supporting arms."

During one of these limited attacks, they were given a hot reception. "We raided a school complex in the center sector and received heavy RPG and small-arms fire," Throckmorton recalled. "We flexed a section of Abrams to cover the withdrawal and brought in Reaper [call sign for the AH-64 Apache]." The helicopters hit the building with 30mm-cannon fire and a Hellfire missile, which brought it down. "The aircraft took several hits from small-arms fire," Throckmorton recalled, "but nothing severe." The company continued to receive mortar fire "every three to five minutes."

The no-fire zone around the mosque was the biggest problem for the company during its forays. "We have been very limited in where we can attack and the enemy has figured this out," Lieutenant Throckmorton complained. "They use this safety zone to evade our fires. This political crap is endangering the troops!" He emphasized, however, "We understood the importance of the shrine and never fired if it would pose a danger to the mosque." The company went to extreme lengths to coordinate fires close to the exclusion zone. "When the angle was bad for one platoon, we might use another if it had a better angle, or we might use a different weapon," Throckmorton said. Fortunately, the battalion's vehicles were equipped with the Force Battle Command Brigade and Below (FBCB2), a Blue Force tracking technology. "I could see where everyone was," Throckmorton explained. "I could determine their weapons' geometry and prevent blue-on-blue [friendly fire] incidents. It gave me great situational awareness and was absolutely invaluable during the fight in the city."

On August 17, militia mortar teams targeted the company's command post, hitting it with a barrage of 60mm and 82mm rounds. Specialist Keith Dow was lucky to survive one close round. "We were doing two-hour shifts and . . . I was trying to keep myself awake. I bent over to get a piece of paper. As soon as I did, all I felt was something like a horse kicking me in the chest, and I saw a bright light. I didn't hear it or see it or anything else. Then I'm on my back, and all I can taste is gunpowder. It was a strange feeling. I didn't know what happened, and it felt like my head was blown to pieces." A mortar round had exploded just outside the window. "Our medic checked me out; I just got a couple of scrapes and bruises," Dow said. "The blast rang my chimes, and I couldn't hear for a day and a half, but the big refrigerator we had put in the window saved my life."

Force Battle Command Brigade and Below (FBCB2)

The Force Battle Command Brigade and Below (FBCB2) tracking technology is a GPS-enabled system that provides commanders with the location of friendly forces by displaying tactical symbols on a monitor: blue symbols for friendly forces, red for enemy forces, and green or yellow for neutral forces. The system consists of a computer, a satellite terminal and antenna, a GPS receiver, command and control software, and mapping software. The system displays the location of the host vehicle on the computer's terrain-map display, along with the locations of other platforms in their respective locations. The system allows users to input or update operational graphics.

John Bruning wrote in *The Devil's Sandbox* that several vehicles equipped with the Blue Force tracker had been stolen by Iraqis insurgents, who were using them to locate and ambush Americans. He reported that 2nd Platoon, Bravo Company, was lured into one such ambush and suffered several casualties, including one soldier killed in action.

Captain Glass took the hint and displaced his headquarters to a building just south of Phase Line Christy, on their northern boundary. "The move went well," Lieutenant Throckmorton said. "We settled in for the night. Most of us got one to two hours sleep." Gunnery Sergeant Dailey and his sniper team also displaced during the night: "The company commander gave us a fire-team as security and threw us in the back of a Bradley, which dropped us off several blocks from a ten-story hotel."

The men made their way to the building without incident. Dailey and a staff sergeant climbed up an outside ladder to the roof while the rest of the team chipped "mouse holes" in the walls of the lower floors to shoot from. "I was manning the M11 sniper rifle as the sun came up," Dailey said. "My partner was observing. As soon as it got bright enough to see, I spotted a man walking down the road with an RPK [Russian light machine gun] over his shoulder. My original intent was to observe, but I couldn't allow the target of opportunity to pass, so I took the shot. I hit him in the upper torso, and he dropped like a stone."

Dailey shot another fighter before the militia could react. The shot scattered the remaining fighters, but they quickly figured out where the snipers were located. "They brought automatic weapons fire on us," Dailey recalled. "We jumped up and ran to a small house on the elevator shaft and waited for the firing to die down." When there was only an occasional shot, the spotter made a run for the outside ladder and quickly descended. "My

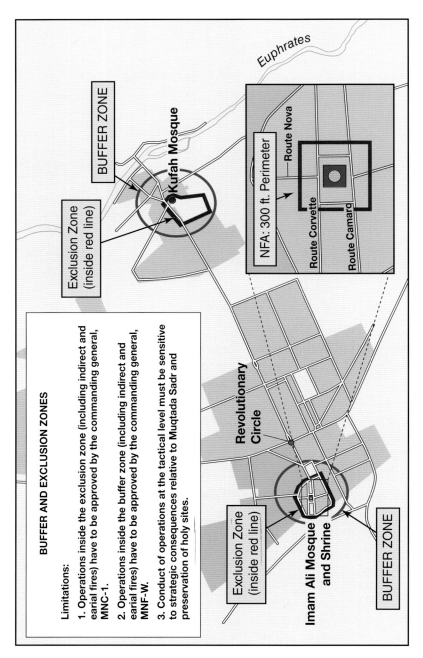

Buffer and exclusion zones were a sore point with the maneuver battalions because at times the zones severely limited their ability to fire and maneuver freely. The militia soon realized where the zones were located and knew it could fire from them without danger of retaliation. *Patricia Isaacs, from an 11th MEU operational slide*

teammate was spotted, and the fire picked up again, forcing me to lie low," Dailey said. "When it died down, I picked up the sniper rifle and dropped down the ladder. It was a long drop!" Dailey and his men made use of the mouse holes in the upper floors for the rest of the day. Militia counter-snipers continued an intermittent fire. Their bullets struck the walls, but failed to penetrate the bricks.

The next morning, Throckmorton and a section of tanks pushed forward to Phase Line Christy and engaged several fighters carrying RPGs and AK-47s. "One of them put a tracer round through my CITV [commanders independent thermal viewer]," Throckmorton said nonchalantly. "Once on Christy, we engaged several bad guys." First, a sniper team reported that two enemy fighters were hidden behind a dump truck. "We moved forward and put an MPAT [multipurpose antitank] round in the truck and the bad guys," Throckmorton said. Later, the snipers identified a mortar-firing position behind a couple of walls. "We fired our coax to get the main gun on line. The snipers adjusted our fire . . . and when we were on target, we put another MPAT through the walls and took out the mortar team," said Throckmorton.

Two days later, Cougar reengaged the area near the schoolhouse that had been destroyed three days earlier. Lieutenant Throckmorton traveled with one platoon, while Captain Glass went with the other. At one point, Throckmorton pushed down a wall with his tank and drove through the wreckage to clear a passage for the Oregonian dismounts. The debris, particularly reinforced concrete, sometimes caused problems. "Rebar would go right through you," a soldier explained. "A lot of buildings that were blown up or knocked down had rebar hanging down or sticking out from the concrete." Piles of inch-thick rebar were also strewn about the area, waiting to be pulled into the tracks of a tank or Bradley, putting it out of action until it could be cleared. "We had to call a welder a couple of times to get it out," Glass recalled.

The company took scattered small-arms fire, but within an hour had secured the place. That evening was relatively uneventful. "After prayers, we listened to the folks at the mosque chant," Glass recalled. "Supposedly al-Sadr agreed to the terms of an agreement the government presented him. However, we still hammered the area around the exclusion zone with artillery and the AC-130 gunship."

A young Iraqi boy who seemed to hang around their position all the time caught Throckmorton's attention. "I told the Special Forces about him, and they snagged the kid and took him away. Later, I saw them again and asked about the boy."

Lieutenant Michael Throckmorton's sixty-ton Abrams breaches a wall for Team Cougar's dismounts. *Capt. Michael Throckmorton, U.S. Army*

"Oh, man," Throckmorton was told. "The kid was selling you down the river. He was an informer for the militia." The story turned out well. The boy was "turned," and he fingered five militia fighters and pointed out several weapons caches. The last time Throckmorton saw the boy, he was working for the Special Forces.

TEAM COMANCHE: 2ND BATTALION, 7TH CAVALRY REGIMENT

Captain Jason Toepfer's Team Comanche launched heavily armed forays toward the west, down Route New York along the southern edge of the cemetery. "That's when all hell pretty much broke loose," Staff Sergeant Van Horn recalled. "We had multiple RPGs being fired at the same time. We were engaging mainly with 25mm HE [high explosive] straight ahead at the buildings just on the outer part of the inner ring." The attacks took the company directly toward the mosque and the no-fire zone.

"We would never fire anything that would mess with the mosque," one soldier explained. "It was clear that it was important." The soldiers understood the significance of the shrine, but it was difficult to understand the operational pauses.

"In the middle of the gunfight, we were told to stop the attack and pull back for the first round of the peace talks," Van Horn complained. The

GROM snipers reported "significant enemy activity, including snipers, mortar teams, and observation posts." Their attached JTAC targeted the militia positions for air strikes, but had to wait because of the cease-fire.

TEAM APACHE: 2ND BATTALION, 7TH CAVALRY REGIMENT

When the negotiations failed, Twaddell's company finally got its wish to be the battalion's main effort. Rainey ordered the company to attack north to Phase Line Christy, its limit of advance (LOA). "After two days in position, we were excited to be on the move," Twaddell recalled. The company attacked with its standard formation: Bradleys up front, closely followed by the dismounts in armored Humvees. "We took long-range small-arms fire, sporadic mortar fire, and a lot of RPGs," Twaddell said. His armored vehicles were like magnets. The militia couldn't resist firing at them. Several of its RPGs were right on target, including one that struck Twaddell's Bradley. "It was the fastest thing on this planet!" he exclaimed after seeing it streak toward him. "It didn't explode, but it left a gouge where it hit our reactive armor. Several of my Brads were also struck, but none of the RPGs exploded. I couldn't understand why, unless the militia forgot to arm the warheads."

As the company advanced into the city, the roads were wide enough for two Bradleys abreast, but in the residential areas they got narrower, restricting the tanks' mobility. The militia fighters were also getting smarter. They started to use a building's upper stories to launch RPGs. Before the Bradleys could locate them and respond with their 25mm cannon, the enemy had fled to another position.

The company's Oregon National Guard platoon found an unfinished, five-story hotel that dominated the surrounding area about two hundred meters short of the LOA. Alpha Company's first sergeant named it the Apache Hilton. The hotel overlooked an open-air market that had been turned into a mass of twisted metal by an AC-130 after it was discovered the militia was using it as a base of operations.

"The insurgents would run across with RPGs and rifles," Spc. Spike Olsen explained, "and we laid them out day after day."

The hotel fronted toward the west, giving it an unparalleled view of the Imam Ali mosque and the buildings around it. The soldiers quickly took advantage of the terrain by establishing two machine-gun positions on either end of a long hallway. Within minutes, they spotted several militiamen dodging through the wreckage. They took the enemy fighters under fire, killing several. The soldiers turned the market into a shooting gallery, so the guardsmen nicknamed it the Bone Yard.

With the hotel secured, Twaddell moved in and set up his command post in the basement. Team Apache's capture of the building placed it in a position to interdict the militia's lines of communication and restricting the enemy's freedom of movement. "We had established a noose around the mosque," Twaddell said, "and now we were going to start choking them [the militamen]."

The fight was not all one-sided. The militia targeted the hotel with an occasional mortar round. Staff Sergeant Kevin Neal, a Det One sniper, said, "[I was] manning a radio when a mortar round landed on top of the ledge of the building, twelve feet from me and another Marine. It blew the window glass out, and I got some debris blown into my right hand. I was lucky because a blouse on my shoulder took most of it, although I lost my hearing for about an hour. Another one of the team took some glass to his head and face, but they were superficial wounds."

The hotel's upper floors provided excellent positions for the company's attached battalion and SEAL sniper teams. The combined teams played

An open-air market that was destroyed in the fighting. The Apache Hilton overlooked the wreckage, which was called the Bone Yard because of the number of militiamen that were killed trying to move through it. *Maj. Edward Twaddell, U.S. Army*

havoc with the militia, who consistently failed to understand how far the snipers could "reach out and touch someone." Staff Sergeant Demuth said, "Sgt. Justin Franks shot a man at or around 1,400 meters with a modified Remington .308."

Sniping was not confined to the U.S. forces, however; militia counter-snipers also moved into the area. The American snipers spent a considerable amount of time trying to locate them. "We had sniper duels that would make the hairs on your neck stand up," Demuth recalled. "Bricks would shatter on you without warning from a sniper bullet." One of the soldiers' favorite tricks was to place a helmet on a stick and hold it in a

Navy SEAL sniper in his "hide." He is looking through his spotter scope. His rifle, an MK-11 7.62mm M-16 with suppressor is resting on its bipods at his feet. *1st Lt. William Birdzell, USMC*

A typical street in Najaf, as seen through a sniper scope. The militiamen often piled barriers in the streets so they could cross without being seen. *Lt. W. Douglas Moorehead, USN*

window, in an attempt to smoke out the Iraqi snipers. Lieutenant Colonel Robert Kelly, 5th Special Forces Group, said that most of the militiamen were not good shots, but there were some who were: "In Najaf we ran into some very good enemy snipers. We got into some pretty intense sniper-counter-sniper fights. It's like a little war within itself."

Lieutenant Campbell's scout platoon displaced from the abandoned hotel to the Apache Hilton. "We colocated with about a half dozen SEALs on the rooftop," Campbell recalled. "There was lots of shooting from the hotel, as well as into it. Our sniper hide in the elevator shaft on top of the roof had something like 100-plus bullet holes in it by the time the fight was over." The "hide" over-looked an alley that the militia was using to move to another position. Several militiamen had been killed using it. "Our guys got some really good shots from this location," Campbell said. "One time I heard one of my guys exclaim, 'Holy shit!' and then start breaking out laughing." The sniper had seen a man swan dive across the opening, hit the street, and roll behind a building on the other side. "Apparently, the bad guys had lost so many men crossing the alley that they began tossing their weapons across the open area, and then do a running dive across—pretty entertaining for the snipers," Campbell marveled.

One of SEAL team members on the roof was a qualified air controller and brought in several air strikes, including one from everyone's favorite AC-130 gunship, Basher. He called in four fire missions. His first mission, two GBU-12 (five-hundred-pound, laser-guided) bombs hit the top of a building, causing two large secondary explosions. The second and third missions were against the same target. Reports indicated that twenty militiamen were killed in the

Anti-Coalition Snipers

An assessment from the U.S. Department of Defense's National Ground Intelligence Center (NGIC) noted, "The prewar Iraqi Army had approximately 3,000 'trained' snipers; however, the prewar training these designated snipers received is questionable, since the incidents of insurgent sniper attack reported generally exhibit a poor shot-to-hit ratio." The assessment cited a report from Najaf that "a sniper fired more than 80 rounds over the course of 8 hours at U.S. forces, but this sniper's firing did not result in any casualties." The NGIC summarized its report by noting, "There is evidence of some true snipers operating in some insurgent groups, which is exhibited by spikes in single shots to the head and torso. A possible source of these true snipers might be the influx of experienced veterans from the Iran-Iraq war."

bombing. The last target was several militiamen carrying rifles and RPGs. Basher engaged them with its minigun, killing fifteen.

"I loved Basher," Twaddell recalled, "particularly the aircraft's female weapons controller. I'd marry her in second." The gunship was very effective in keeping the militiamen from moving about the battlefield at night and resupplying.

During the three days the company occupied the hotel, it experienced its second operational pause because of the resumption of negotiations. When they failed, Alpha received word to tighten the ring around the Imam Ali mosque. Twaddell launched several probes toward the mosque. Rainey accompanied one of them. Author John Bruning wrote in *The Devil's Sandbox*, "They drove straight into the teeth of a Mahdi defensive position and Rainey's Bradley took an RPG and three near misses. Luckily, everyone emerged unscathed, and Rainey's gunner killed at least one of the Mahdi rocket teams."

After returning from one foray, Twaddell learned that the Iraqi 36th Commando Battalion had arrived and was scheduled to make the final assault on the shrine. "The plan was to open a breach, and the Iraqis would go in and take the mosque," he explained. "If things got tough, we would provide fire support."

U.S. Army snipers scan the area for Mahdi militiamen. Note that the snipers are positioned well back in the room, away from the windows. The rifle is the M24 sniper rifle with a Leupold MK.4 fixed-power scope. It has an effective range of 800 meters. *Defenseimagry.mil 061019-A-7603F-149*

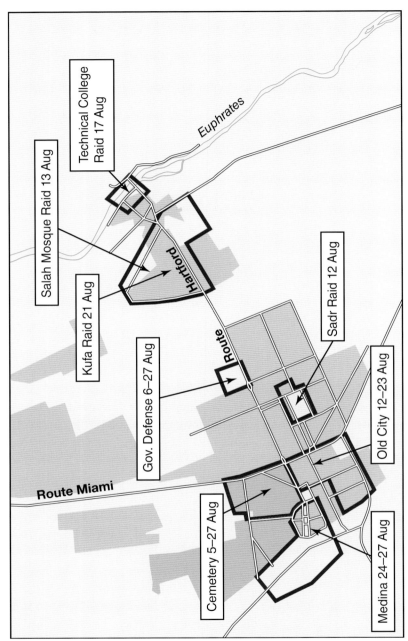

The major offensive actions against the Mahdi Militia in Najaf. *Patricia Isaacs, from an 11th MEU operational slide*

CHAPTER 12

Endgame

11TH MARINE EXPEDITIONARY UNIT
(SPECIAL OPERATIONS CAPABLE)

WITH THE FINAL ENDGAME in sight, the MEU needed to find the best route for the assault on the shrine. "We had done numerous planning sessions on how we were going to get the Iraqi forces into the shrine without excessive casualties," Moran explained. "The initial plan involved pushing two armored cavalry companies down the north-south road (Route Nova) that ran on either side of a huge underground parking garage to open breach lines. The battalion would then isolate the shrine and transport the Iraqis into the area to clear it. For political reasons, only Iraqi forces would do the actual mosque assault."

Iraqi forces continued the build up. From August 19 to 21, four hundred men from the 2nd Battalion, Iraqi Intervention Force (IIF), and seventy-five men and five U.S. advisers from the 1st Brigade

Mockup of Imam Ali shrine that was used to orient the Iraqi forces tasked to take it down. *11th MEU operational photo* headquarters closed on FOBs Echo and Duke. Even with the additional forces, the plan was considered to be a very high-risk operation. "We couldn't guarantee that the Iraqis would not take excessive casualties in the movement to the objective," Moran said. "The area was about as heavily built up as you can get—defensive barriers, IEDs, antiaircraft guns, so many places for the enemy to hide. It was extremely dangerous."

On August 22, a rehearsal-of-combat (ROC) drill covering the planned assault of the Imam Ali mosque was held at FOB Duke for the senior commanders at MNF-I and I MEF. "The Iraqi defense minister, Lieutenant General Metz, Lieutenant General Conway, and Brigadier General Hejlik were all there," Major Butler recalled, "plus about 150 to 200 other soldiers and Marines—pretty historic." Rainey and Miyamasu commented that they had seen a steady increase in the quality of the militia and that the enemy fighters seemed to be more determined and professional. The brief went on for over two hours. "It was a good brief," Butler said, "but the general [Metz] didn't give us a thumbs up for the final push." The senior commanders thought the plan was dubious at best. To test its feasibility, Miyamasu's battalion was directed to conduct a limited attack from the western side of the city to determine the enemy's strength.

Butler recalled that the meeting broke up when Metz stood up and emphasized, "This is the tip of the strategic spear for the entire theater."

1ST BATTALION, 5TH CAVALRY REGIMENT (BLACK KNIGHTS)

If we take fire from it, we destroy the whole building.
—Lt. Col. Myles Miyamasu

In the early morning hours of August 12, the 1-5 Cav kicked off a limited attack on an underground parking garage and the three westernmost hotels in the Old City. Intelligence reports indicated that the garage was the militia's storage facility, assembly area, and base of operations to support its men in the area of the shrine. "Video feeds from UAVs showed [that] hundreds of guys come out of there and run to where the fighting was," Mayer recalled.

The MEU also had an attached signals-intelligence unit (two officers and twenty-six enlisted men) from the 3rd Radio Battalion, which monitored the militia cell-phone calls. "The militia forgot all about security once the fight started," Hejlik noted. "That's what gave us the intelligence for the authorization to take down the hotels and the parking garage." A detachment from

MCSOCOM Det One provided snipers, fire coordination, command and control, and intelligence support.

"A full spectrum of battle-space capabilities," said Col. Robert J. Coates, Det One's commanding officer. "The snipers kept them down in the day, and fires kept them down at night." It was reported that his snipers logged "kills" from as far as 1,300 to 1,400 meters away. Detachment One was able to provide advanced imagery, data, and signals intelligence. "They [the 11th MEU] got intelligence products . . . that they had never, ever seen before," Coates reported.

Master Sergeant Ryan Keeler, Det One's communications chief, said, "When we showed up, the maps they had were like the maps you buy at the gas station. We sent back requests, and a day later . . . we were able to print them off and give them to the units we were supporting. They couldn't believe the photo imagery that we were able to get, one block over."

The parking garage ran parallel to the main east-west road. The route was also lined with four-story hotels, whose windows overlooked the two main roads, designated Route Corvette and Route Camaro. Despite its disadvantages, the western approach was favored because the roads were easy to traverse and ran through a less dense section of the city. Badger's Alpha Company (Mad Dog) was tasked with going in and destroying as much infrastructure as it could in thirty minutes. "Mad Dog had six tanks, four Bradleys, and four M114s to use," Miyamasu said. "His [Badger's] specific task was to put [at least] three tank rounds into the first three hotels on the northern approach [Route Corvette] and to fire tank rounds into the underground garage."

Mayer was particularly interested in the 1-5 Cavalry's foray because his battalion had been tasked with protecting the Iraqi Intervention Force for the final assault on the Imam Ali mosque. "We looked at everything," he recalled. "If you come from any other direction, the roads are heavily IED'd, mined, reinforced, and well fortified by the enemy."

Moran decided to accompany the attack force: "We tagged along with them to get a look at it and to find a road that was the best access point into the western side of the shrine complex." The battalion packed its company commanders and independent platoon commanders into two LAVs, while the command group—Mayer, Moran, and the air officer—was crammed into an armored Humvee.

The convoy drove west through the cemetery to the escarpment, a 100-foot cliff that bordered on the dried up Sea of Najaf, and down a narrow dirt road that wound its way to the extreme northwest corner of the Old

Unmanned Aerial Vehicles (UAVs)

Unmanned aerial vehicles (UAVs) proved their worth during the Persian Gulf War. In one memorable incident, Iraqi troops on Faylaka Island surrendered to a low-flying Pioneer UAV that had been launched by the battleship U.S.S. *Wisconsin*, which was still over the horizon. Fearing they were going to be targeted by the ship's sixteen-inch guns, the Iraqis waved white handkerchiefs, undershirts, and bed sheets. The Pioneer operator asked the ship's commanding officer, "Sir, they want to surrender. What should I do with them?"

After the war, upgraded UAVs were used during the air campaign and subsequent peacekeeping operations in the Balkans. They provided surveillance over areas that were deemed too hot for manned aircraft and

An MQ-1 Predator unmanned aerial vehicle (UAV) serves in a reconnaissance and forward-observation platform and can also fire two AGM-1114 Hellfire missiles. In Najaf, it was used for observation. *Defenseimagery.mil 080612-F-5957S-243*

City and the Ring Road. Private First Class Cosby was in the lead Abrams (call sign Blue 2): "There was no visibility, so we missed our turn, had to turn around and go back. Once we got on the road, there was a steep grade leading into a dirt road and then around a curve that took you pretty much right into the city. It was not guarded at all. There was a lookout tower, but nobody was in it." As Cosby's tank passed through a defile, its commander spotted eleven daisy-chained IEDs. "We didn't want to shoot it with coaxial and just damage it," Cosby said. "We wanted to disable it completely." His were so effective that they forced Serb forces into hiding. The UAV really came of age in Afghanistan, when weaponized versions were deployed with Hellfire antiarmor missiles against Taliban and Al-Qaeda targets.

During the battle for Najaf, the MQ-1 Predator was used for reconnaissance missions over the city. "The UAV was a great piece of gear," Lt. Col. Gary Johnston emphasized. "I mean absolutely phenomenal. We had live feeds day in and day out . . ." He just happened to be watching the UAV feed of one of the hotels targeted in the final battle when the building was taken down by a pair of 2,000-pound precision-guided-munition (PGM) bombs. "It was night time, and I saw the explosion, and I said, 'My God, where's the mosque?' There was this huge cloud of smoke, and I couldn't see it. 'Where's the mosque? Where's the mosque?' I exclaimed. Finally, the cloud dissipated, and I could see it, which was a huge relief. I was asked if we wanted to reattack the hotel, but there was no need. It was gone! The bombs plus the large amount of munitions stored in it [the hotel] leveled the building and killed quite a few militia that were using it as a headquarters and storage facility."

The MQ-1 Predator is a medium-altitude, long-range aircraft that operates much like any other small plane. Its 100-horsepower engine turns a driveshaft that rotates the aircraft's two-blade, variable-pitch "pusher" propeller at speeds of 135 miles per hour up to an altitude of 25,000 feet. The Predator can carry a payload of 450 pounds and can loiter over an area for twenty-four hours, fully loaded. The UAV can provide real-time imagery using its sophisticated monitoring equipment. It has a full-color nose camera, a variable-aperture camera (similar to a traditional TV camera and its main set of "eyes"), a variable-aperture infrared camera for low light and night viewing, and a synthetic aperture radar (SAR) for seeing through haze, clouds, or smoke. The aircraft can carry two AGM-114 Hellfire missiles that, when fired, hone in on a laser beam illuminating the target. It is controlled by a pilot with a standard flight stick and associated controls, which transmit commands over a C-Band line-of-sight data link or a Ku-Band satellite link for long-range missions. The pilot uses the aircraft's sensors to control it.

tank pulled aside, and a Bradley took the IED under fire with its 25mm cannon, destroying it.

"Right past that," Miyamasu said, "there was another IED chain. Two of those were destroyed, leaving enough room to allow access to the western approach."

As the first four vehicles turned onto the road, "everybody started taking RPG and sniper fire," Cosby exclaimed. "Literally, one second there was nothing and the next, boom, boom, boom!"

Moran watched in fascination: "I was sitting on top of the plateau and seeing RPG after RPG fly from the center of the city out toward Ring Road . . . [M]ortar fire and RPGs. [It was] just completely intense—more so than any I had seen in previous fights."

Mayer recalled, "It was an incredible amount of fire, mortars were just raining down on us. My machine gunner shot over three thousand rounds. I sat there in my Humvee and watched RPGs bounce off the tanks. I thought, 'Holy smokes, these guys aren't getting weaker. They're getting stronger!'"

Suddenly, Badger received bad news: "One of my tanks got hit with an RPG on the left side of the sponson box [big storage box], which penetrated the armor about three or four inches and set it on fire."

Unaware that his tank had been hit, Beams recalled, "It kind of rocked us a little bit, and we heard a thud. One of our fire-extinguisher Halon bottles went off. We kind of stopped for a second, trying to figure out why it went off and wondering if we were on fire." Within seconds, Beams received a radio call. "Lieutenant Schaffer called, and he's like 'Blue 2, this Red 1. Are you guys OK? You just got hit with an RPG!' It kind of made us flip out a little bit," Beams said drolly.

Marine Corps Special Operations Command Detachment One (MCSOCOM Det One)

Marine Corps Special Operations Command Detachment One (MCSOCOM Det One) was a pilot program initiated to assess the value of assigning Marine Corps special-operations forces to the United States Special Operations Command. The unit was activated in June 2003. It consisted of approximately ninety Marines and Corpsmen organized into four sections: a reconnaissance element (thirty men), an intelligence element (twenty-nine men), a fires element (seven men), and a headquarters element. Det One deployed to Iraq in 2004, where it was employed in direct-action missions (pursuing high-value targets in Baghdad), coalition support, and battlefield-shaping operations. It also provided sniper support, fires coordination, command and control, and intelligence support to the 11th MEU during the battle of Najaf. The detachment completed its seven-month deployment and returned to the United States. The unit was disbanded in March 2006, after proving its "proof of concept." Det One has been succeeded by the 2,700-man United States Marine Corps Forces Special Operations Command (MARSOC).

By this time, the sponson box was on fire and small-arms ammunition was cooking off. "We kept trying to put it out, but we couldn't," Beams explained. "Finally, we had to have the infantry guys dismount with their fire extinguishers and help us." Despite the fire, Beams's crew continued the fight. They learned the next day that the jet from the exploding warhead had penetrated about five inches into the armor. "It didn't go inside," Beams said thankfully, "but it did a number on us, I can say that much." His bad luck was not over.

"My tank commander's sights went out, and he couldn't see," Cosby said. "We were trying to maneuver the tank and not kill any friendlies and still shell the buildings. It was the craziest time!"

While the tanks and Bradleys fought it out on the ground, Basher flew overhead, waiting for permission to attack. "It took about twenty minutes to get the release authority after Basher identified several mortar tubes that were firing on the convoy," Miyamasu complained. Finally, after expending "a ridiculous amount of ammunition," Badger requested permission to withdraw. "We pulled out after thirty minutes with no injuries and having killed thirty to forty militiamen," Miyamasu recalled,

As the force withdrew along an alternate route, Miyamasu brought Basher back in: "It was able to acquire a five-man machine-gun team attacking Alpha Company's trail element. Basher killed them with its 105mm cannon and minigun." Helicopter gunships also joined in, destroying a mortar position and killing a two-man RPG team. "It was almost a kind of free-for-all—a target-rich environment," Stauch said. "In that half-hour, we fired TOWs, over seventy main-gun rounds, hundreds and hundreds of 25mm rounds."

Lieutenant Colonel Mayer said it was awesome: "It was the most intense firefight I have ever seen. The city seemingly erupted . . . [T]he tanks roared back, shooting their entire basic load of ammunition."

HEADQUARTERS, 1ST BATTALION, 4TH MARINE REGIMENT

The intense enemy opposition during the 1-5 Cav's foray proved that a direct assault into the city was not feasible. The assault force had to pass through the enemies' stronghold, the densely urban Old City, which the 1-5 Cav had proved to be a formidable task. The second major concern was that the route ran straight toward the shrine, and support firing was severely restricted for fear of damaging the holy site.

"General Metz and General Conway decided that we were just going to squeeze the enemy by taking limited objectives on the outer perimeter of the Old City," Moran explained. "We would just tighten the cordon, little by little, all the while shrinking the no-fire zone and the restricted-fire area that surrounded the shrine." A battalion report noted, "The planning was agonizingly careful, involving several days of nonstop work. It was not without disagreement, as planners considered various options." The new plan envisioned 1/4 attacking from the west side of the Old City to seize a toehold north of Route Corvette. Once it was seized, the battalion would operate from there until the way was open for the thrust eastward through the dangerous hotel–parking garage complex.

The attack was slated to begin at 2230 on August 24, led by the battalion's tank platoon, reinforced with a platoon of the 1-5 Cav's Bradleys, and followed by an engineer sweep. Alpha and Charlie Companies would follow in AAVs. The battalion plan noted, "At the intersection where Ash meets Ring Road, Charlie Company would deploy south and occupy two buildings designated number 60 and number 77. The multi-story buildings would serve as base for the toehold and cover the movement of Alpha Company along the northeast section of Ring Road west to building number 61," an old hotel that was being refurbished. Charlie Company's objective, a two-building complex, overlooked the entire western side of the Old City. Moran said, "Each of the buildings was basically an enemy-platoon-sized strong-point from which the militia could pour heavy fire on the two east-west roads [Routes Corvette and Camaro]."

The reinforced tank platoon, with four Abrams in the lead and the Bradleys following in support, started about a half-hour before the infantry-laden AAVs. After a one-minute artillery barrage by Romeo Battery on the northwest portion of the road network, Thomas pushed his vehicles forward. "We were immediately engaged by IEDs, RPGs, small-arms and automatic-weapons fire," he remembered. "One IED struck my lead vehicle. It was a homemade claymore with large ball bearings that went through the armor on the skirt, forcing it to withdraw. The tank barely crawled back to the assembly area."

One of his tank commanders passed out with heat exhaustion. "Even though it was nightfall," Thomas explained, "it was about 140 degrees inside the tank, even at open protective, with hatches partially open." Another tank was struck by an armor-piercing RPG. "We were lucky," he exclaimed. "It went through our ballistic skirt, which is nine hundred pounds, then through the track until it reached the last link, where it stopped. If it had hit a little lower, it would have gone into the fuel tank." This tank also had to limp back to the assembly area. The platoon was down to two tanks, but it had cleared out the enemy fighters.

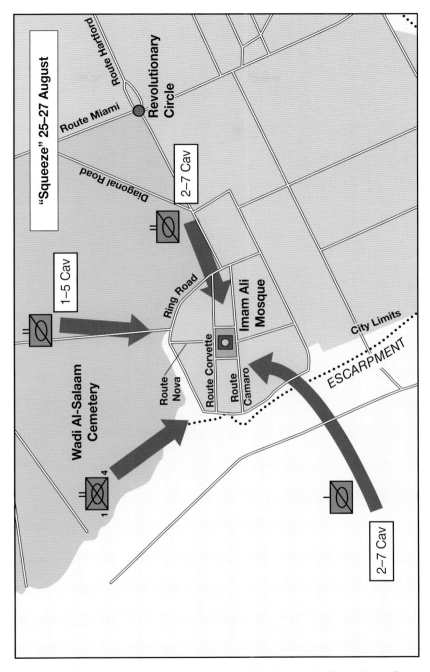

The squeeze plan developed to tighten a cordon around the shrine, rather than make an all-out assault. As the U.S. forces advanced, the no-fire zone would also be reduced, allowing greater freedom of maneuvers and fire support. *Patricia Isaacs, from an 11th MEU operational slide*

CHARLIE COMPANY, 1ST BATTALION, 4TH MARINE REGIMENT

Charlie Company kicked off its attack on schedule. The company was crammed into several AAVs for the uncomfortable ride to the objective. The AAV was designed to accommodate twenty-one combat-equipped passengers plus three crew members, but not necessarily in comfort. With the hatches closed and every inch of space crammed with extra equipment, ammunition, and weapons, the vehicle can be extremely claustrophobic and uncomfortable. The engine's noise, the vehicle's constant jerky movements, and the threat of enemy fire added an extra dimension of distress.

Sellers was not happy as the convoy rolled into the city. "I was in the TC [tank commander] hatch of the AAV, and I couldn't see anything," he recalled glumly. "I asked one of the men what he saw. He replied rather drolly, 'I see buildings.'"

"Oh great," Sellers had thought sarcastically. "That's all I need to know!"

The convoy initially proceeded against token militia resistance—scattered mortar fire and fifty-five-gallon drums of ignited fuel that were rolled down the escarpment.

Wallace was in another AAV, and he was also unhappy. "Our platoon sergeant couldn't fit in the TC hatch, so I was the lucky one that got it," he complained. "The whole time we're moving to the objective I'm thinking, 'Damn, how am I going to get out of this thing?'" He didn't want to climb out of the top because "if these guys we're going to fight have any sense, they're going to shoot at the vehicle." As the AAV stopped and dropped its ramp, Wallace solved his dilemma by squeezing out through the rear hatch. "I was one of the last ones off," he said, "and as I got out, it was complete confusion for the first minute or so. All the vehicles stopped close together, and everybody was mixed in with each other." The company was strung out along the street. "Literally our whole company was along the sidewalk," Wallace exclaimed. "The whole company!" He scrambled to find his squad. "I'm yelling for my guys, 'Where are you at? Where's this guy, where's that guy?'"

Somehow in the crush of men and vehicles, Sellars found his men. "My Marines were in kind of a 360 [circle], and they didn't know what to do," he said. "I yelled 'Follow me!' and just like in the movies, they jumped up and followed me into the first building [number 60]."

They kicked in a door and came face-to-face with an old woman. "Luckily, nobody shot her," Sellars exclaimed. "She looked at us with an expression that said she'd been through hell. Her house was on fire, armed

Building number 77, one of Charlie Company's nighttime objectives. The building was defended by several militiamen. The company suffered several casualties clearing the building. *Maj. Michael Irwin, U.S. Army*

A Bradley, as seen through a night-vision device. The round white ball in the left is a 25mm round exploding. *Defenseimagery.mil DF-SD-07-29290*

strangers had invaded the shambles of her home, guns were going off, and everyone who came in had pointed their weapon at her." There was nothing that Sellars' platoon could do at the moment, so they hastily filed out.

"We run around and go to the next building, but it's also on fire," Sellars recalled. "Finally, we go in one that's pretty well blown to shit."

Wallace vividly remembered clearing the building: "Corporal Jenkins cleared the first floor. I went up the second, and then Jenkins followed. We bounded from one floor to the next until we reached the top deck, where we set up security."

Thomas's remaining vehicles—two Abrams and four Bradleys—were still taking a large amount of fire, from both small arms and RPGs. "We fired our main guns into almost every single building because we were taking fire from them all," he said. The Bradleys stayed on Route Camaro, while the tanks remained on Route Corvette. The militia had set up makeshift roadblocks on Corvette. "There were large, twenty-foot containers, piles of dirt, bricks—anything they could use," Thomas said. "We fired obstacle-reduction rounds to clear them." The Bradleys used their 25mm and TOWs against the militia positions. At one point, Thomas was notified by the 2-7 Cav that the militia was fleeing from their advance toward his position. "We would engage them with coax, the .50-caliber, or the main gun if they got behind a wall," said Thomas. "We would kill them as they ran across the street—so many that their bodies stacked up—but they kept coming."

Forceable entry, as seen through a night-vision device. *Defenseimagery.mil DM-SD-06-03067*

After clearing the platoon's assigned building. Captain Morrisey pulled Sellars aside, pointed to the next building, and told him to check it out. "I took a fire team with me, kicked in the door, and rushed into a wide room that had some construction off to the right side," " Sellars said. He immediately noticed several bags that looked like big sandbags. "We moved to the back of the room and as I bent down to pick up an Iraqi bayonet, a deafening explosion erupted!" he said. The room immediately filled with a heavy dust and the acrid smell of cordite filled their nostrils.

"We're coughing and we can't hear, but we're screaming at each other to 'Get out! Get out!'" Sellars said. One of his men was bleeding from facial wounds. "My point man looks at me," he recalled. "He's bleeding, and I said, 'Frag it. Throw a hand grenade in.' He's all excited and pissed off because he just got hit, so he pulls the pin, stands in front of the door, throws, and just kind of watches it. I yelled, 'Get out of the way, you dumb ass!,' pull him out of the way, and boom, it goes off." Minutes later, the second platoon arrived. "I send [the] second platoon in," Sellars said with relief. "Just go," he told them. "It's your building, have at it."

The second platoon immediately ran into trouble. "You could tell it was mass confusion down there," Wallace recalled, "because they had taken four or five casualties all at once, and they're stuck."

Sellars said, "It sounded like the firefight from hell by the sounds on the radio. You've got screaming, and everybody's going ape shit!" Two militiamen

Working from the top down. *Defenseimagery.mil DM-SD-06-01459*

had taken refuge on the ledge of the basement. "They had thrown a grenade up and wounded some of the second platoon [four Marines]," Sellars said. In turn, the Marines threw several hand grenades into the basement, which killed the two enemy fighters.

In the meantime, Wallace ran over with his squad to help out. "We got in there, and it was totally confused," he recalled. "It was a bad situation . . . I tried to help, but the other squad leaders said they had it under control."

Jenkins was concerned because the other platoon was using NVGs, while his men were using flashlights attached to their rifles. "With NVGs and the infrared flashlight [red illumination that can only be seen in the NVG], you can't see anything," he explained, "You have complete tunnel vision, especially if there's no light in the building. You have to have a little bit of light for them to work."

Wallace agreed. "They couldn't see anything," he said. "Our flashlights were flooding out their NVGs. They're like, 'Turn off your flashlights!' It was a bad deal all around." Wallace watched as a sergeant "pushed his guys down the stairs, doing the best he can, because it was really chaotic."

The second squad's Pfc. Ryan Cullenward was the lead man and was tasked with fragging the first room of the basement. As he rushed around the darkened hallway corner, he ran head on into a fighter preparing to fire an RPG, and they both fell to the floor.

"The two literally fell on each," Sellars related, "and the Marine couldn't get his weapon, so he dragged his bayonet out and stabbed the Iraqi to death!" Another Iraqi tried to intervene, but was shot to death by the other members of the Marine's fire team. "The Marine stood there with his bayonet," Sellars observed, "looking a little dazed by what he'd just done." Meanwhile, the rest of the second platoon finished clearing the building and pulled out, leaving Sellars's platoon as the sole occupants, except for "two dead guys on the third deck and two dead guys in the basement."

The first platoon set in for the rest of the night. "We set up our little defensive position and just hunkered down for the night," Wallace recalled. For the rest of the evening, he could hear the army "hammering the hotels and the underground parking garage." Helicopter gunships and fixed-wing aircraft also pounded the militia positions.

"The biggest thing about that night," Sellars remarked, "was when Basher came on station. I heard Captain Gibbons talk to it all night, and it's just eating them [the militia] up all night."

Bronze Star Citation

Private First Class Ryan D. Cullenward

For heroic achievement in connection with combat operations while serving as rifleman, 2nd Platoon . . . in Najaf, Iraq from 24 August 2004 to 27 August 2004. Cullenward displayed exceptional courage, dedication, and leadership during C Company's attack of a Mahdi Militia strongpoint in the old city of Najaf. While clearing a hotel just three hundred meters from the Imam Ali Shrine, he engaged in hand-to-hand combat with an enemy militiaman who was preparing to fire an RPG at second squad. Unable to engage the enemy with his rifle, he quickly wrestled the militiaman to the floor and began to deliver a flurry of punishing blows with his fists. He finished off the enemy with mortal thrusts of his bayonet . . . [His]action resulted in the death of one enemy fighter and undoubtedly saved the lives of every Marine in the immediate area. His courage reflected great credit upon himself and were in keeping with the highest traditions of the Marine Corps and the United States Naval Service.

Moran recalled, "From his position, Gibbons was able to direct the precision bombing of over half the hotels that intelligence told us were militia occupied. He was a busy guy, dropping five hundred- and, at times, two-thousand-pound bombs."

Sellars was in a good position to observe the results: "We finally got approval to bomb the parking garage. When the bomb hit, secondary explosions blew debris out of every single opening."

To make sure the aviators knew his location, Sellars marked his position with MRE heaters. The AC-130's optics were so good that the aircraft could plainly see them and differentiate their heat signatures of those of the militia that were trying to infiltrate the area. With Basher overhead, the night passed relatively quietly, with only "pop shots and a few RPGs," Sellars recalled. Overnight, he had his platoon dig mouse holes in the walls for visibility. "You could hear somebody with a sledge all night long," he said.

As dawn broke, sniper activity dramatically picked up. Sellars said, "They were very good. They put several rounds right through the thin masonry wall above our heads." At one point, one of his men was shot through the heel of his boot. "I put him in an oval hole at the base of the wall," Sellars said. "It was only a foot tall, and I thought it was a very good protected position; however, the sniper put a round right through the hole." The sniper pinned the man down. "We couldn't find the enemy sharpshooter, even our own snipers. The guy was good." Sellars was forced to evacuate the rooftop position. "It was like a movie, 'Get off the roof! Stay low!'" he said. "We lay down covering fire by just stepping out from the corner and firing indiscriminately at the rooftop where we thought he was, just so we could get the wounded man off the roof."

To add insult to injury, the militia started mortaring Sellars's building. "One of my Marines was staring out the backside of the building when a mortar round landed right in front of him," he recalled. "The man just sat there for a few minutes, totally freaked out by it." Sellars thought that at one point his building was hit with friendly mortar fire. "Never quite proven," he reported, "but I guarantee it was ours. We ended up calling off the fire. None of my guys were injured from it, luckily."

ALPHA COMPANY, 1ST BATTALION, 4TH MARINE REGIMENT

While Charlie Company seized its objective, the AAVs carrying Alpha Company moved into the cemetery, where Sotire met Mayer for last-minute instructions. "We linked up in the dark," Sotire recalled. "Mayer spread a map out on the hood of his Humvee and used his flashlight to point out the buildings he wanted us to seize."

As they talked, mortar fire impacted the area around them. "Mayer and the command group [were] just outside the cemetery when two 82mm mortars landed about fifty meters away," Zjawin recalled. "Mayer just continued the brief like nothing had happened!"

Within a few minutes, the company was on its way to its objective: a series of buildings about two hundred meters east of their sister company. The move placed Alpha considerably closer to the mosque.

Zjawin was in the commander's hatch of the lead vehicle, looking for an infrared marker on the side of a building, which marked it as the objective. He spotted it through his NVGs and ordered the driver to stop and drop the ramp. "I saw three people run out, and I started shooting," he recalled. "An RPG streaked by my head. 'Get out of here,' I thought and tried to climb out of the hatch. My gas mask got caught, and I literally had to break the strap to get free . . . [But]in the process, I fell off the trac. Two of my men grabbed me and pulled me to cover. They asked me if I was hit. I was embarrassed as hell."

As his platoon raced into the building and started clearing it, Smith's 1st Platoon set up security. Suddenly, an RPG exploded against a corner of the building, blowing shrapnel into the Marine position. "First Platoon lost a machine-gun team," Zjawin recalled somberly. "One man lost half his face, another most of his hand, and the team leader took fragments all up and down his legs." Within seconds, Alpha Company had taken its first serious casualties and was no longer seemingly invincible. (The Marine's face wound was eventually repaired by reconstructive surgery and "looks OK" according to Zjawin.)

Zjawin's platoon succeeded in clearing the building and "that's when things got real interesting." After the sun came up, the militia snipers started peppering the building.

"We start taking fire from everywhere," Sotire recalled. "We're basically surrounded by higher buildings, and everyone knows where we are. It seemed like the objective was directly in an enemy kill zone." He quickly learned that their building was a terrible defensive position because the walls were only one brick thick and bullets were passing straight through.

"Many of the buildings in the Old City had ancient walls made out of dried mud," Lieutenant Colonel Mayer said, "so rounds just passed through them like butter." Everyone was forced onto their stomachs close to the sides of the room, where a thicker layer of concrete rose about a foot off the floor. "I remember vividly talking with Bruce Sotire just after sunrise," Mayer said, "and 14.7mm holes started punching through the brick walls, allowing sunlight to stream through . . . [E]veryone in the room looked at the increasing number of holes in amazement for a few long seconds before hitting the deck."

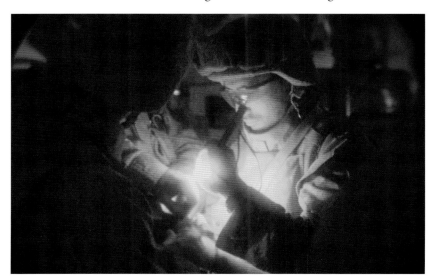

A navy corpsman works on a wounded Alpha Company Marine by the light of a flashlight.
Defenseimagery.mil DM-SD-07-15211

Sotire recalled, "We're all down trying to pinpoint the militia snipers, but they have us. We can't maneuver because they have the alleys covered by grazing fire, and we don't know where the snipers are." Enemy fire increased as more and more militiamen joined the fray. "We take our first KIA," Sotire related. "Lance Corporal Alexander Arrendondo was looking out a window, trying to spot the source of the fire, when he was shot in the head and killed instantly."

Zjawin was on an adjacent roof when the first incident occurred: "I yelled at him [Arrendondo] to get his head down. The next thing I knew, he took a round in the forehead." Two others were wounded, including the company first sergeant.

The daylight move had been costly. The enemy had observed the company and targeted it almost immediately. From that time on, Mayer said, he "directed the companies to breach interior walls so the Marines could move from building to building without giving away their position by going outside."

The heavy fire forced Sotire to pull his men off the roof. Before everyone could evacuate, Pfc. Nicholas M. Skinner was shot in the upper chest and mortally wounded. At this point, the gloves came off, and the exclusion zone was reduced to allow Sotire to bring in close air support to suppress the sniper fire. "I knew which buildings they were in," he said, "and we started dropping them one right after the other."

Zjawin said, "[I watched] JDAMS land right in front of my position, taking down buildings only 200 to 250 meters away. They swayed as they blew up." The militia pulled back, allowing Alpha Company to regain the initiative. By nightfall, the company started conducting squad-sized patrols.

"We had good success," Sotire remembered. "We expanded the perimeter another two hundred meters."

Zjawin recalled, "I took a friendly fire casualty that night trying to clear out a building. We're out in the street and about ready to make an entry into a building when my point man takes all sorts of automatic-weapons fire. A bullet hit him in the helmet, creased his head, and lodged in the back of the headgear." The stunned Marine dropped his weapon and staggered down the street, completely unaware of what happened or where he was. Zjawin remembered that he was "just a mess!" Zjawin later reconstructed the incident. "I could see how it happened," he explained, "He [the shooter] saw movement and opened fire, lighting up my point man." It was a miracle that the Kevlar helmet saved the point man's life.

By the second day, the enemy bodies were starting to decompose. Zjawin had them moved to a corner of the building, but it didn't help the smell. "One night living with those bodies ain't that bad," Wallace explained. "However, it's hot in those buildings, and the flies are thick, and we're just dying from the smell."

Sellars said, "We finally decided that we just can't take the dead guys anymore."

Jenkins detailed two Marines and two corpsmen for the grisly assignment. "They wrapped them up in blankets and dragged them up the stairs," Jenkins said. "It was bad, very bad." The remains were taken into the courtyard until they could be picked up and buried.

That night, Sellars checked on one of his sentries. "You see anything out there?" he asked.

The man replied nonchalantly, "Besides the dog running around with the dead guy's arm in his mouth? No, I haven't seen anything, sir." The sentry pointed to the animal.

Sellars was completely taken back by the macabre sight. "The dogs had just eaten dead guys," he said, "and you're like 'Crap, this is not cool at all!'"

HEADQUARTERS, 2ND BATTALION, 7TH CAVALRY REGIMENT (GHOST BATTALION)

[Fighting in Najaf was] tackle football in the hallway, with no roof on the hallway.

—Lt. Col. James Rainey

Rainey's battalion continued to tighten the ring in the Old City by selecting key objectives, usually schools or factory complexes. "We were essentially doing an urban version of island hopping," Major Karcher said. "You can't be everywhere, so you decide what you want to control." Rainey was constantly on the move from one company to the other. He traveled with Major Karcher in two Bradleys with only two soldiers for security.

"Their gunners were the best in the battalion," Captain Conley recalled. "The sergeant major rode in the back of Rainey's Brad along with a medic and an interpreter."

Captain Throckmorton said that Rainey "came down all the time to visit . . . and was on the net with me constantly. As a result, I always knew what he expected. I knew his intent and that he would support us. He was a great guy to work for."

TEAM COUGAR, 3RD BATTALION, 8TH CAVALRY REGIMENT

On August 19, Captain Glass launched a night attack against several buildings near the exclusion zone that were reported to be a militia barracks and weapons-storage area. The attack was in conjunction with the 1-5 Cav's attack from the north. "The CO took the White Platoon [2nd Platoon] and an armored bulldozer," Throckmorton said. "The tanks were to use their main guns to force a penetration into the buildings so the bulldozer could clear a section." The militia reacted violently, showering the intruders with salvos of RPGs and automatic-weapons fire. "We took a pounding from both sides

An Alpha Company, 1/4, Marine standing guard while his buddies sleep. Note the bullet holes through the thin mud-brick walls. *Defenseimagery.mil DM-SD-05-14308*

of the road," he recalled. "The weapons-system officer on board saw what needed to be done and authorized a fire mission. Basher saved our bacon."

The AC-130 fired its 40mm-cannon and 105mm-howitzer rounds down both sides of the road, within fifty meters of the tanks. In addition, AH-64 Apaches hit the militia with 30mm chain guns and Hellfire missiles. Glass's tanks also fired sixty-six MPAT 120mm main-gun rounds. "It was amazing," Throckmorton exclaimed. "All told, we hammered the enemy for over two and a half hours." Through it all, the mosque loudspeakers kept up a steady harangue.

From August 24 to 27, the company operated out of another school-house. On the evening of August 24, Throckmorton accompanied 2nd Platoon on an attack against a militia-held schoolhouse. He recalled, "As we pulled up to Ring Road, a mortar round landed about fifteen feet away. It knocked my loader pretty hard. He cut his cheek and had a numb arm for a few minutes."

After reaching the school, the dismounts entered it. "We were set to clear the building," Sgt. Chad Overman recounted. "The Bradleys first secured a perimeter, and the Humvees drove in there and dropped us off. We crossed the street and went into the building. Spc. Brian Hill actually shot an RPG guy. All you could see was his head, and he hit him. It was a two-hundred-meter shot."

Throckmorton said, "While clearing the building, three soldiers were wounded by a hand grenade." A medic, Sgt. Cody Wright, treated

Looking through a tank driver's view port down a debris-laden street in Najaf. Note the barrel of the tank's 120mm cannon. *1st Lt. William Birdzell, USMC*

the injured. Throckmorton added, "It could have been a lot worse. We were really lucky. I was surprised by the small number of casualties. I expected major gunshot wounds, . . . but nobody was injured as bad as I thought."

The attack force withdrew, and as it passed the northern entrance to the mosque, "four IEDs exploded but did not do any damage," Throckmorton said.

Gunnery Sergeant Dailey's Det One snipers set up in the upper floors of the schoolhouse. "We started taking fire from a 12.7mm antiaircraft gun that penetrated the eight-inch-block wall," he said. "It got our attention!" The Marine snipers also identified their opposite number as a cagey militia sniper. "He had obviously done his homework," Dailey said. "He pulled a brick out of the wall and then replaced it after shooting." The Marines could not spot the sniper's location, so they teamed up with their counterparts. "The army snipers brought up their .50-caliber Barrett and placed it alongside ours," Dailey said. "We both fired ten rounds with exploding tips into the wall . . . and collapsed it. No more militia sniper." Countersnipers were not the only thing Dailey had to worry about: "My JTAC and I were on a balcony when a mortar round exploded close by. He was blown through the air, and I went ass over teakettle!"

TEAM APACHE, 2ND BATTALION, 7TH CAVALRY REGIMENT

Alpha Company 2-7 (Team Apache) launched a night attack as Basher provided heavy fire support with its miniguns and cannon overhead. "The

Oregon National Guardsmen dismount from a Bradley to clear a building. One guardsman provides security for the others as they advance on the building. Note the personal gear hanging from the Bradley. *Defenseimagery.mil DF-SD-05-04703*

bad guys were within twenty meters of us," Twaddell recalled, "until Basher took them out."

In some instances, the militia fired on the company from a building's second story. The company used a leapfrog maneuver to deal with the threat. Dismounts would clear the building under the protection of the Bradleys, remount, and continue forward, repeating the maneuver as needed. Twaddell controlled the movement from a Bradley. "It was an anxious time for me," he recalled, "maintaining tactical control and accountability at the same time. I had one staff sergeant take a round in the leg and several men with minor shrapnel wounds that were returned to duty almost immediately."

Sergeant Cody Wright was medic attached to the company. "We didn't have anything major until the final assault," he said. "A couple of guys got minor shrapnel wounds from an RPG. We fell back a little to a house to get some cover. A team member went into the basement that happened to have a couple of hostiles. One threw a grenade, and that's when we received the worst of the casualties."

Alpha's advance continued until it reached the ring road. "We backed off about fifty to a hundred meters to a building that gave us good observation and protection," Twaddell said. When the sun came up, the company was firmly established in a position for the final assault on the shrine. The SEALs established a new observation post and immediately exchanged fire with the militia. Eight enemy fighters were reported killed in action.

1ST BATTALION, 5TH CAVALRY REGIMENT (BLACK KNIGHTS)

On August 23, cease-fire negotiations curtailed offensive operations. The battalion report stated, "In the days following the 20 August 'offensive cessation,' there appeared to be progress made on al-Sadr's acceptance of a ceasefire. It broke down, however, over conditions of turning the shrine over to Grand Ayatollah Sistani."

Beams recalled, "We were told not to engage unless they shot at us. We really didn't want to, you know."

Badger echoed Beam's thoughts: "It was very frustrating for the 1st Cavalry soldiers because they wanted to end it."

After a few hours, the negotiations broke down again, and the 1-5 Cav charged into the city for the second time on the August 24.

"I had Charlie Company [Commando] take the lead into the outer ring road," Miyamasu explained. "I directed him to look for VBIEDs [vehicle-borne improvised explosive devices] and destroy them with the Bradley's 25mm cannon." McFall's Charlie Company crossed the line of departure (LD) at 2130. "Commando led with a tank and a Bradley section," Miyamasu recalled.

"It's the first time we used tanks in over a year," McFall said, "so it was interesting." As Charlie crossed the LD, Bravo Company moved to a support-by-fire position.

As Sgt. 1st Class William Ferguson's lead tank went around a corner, an IED exploded, stripping a few nonessential items off the outside, but nothing critical. "He then identified a concrete barrier surrounded by concertina wire," Miyamasu recalled. Because the shrine was located directly ahead, the tank couldn't use its main gun to destroy the barrier, so Miyamasu decided to employ Basher. "It used its gun on the barrier, which caused a pretty significant secondary explosion," he said, "and paved the way for our attack on the final day."

With the barrier destroyed, the tanks opened fire on buildings from which they were receiving fire. McFall estimated that his two tanks "unloaded, forty to fifty [main-gun] rounds." After suppressing the enemy's fire, Charlie Company withdrew to refit.

With Charlie Company engaged, Bravo Company "started finding daisy-chained IEDs running along the roads," said Keahtigh. "There would be five AT [antitank] mines with 155mm shells underneath—twelve or more in a row. We overran them so quickly the militia couldn't get to the batteries to hook them up." While pulling back from the raid, Keahtigh observed three mortar rounds impacting an intersection. "They dropped another three two minutes later," he said, "and then one round every two minutes." He realized the militia had trained its mortars on the intersection and were waiting for an opportune moment to fire a lethal barrage. "That's when we learned they weren't just untrained militia," Keahtigh said. "They were learning to fight."

On August 25, the 1-5 Cav conducted an attack in conjunction with the other two battalions—1/4 in the west and the 2-7 Cav in the east—to seize a foothold on the northern approach. The objective of the multibattalion attack was to squeeze the militia into a smaller and smaller area, as well as to set the stage for the final assault on the mosque with Iraqi Intervention Forces. Alpha Company was again tasked with leading the task force into the city. "We were going to attack north to south to gain an initial foothold by seizing a four-story building with Schaffer's 1st Platoon, supported by an engineer squad," Badger explained. "We went in with a tank and Bradley combination. As soon as we turned the corner, we came into very, very heavy contact and had to shoot our way past it." The column pushed on past buildings that had been reduced to "rubble from artillery, bombs, and tank rounds for the past three weeks," Badger observed. "We got to one that was still habitable, and my dismounts pushed off to secure the building."

Initially, Schaffer was told it was a two-story building. "The lead tank reported, 'I think I've got a two-story building on my left that looks good,'" Schaffer recalled. "I'm hearing Captain Badger say to me on the radio, 'Roger, go ahead Red 1.' So we roll up and dismount. It's pretty surreal—buildings on fire, people running around, shrine . . . all shadowy." Schaffer soon found that instead of two stories, the building was six or seven stories high and contained over three hundred rooms. Schaffer's men burst in, throwing hand grenades and firing shotguns and rifles in a "close-quarter fight, straight up and intense." He said, "We killed six guys going in through the ground floor and the mezzanine offices. We took four enemy prisoners, who were hugging a propane tank, their weapons stacked near them." Within minutes, Schaffer realized he didn't have enough men to clear and hold the building. "I called Badger and said, 'Send me up the engineers.'" There was a platoon of engineers from the South Dakota National Guard attached to the company, which Schaffer used to secure the entrance points while his infantry cleared the rest of the building.

Schaffer stood on the roof at dawn. "Daylight breaks, and we're like, 'Wow, we're only about a hundred meters from the shrine!' It was huge. We're like, 'There it is, after all this time.' And I'm thinking, 'Why don't we just go up there and take it?'"

Within minutes, Bravo Company arrived. "I came in at 0500, following my two Bradleys," Keahtigh remembered. "My Humvee got hung up on a piece of sidewalk, and we jumped out. RPGs were whizzing by. We're shooting; they're shooting!" Keahtigh thumbed a ride in one of the Bradleys. "When they dropped the ramp, it was a lot like training. You have an idea where you're going, but you're kind of lost a little bit, and the rounds are going off."

Keahtigh and his small team ran into the building: "I linked up with Lieutenant Schaffer, who gave me the lay of the land." In the meantime, his men were rushing in, out of the line of fire. "I pushed my second platoon to the upper floors and to the roof, where they started setting up," he said. "My first platoon came in. I gave them the bottom floor and told them to look for a breach point into the next hotel, as we were going to push south towards the mosque."

Within minutes, the men on the eastern side of the building came under accurate sniper fire. "One sniper got two of my boys that were no more than twenty meters away," Keahtigh said regretfully. "They were difficult to spot, but I finally found their position. I had to use a mirror to jump out and look." He had a tank fire its main gun into the second floor of the sniper's building, which collapsed it. "We learned quickly that we needed to use a weapons system that would do some real damage," he explained.

By this time, Keahtigh's entire platoon was fully engaged—1st Platoon on the bottom and second floor, 2nd Platoon on the third and fourth, and the company snipers on the roof. Suddenly Keahtigh was notified by radio that one of the snipers was wounded. "Sergeant Ayers got shot in the hand, and it was bleeding so heavily," he recalled. "You would have thought it was real bad." Then another sniper was hit on the roof. "My personal security guy, the XO's [personal security man], and a medic run out and pull Ayers to cover," he said proudly. "They were all on the roof taking fire. You could see the rounds skipping off the concrete, but they got him to safety."

Keahtigh tried to comfort one of the wounded men. "He's lying there, screaming in pain," he recalled. "I always told them to put some Skoal on the hurt, and they'd be all right. So I bent over and said, 'How you doing?' and he replied, 'I'm in pain, sir.' I said, 'Man, I'm going to put some Skoal on that and make it feel better!' And he starts laughing." The wounded men were placed in an armored ambulance and safely evacuated.

Keahtigh brought up a tank and Bradley to support the assault into the next building. "The targeted building was the decisive piece of terrain," Miyamasu explained. "It was five stories tall and dominated every single building."

Keahtigh signaled the vehicles. "They pushed forward," he said, "and immediately got pinged with RPGs." In addition, the militia started dropping 120mm mortars. Shrapnel from one of the explosions blew through the Bradley's night sight and injured the gunner, forcing it to withdraw. An electrical-system failure took the tank out of the fight. Another Abram-Bradley combination replaced them. Keahtigh's 1st Platoon was ready to go.

"They're anxious, even a little nervous," Keahtigh recalled.

On trooper asked, "Sir, what does it look like?"

Keahtigh responded, "The tank and Bradleys are going to blow a hole in the wall, and then you're going to assault that next hotel."

"That's it?" The trooper wasn't convinced that it would be enough. After carefully studying the wall, Keahtigh decided not to use a high

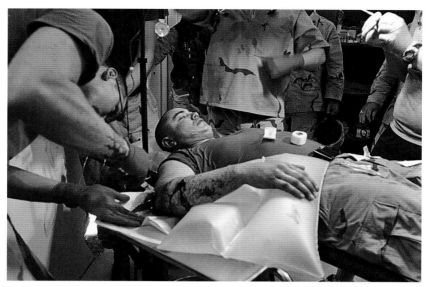

U.S. forces developed detailed plans for the swift evacuation of casualties. Most of the wounded were loaded on whatever vehicle was handy and taken to a forward medical aid station. After initial treatment, they were then evacuated via helicopter to the rear for more extensive treatment. *Defenseimagery.mil DM-SD-07-04083*

explosive, because he thought it would bring the whole building in on top of them.

Within minutes, the second Bradley took several RPG hits, which set off the Halon system, forcing the tank to pull out. Another Bradley was ordered into the fray. Keahtigh coordinated its fire with the tank to pin the enemy down and launched the infantry assault. "The first squad took off with eight men, and then the rest of the platoon," he explained. "They secure the first floor and start systematically taking the building down."

The assault platoon reported one man wounded with two bullet wounds in the arm. "Doc puts him right in a Bradley, and *boom*, he's gone," Keahtigh recalled. "And eight minutes later he's at the aid station." The building was quickly secured. The company was ordered to stand fast and prepare to defend the building. "And that's when the counterattack comes," he said. "We started using aviation."

Miyamasu recalled, "We were passing aircraft regardless of the call sign directly to Darren [Keahtigh]. He employed fires on buildings in and around the one he was in." As the aircraft made their runs, one of the helicopters was hit and forced to return to base. The combination of air, automatic weapons, and mortars enabled the company to gain fire superiority.

Charlie Company, in the meantime, had relieved Alpha (Team Apache) and was positioned to cover the main road to the mosque. "I directed Captain McFall to push his tanks and Bradleys as far south as he could without crossing the intersection near the Imam Ali shrine," Miyamasu said. "So we were basically fifty meters from the shrine in violation of the exclusionary zone."

McFall described the deployment: "I had a Bradley on the west side of the ring road, a Bradley on the east, and a Bradley looking down the middle to cover the rear. I was positioned right in the middle. The only thing protecting us was our gun truck." His infantry dismounted and cleared the closest building. In the process, two militiamen tried to escape down an alley, but were shot and killed. One of McFall's men was shot in the arm while crossing a street and had to be evacuated.

His position was soon under mortar fire. In response, Apache gunships were brought in. "Literally, they fired their 25mm cannon right in front of me," McFall exclaimed. "It almost hit my gunner!" There was little choice. "We had Marines about a hundred meters west and 2-7 Cav on the east. It was a very restrictive fire area," he explained. Charlie Company continued to maintain its position until 1500, when it got the call saying a cease-fire was in effect.

Correspondent Phillip Robertson was able to sneak past the American lines and talk with one of al-Sadr's lieutenants. "Sheikh Ahmed Shibani, one of Sadr's spokesmen, probably fourth or fifth down the organizational chain, said a letter had been sent to the Iraqi government offering to lay down our arms, vacate the shrine, and become a political party," he wrote. Robertson quoted Shibani as saying, "We made the offer, but we don't trust the Americans."

CHAPTER 13

Cease-Fire

I think they're tired of us beating up on them.

—Lt. Col. Myles Miyamasu

1ST BATTALION, 4TH MARINES

THE BATTALION MAINTAINED ITS position in the Old City, preparing to conduct Operation Thunder Road, the final assault on the Imam Ali shrine, designated Battalion Objective A. Wallace remembered, "There were rumors floating around, 'Hey, you're going to keep pushing forward, toward the mosque.' The lieutenant came around and told us, 'We're just going to start bounding and clearing out these hotels all the way down.'"

Wallace gathered his squad and gave them the word: "I briefed my Marines, and they mumbled, 'Damn, this sucks!'"

The intensely violent army and Marine attacks had taken a huge toll on the militia's willingness to continue the fight, however. "We knew we were running out of time because of Sistani's return," Lieutenant Colonel Mayer said, "so we intended to kill as many of the militia[men] as we could before he arrived, hoping that we could execute Thunder Road and finish Sadr for good."

On August 25, the *Los Angeles Times* reported that "al-Sadr was ready for any peaceful solution aimed at solving the problem." The paper also noted that al-Sadr's support was declining and that militiamen were "slipping away."

Lieutenant Colonel Rainey noted, "This [August 25] is the first day we have not seen a lot of enemy coming at us."

Lieutenant Colonel Johnston heard that a senior Mahdi leader was ready to give up. "Shibani [Ahmed al-] was apparently inside the mosque and said, 'I'm ready to come out.' He was told, 'No way. The sun's down, and if you come out, you'll never make it.'" Johnston thought this might be just another stalling tactic: "We didn't know if this was one of the typical, 'Yeah, I want to come out,' ploys."

That night the MEU dropped a lot of ordnance. "We basically lit up the whole world that night and did a lot of preparation for the following day's attack. I think that was pivotal because the call was made to Sistani by al-Sadr, 'Help me! Get me out of here and [let me] save face,'" Johnston mocked.

Lieutenant Colonel Mayer recalled, "It was an awesome display of firepower. We did our best to level every hotel and building leading to the shrine."

Rumors abounded that a cease-fire was imminent. "On the twenty-fifth, we learned that Sistani was coming from Basra," Mayer recalled. "He had been in London for heart surgery and had returned to end the fighting." Al-Sistani flew to Kuwait and then motored to Basra.

"We helped ensure Sistani's security when he spent the night in Basra before heading up to Najaf," British Major Neal Croft recalled. "When he left early the next morning, he had a following of more than ten thousand people, which was an incredible sight." The procession slowly made its way northward, greeted by hundreds of thousands of cheering Iraqis, proving that Grand Ayatollah al-Sistani was the undisputed religious leader of the Shiite faithful.

On August 26, Sistani arrived in Najaf and immediately began to work out an agreement with al-Sadr. A spokesman for Ayatollah said, "We have started contacts with Muqtada al-Sadr, and in the coming hours, we are waiting, hoping that we will succeed in saving the city from destruction."

Within hours, the news media announced that an agreement had been reached. Reuters reported, "Iraq's most revered Shiite religious authority [al-Sistani] has agreed to a 'very positive' deal with rebel cleric Muqtada al-Sadr to end a three-week uprising by Sadr's militiamen in the holy city of Najaf."

The Associated Press went on to report, "The plan calls for Najaf and the city of Kufa to be declared weapons-free cities. All foreign forces would have to pull out of Najaf, leaving security the police and, the Iraqi government would have to compensate those who were harmed by the fighting." The Mahdi Militia fighters were allowed to walk out and lay down their weapons.

"That's kind of the way things ended," Johnston said. "We held back and the political process went into effect." The agreement was the "right thing

U.S. forces were within a hundred meters of the Imam Ali mosque when the cease-fire agreement was signed. Grand Ayatollah Ali al-Sistani accepted the keys to the mosque from al-Sadr, after the latter promised that his Mahdi Militia would lay down its weapons and evacuate the city. *Maj. R. Bruce Sotire, USMC*

to do," Johnston believed. "If we or the Iraqis had gone in [mosque], there would have been a lot of damage to the shrine and cost many innocent lives because there were women and children in there."

Lieutenant Sellars went around passing the word. "I remember lying there that night half asleep, sitting there in the dirt with the dead bodies just reeking, and I hear the lieutenant walking around," Wallace said. "I heard him say, 'They're talking about a cease-fire,' and that woke me up. 'What do you mean a cease-fire? What's going on, sir?' The officer replied, 'We're going to hold off on the mission until we see how the cease-fire goes.' So I was like, 'OK!' That sounded a hell of a lot better to me than going in."

At 1515, General Casey issued Frag Order 582 directing an end to offensive operations to allow Iraqi political and religious officials to remove the Mahdi Militia from the shrine. "When the cease-fire went, 1/4 was within a hundred meters of the western side of the mosque," Mayer said, "1-5 was within a hundred meters of the northern side, and 2-7 was within a hundred meters on the east. We saw that the militia was pretty well whipped." Mayer was disappointed, to say the least. "We had been slugging it out for three days . . . and had lost Marines and soldiers. We felt the decisive blow would have gotten Sadr and all his henchmen."

Major Butler was in agreement. "Everyone I spoke with at the time was extremely frustrated and upset. We felt as though we'd delivered a steady pounding on Sadr's forces for three weeks and were about to deliver the final blow for a complete victory. But instead, Sadr and his thugs escaped."

Reuters reported, "Thousands of chanting Iraqi Shiites have entered the sacred shrine, greeted by rebels who have reached a peace agreement. The supporters of Sistani kissed the outer wall of the Imam Ali mosque before the militants allowed them in. Armed with AK47 assault rifles, teenage fighters loyal to al-Sadr spilled over the alleyways leading to

Iraqi Resistance Report

The U.S. puppet governor of an-Najaf, Adnan az-Zarafi, declared that the "crisis" between the Jaysh al-Mahdi and the U.S. invaders had ended. Az-Zarafi told the press that the U.S. side had agreed to three conditions laid down by Muqtada al-Sadr.

the gold-dimmed mosque. An order from Sadr, telling his fighters to lay down their arms and join the pilgrims, was read out over the mosque's loudspeakers."

One unrepentant fighter said, "We will support whatever Ayatollah Sistani and Sayyed Muqtada have agreed. But we will still slit the throats of the Americans."

Corporal Wallace watched from a rooftop position: "Immediately after the announcement, they [militiamen] just came out. I mean, you could just see them sitting on top of buildings with AK-47s in their laps."

It took some time for word of the cease-fire to make its way down to the last man, however. "I'm going to say that four Mahdi militia[men] probably got smoked after the cease-fire was announced," Sellars speculated. A sudden stillness blanketed the area—no shooting or explosions, no sounds of diving aircraft. "It's the strangest thing to go from looking for someone to kill to seeing them on the street, and you can't shoot them," he said, not quite believing how fast events had transpired.

Within a short time, the city's residents started returning to their homes. "Ten minutes after we found out about the peace treaty, then people were walking down the road with their bags and stuff, coming back to their homes," Wallace exclaimed. "It was just tripping me out!"

Sellars was also amazed. "You've got people on the streets, walking around, looking for their dead Mahdi Militia relatives, or the dead relatives that were in the buildings," he said. "Everybody's just happy as can be—one of the oddest things. Everybody drives up or walks up just happy, completely happy . . . [There is] a lot of waving, a lot of kids coming out to see us."

The Mahdi militiamen took the opportunity to mingle with the city's residents. "We could tell who used to be the fighters," Sellars explained. "They were the young males who just stand there and refuse to acknowledge our presence, even with a scowl. They acted like we weren't even there."

The agreement stipulated that the militiamen were to lay down their arms and evacuate the mosque. "As we watched, they were literally loading

The Imam Ali mosque, as seen through a sniper's "mouse hole" during the final days of the battle. When the fighting ended, the three U.S. battalions were within a hundred meters of the shrine and ready to launch the final assault. *Capt. Michael Throckmorton, U.S. Army*

weapons in the back of vehicles and in donkey carts to save as many as they could," Mayer recalled. He was ordered to set up traffic-control points to stop the flow of weapons out of the city. "I don't think the militia took them out," he speculated. "They hid them in the houses of sympathizers in the southern part of the city to get them at a later date."

Al-Sadr's office was suspected of containing substantial amounts of ordnance. "We were a part of a raid [on the office] by army Special Forces and the platoon from the Maritime Special Purpose Force," Borneo crowed. "We planned it for two days, and it was super successful! They went in and cleared the building, seized seven tons of weapons, and captured two of al-Sadr's key lieutenants and forty others without firing a shot." The haul included new AK-47s, RPGs still in plastic, antipersonnel and antitank mines, and hundreds of pounds of explosives. "It was a gold mine!" Borneo exclaimed.

The raid eliminated one of al-Sadr's key stay-behind cells. "If it had not been removed, the Iraqi police would not have gone into the area because they were still intimidated," Johnston pointed out, "They knew where the weapons and ammunition were stored, and once we rolled in there and captured the militia, they would point out all sorts of caches."

The caches were not the only problem; unexploded ordnance also littered the area. "Our EOD guys were extremely busy," Johnston said. "It was dangerous. At one point, they had to take out some five-hundred-pound bombs that didn't detonate. It took them four days to go through and clear the Old City of weapons and ordnance."

Explosives were not the only things that were discovered; the Iraqi police and ING found evidence of torture. General Amer Hamza al-Daami, deputy police chief said, "We entered the building which was being used as Muqtada Sadr's court, and we discovered in the basement twenty-five charred and bloated bodies of police and ordinary civilians. Some were executed, others were mutilated, and others were burned."

Alpha and Charlie Companies were withdrawn to FOB Duke for rest. Bravo Company was moved to an advance assembly area for a day in case the cease-fire broke down, and then it too was withdrawn. "We were on edge," Sellars recalled. "I just didn't have much faith that the cease-fire would work. I anticipated, 'Oh, now they'll attack the police station like they did the first time around, and we'll be back at it again.'"

With the fighting over, "the Iraqi police and the ING were all over the place," Sellars observed. "They secured the mosques and the government buildings." In a strange turnabout, the ING had to be called out to protect al-Sadr. "The ING had to go downtown and disperse a crowd that had gone there to kill the man who they [the ING] had been trying to kill a week before," Sellars said.

From left to right: Lieutenant Colonel Mayer, Cpl. Erik Smith, Lt. Scott Cuomo, navy Chief Warrant Officer Matthew Middleton, and Lt. William Birdzell on the night the cease-fire went into effect. The Imam Ali mosque is in the background. *1st Lt. William Birdzell, USMC*

1ST BATTALION, 5TH CAVALRY REGIMENT (BLACK KNIGHTS)

Miyamasu received a call late in the evening of the twenty-sixth. "Colonel Haslam told me that Ayatollah Sistani had brokered an agreement with al-Sadr," Miyamasu recalled. "At 1000 the next morning, the militia would be allowed to leave the city." He quickly passed the word to his company commanders.

Keahtigh's Bravo Company was holed up in a building overlooking the mosque. "After the cease-fire, we watched them [militiamen] taking weapons from the mosque, and there was nothing we could do about it," Keahtigh said.

For Keahtigh, though, the fight was not over. "Lo and behold, a fire started in the building, and that's where I learned to fight fires," he said. "I don't know what sparked it, but black smoke started filling the building. The heat was intense; I could feel it on my face." Many of his men were asleep and scattered throughout the floors and rooms of the building. Adrenalin pumped through his bloodstream as he dashed up the stairs. "The only thing I could think of was if someone were to die from smoke inhalation," he said. "I just couldn't live with that . . . [C]ombat is one thing, but to die from something like this . . . it would be stupid."

Keahtigh ran from room to room shouting, "Get out! Get out!" He said, "I hit one room and there were three young studs still sleeping. I got them

A weapons cache discovered by U.S. forces. The trove includes RPG warheads, 82mm mortar rounds, rocket boosters, and antitank rockets.
Defenseimagery.mil DM-SD-07-17328

up and pushed them out of the room toward the stairwell. And then I went to the next room, kicked open the door, and it's full of smoke. There's one of my men sitting up on the bed, but he wasn't all there. He's giving me that dazed and confused look. I got him up and pulled him out." By this time, his men had gathered on the first floor. "We all got downstairs," he said thankfully. "My NCOs gave me a thumb's up; everybody was accounted for." His men grabbed fire extinguishers and water bottles to put out the fire. "I put a lieutenant in charge," Keahtigh said, "and eventually we got the fire out."

The next morning, a delegation of Iraqis asked to bury their dead. "We had already wrapped them [the bodies] up in blankets," Keahtigh recalled, "so I said all right, but we'll search them first." One member of the delegation was suspect. "When we lifted his shirt, he still had on black clothes," Keahtigh recalled. "The look on his face told me that he absolutely didn't like us." Keahtigh also remarked that the delegation was surprised that his soldiers had wrapped the remains and treated them with dignity. The bodies were taken to the cemetery.

Stauch remembered, "We witnessed a lot of funerals. At one point, we talked to a local that claimed to have been in charge of digging the graves for all the militia. He showed us which portion of the cemetery was for them. Over the next few days we just watched it continue to grow . . . [T]here were hundreds of bodies coming in there. They got to the point where they were doing mass burials." It was estimated that between 1,200 and 1,500 Mahdi militiamen died in the three-week battle.

By early afternoon, the 1-5 Cav received word to pull back from its advanced position in the Old City. "We didn't have enough transportation," Keahtigh said, "so we walked out . . . the whole length of the cemetery to Phase Line Dodge, where we loaded into Bradleys. As the last man loaded up, I looked around and realized, 'I'm proud of my boys; they stood tall, heads up.' . . . [I]t's a good feeling."

The battalion established traffic-control checkpoints to make sure the militiamen didn't leave with their weapons. "We searched everything," McFall recalled, "carts with bodies, an ambulance—I didn't care."

Schaffer thought, "It was our town at that point. Nobody wanted to tangle with us."

TEAM APACHE, 2ND BATTALION, 7TH CAVALRY REGIMENT

Early in the morning of August 27, Twaddell received word that a cease-fire agreement had been reached with al-Sadr. A news report said, "Rebel cleric Muqtada al-Sadr has officially handed over control of Najaf's Imam Ali shine to a representative of Grand Ayatollah Ali al-Sistani . . . [T]he handover happened at 1330."

"I was in the company CP [command post] when the word came in, 'Withdraw your company no later than 0900,'" Twaddell recalled. "We pulled back to Apache Hilton for the night."

Campbell slept on the roof. "I woke up about daylight and heard a bunch of noise . . . [T]hen the bad guys started to come out from the mosque and lay down their weapons."

TEAM COUGAR, 3RD BATTALION, 8TH CAVALRY REGIMENT

Throckmorton remembered, "Some bad guys didn't get the word about the cease-fire and exchanged fire with the Iraqi police. Fortunately, they were all terrible shots."

Thousands of people, estimated to be as many as ten thousand, were in and around the mosque. Some of them handed in weapons, while others identified weapons caches to the police. Throckmorton recalled "the occasional rifle shot, but nothing like it was."

Captain Glass pulled Team Cougar back to Camp David in stages—the snipers, the Oregon National Guard, and the company trains around 1500, 1st Platoon at dusk, and 2nd Platoon at 2130.

Captain Conley recalled an incident that could have had tragic consequences:

> There was a demonstration of about 1,500 people that came toward the camp. The battalion mortar platoon fell out to keep them away. In addition, the Iraqi police, who were not known for their professional competence, set up a roadblock. Suddenly, one of the police opened fire with his machine gun over the heads of the demonstration. There was instant pandemonium. My soldiers prepared to fire. The demonstrators screamed and scattered in every direction . . . [H]undreds of flip-flops lined the road . . . [T]he tension was palpable. Suddenly, one of my soldiers spotted a chicken in the road, pointed at the bird, and yelled out, 'Look! That's why the chicken crosses the road.' My men started laughing, which broke the tension."

Despite the demonstrators' desperate scramble, there were no injuries.

The battalion pulled back to FOB Duke the next morning, where it waited to see if the cease-fire would last. "We stayed there for about ten days," Lieutenant Campbell recalled, "performing maintenance, playing cards, and generally being bored." He was proud of his platoon and its performance. "We did well standing on our own," he said. "It gave us a great deal of confidence in ourselves and the men in the platoon." When it was obvious the cease-fire was holding, the battalion loaded its armor onto HETs and returned to Taji.

Rainey was rightly proud of what his battalion had accomplished. "The soldiers and Marines that fought with Task Force 2-7 performed remarkably well," he said. "They took the fight to the enemy and destroyed them. We had twenty-nine wounded; none of those soldiers lost their lives. Any time you can accomplish a mission in an urban area for fifteen days and not lose a soldier, there's got to be a large amount of grace from God." It was estimated that the 2-7 Cav accounted for over 350 Mahdi militiamen killed. However, the exact number will never be known, as the enemy recovered its dead and buried them as soon as possible.

Three months later, after Sunni insurgents had taken over Fallujah, Marine Lt. Gen. John F. Sattler called Lt. Gen. Thomas Metz to request reinforcement. "Tom," Sattler began, "I need 2-7 Cavalry . . . ." Rainey's battalion was asked for by name because of the high regard the Marines had for its fighting prowess.

Parting Shots

T HE MAHDI MILITIA REMAINED active in Najaf, despite al-Sadr's guarantee it would disarm and leave. While the militiamen rarely attacked the Marines, they would take on the Iraqi police. On one such occasion, a firefight, a CAAT-Bravo patrol happened to be in the area. The patrol immediately engaged the enemy with small arms and its heavy machine guns. After approximately thirty minutes, the militiamen melted away. There were no friendly casualties.

Three days later, CAAT-Bravo's first section was ambushed while on a local security patrol. The ambush began with the detonation of a remote-controlled improvised explosive device (RCIED), which exploded ten meters from a CAAT vehicle, slightly wounding three of the occupants. The attackers also began firing small arms. As the smoke from the blast cleared, the Marines spotted three gunmen, whom they took under fire with a .50-caliber machine gun, killing one and wounding the others. The after-action report noted, "The three individuals were assessed to be Mahdi Militia fighters, after finding militia propaganda, cell phones [used to trigger the RCIED] and stacks of currency."

Immediately after the cease-fire, the MEU began cleaning up the city and rebuilding its infrastructure. "Within a month, we spent $8.5 million," Lieutenant Colonel Johnston said. "We put the people to work cleaning up the streets. It was remarkable how quickly it was done." Colonel Haslam had joint survey teams (U.S. forces, the Iraqi Security Force, the Iraqi police, and the Iraqi National Guard) go into the city to assess the extent of building damage. A construction contractor would provide the teams and a building owner with a repair estimate; the owner would then present the estimate to the government information center for payment.

Personal-injury and death payments were handled differently. "The claims had to be verified by the local hospital before being reviewed by coalition officers," Johnston indicated. "Initially, some people would come by three or four times with the same death certificate. We'd look at it and say, 'This is bogus, we're not going to pay a twenty-year-old guy that got shot in the chest. He's probably Mahdi Militia.' The most we would pay for death was $2,500." The process worked. In a very short period of time, the MEU paid out over ten thousand claims.

Lieutenant Colonel Mayer recalled, "Col. Haslam and I spent months going door to door throughout Najaf and Kufa, covering any place where we had fought the militia." He described the process. "We would meet at a designated location, lay out a map, . . . determine who would take what neighborhood, and draw a boundary around each sector. We would then walk door-to-door, making damage assessments on every business, home, market, roadside shanty store—practically anything and everything that might have value to one of the residents." The first time, they carried cash, but as word spread that the Americans were paying cash on the barrelhead, "the situation turned into a moblike condition, with crowds so large, nobody could move," Mayer said. After that, Mayer and Haslam handed out chits to be redeemed at the government center. "Over time," Mayer said, "the people got used to our presence and would often have chai [tea] waiting for our assessment details."

Downtown Najaf after the battle. Note the predominance of young men, who days before may have carried rifles and RPGs against American forces. Note also the two women in black and the man standing beside them. A close-up view shows they are carrying camera equipment. They may have been reporters for one of the Arab news media. *Capt. Michael Throckmorton, U.S. Army*

The Marines quickly learned that female Marines and sailors were "huge force multipliers." They talked with Iraqi women and children. "The Iraqi women would open up to them," Lieutenant Colonel Mayer said. "We learned a lot about the city and its residents. Our women were also better at telling if an Iraqi woman was lying and weren't taken in by a female's sad eyes, like most of the male Marines [were]."

Within a few months, the 11th MEU doled out almost $45 million in condolence/compensation payments and for infrastructure repair and construction projects. With this money, eight new schools were built and twenty-four were repaired. The funds also rehabilitated thirty-six police stations and vehicle checkpoints.

"The citizens were very grateful . . . for the concern we showed and the effort we put into rebuilding the city," Mayer said. "Many Iraqis related to us that they blamed Sadr for the fighting . . . and they were grateful to the Americans for expelling him and his thugs . . . [They also] wondered why Sadr wasn't helping to rebuild the city."

While the MEU and the battalion headquarters concentrated on infrastructure projects, Alpha and Charlie Companies went to work training Iraqi National Guard units. Alpha Company returned to Diwaniyah and conducted joint patrols and training for the 404th ING battalion. Similarly, Charlie Company worked with the 405th ING battalion adjacent to FOB Baker. The battalion after-action report noted, "Training the ING proved to be a learning experience . . . seeing the Iraqi soldiers transformed from a group of individuals . . . into a confident fighting force . . . provided a promising glimpse of what the Iraqi military might become in the future."

Irrepressible Iraqi children welcoming Marines after the battle.
Maj. Michael S. Wilbur, USMC

Marines training Iraqi national guardsman after the battle. The training helped give the Iraqis confidence in themselves and their unit.
Defenseimagery.mil DM-SD-08-04155

Lieutenant Colonel Mayer was proud of their training accomplishments. "Barracks were built, sanitary kitchens and food was contracted for, septic tanks [were] installed, uniforms and personal-protection equipment [were] issued, quality noncommissioned and commissioned officers were assigned, and recognition ceremonies were conducted to honor those that fought against Sadr."

By Christmas 2004, the Iraqi security forces were in control of Najaf and Kufa. "Iraqi security forces had the greater urban area secure with checkpoints and roving patrols," Lieutenant Colonel Mayer recalled. "Most importantly, life had returned to normal. Markets were crowded, restaurants full, schools restarted, and commerce flowing . . . [P]eople were friendly toward us."

TILL WE MEET AGAIN

The cease-fire in Najaf closely paralleled the political solution that had ended the fighting in Fallujah three months earlier. In both instances, the U.S. military had the enemy on the ropes, but was not allowed to finish the job because of a lack of political will. In the case of Fallujah, the army and Marines were ordered back into the city seven months after Sunni insurgents established it as a base from which to launch attacks on coalition forces. By letting al-Sadr off the hook in Najaf, the coalition only

Captain Bruce Sotire passes out rubber balls to schoolchildren after the battle. The local citizens welcomed the Marines after al-Sadr's Mahdi Militia surrendered and left the city.
Defenseimagry.mil 041103-M-0095Z-006

delayed the inevitable. In early 2006, al-Sadr reappeared. His Mahdi Militia launched a brutal civil war for power with its Shiite rivals. In addition, al-Sadr supported Shiite death squads that fueled sectarian violence, which spun almost completely out of control. In the bloodbath that followed, it is estimated that thousands of Iraqis, mostly Sunni, were killed.

In 2007, al-Sadr's forces clashed with U.S. and British forces in Sadr City and Basra. The punishing counterattacks forced al-Sadr to flee to the Iranian holy city of Qom. He announced that he would not return to Iraq until after the Americans were gone.

In the March 2010 Iraqi general elections, neither of the two main candidates, Ayad Allawi and Iraq's prime minister, Nouri al-Maliki, achieved the necessary plurality to govern. The March 28, 2010, the *Guardian* reported that representatives from al-Maliki's office had traveled to Qom to meet with al-Sadr: "They [the representatives] had come to seek a détente—and more importantly to find a way, any way, that the exiled cleric [al-Sadr], who maintains an overlord's hold over more than two million Shia Iraqis, would support Maliki being returned to office." As the *Guardian* article stated, "Sadr has been transformed from a pariah into a potential kingmaker."

The political stalemate has allowed al-Sadr to emerge as a key power broker, and with the Iraqi government paralyzed, he may yet rise to prominence. It is possible that sometime in the future, the United States may find itself across the bargaining table with Muqtada al-Sadr.

Battle Time Line

July 31 to August 2

The 11th MEU assumes responsibility for the city of Najaf, excluding the exclusion zones surrounding the Imam Ali mosque and the Old City.

Al-Sadr's Mahdi Militia becomes active outside the exclusion zones, manning illegal checkpoints, kidnapping and conducting harassing attacks on Iraqi Security Forces, and terrorizing the local population.

August 2

A local security patrol from 1st Battalion, 4th Marines (1/4) is attacked by the Mahdi Militia in the vicinity of the city's maternity hospital. The battalion's combined antitank team returns fire and kills an estimated ten militiamen. There are no friendly casualties.

August 5

Early in the morning, Mahdi Militia attacks the main Iraqi police station from positions in the Wadi al-Salaam cemetery. The 1/4 quick reaction force (QRF) responds to the governor's request for assistance.

At 0830, the QRF engages with an estimated 300 Mahdi militiamen in and around the cemetery. The QRF returns fire and requests reinforcement. A mechanized reaction force and helicopter gunship respond in support.

One UH-1N gunship is shot down. The mechanized reaction force reroutes to secure the site of the downed helicopter. Battalion reinforcements deploy from FOB Echo in Diwaniya to Najaf.

The 11th MEU requests additional reinforcement. Multi-National Corps–Iraq (MNC-I) orders U.S. Army   Cavalry and 2-7 Cavalry to report to 11th MEU for combat operations.

At 1900, MNC-I's commanding general authorizes 1/4 to attack Mahdi Militia forces in Wadi al-Salaam cemetery. An estimated 130 militiamen are killed.

The 1-5 Cavalry advance echelon arrives at FOB Duke and is assigned to attack and clear the eastern sector of the cemetery.

August 6

1/4 attacks into the cemetery. Numerous weapons caches are uncovered, yielding thousands of rounds of ammunition, hundreds of RPGs, AK-47s, and improvised explosive devices. Dozens of militia fighters are killed.

August 7

1/4 reaches its limit of advance. The 1-5 Cavalry main body arrives at FOB Duke.

August 8

1/4 withdraws from cemetery to refit and rearm. I Marine Expeditionary Force (I MEF) assumes operational control. Exclusionary zones are reduce to allow for the greater use of fire support.

August 9

The 1-5 Cavalry attacks into cemetery and overwhelms militia defenses.

August 10

The 2-7 Cavalry arrives at FOB Duke and prepares for combat operations in the southern sector of Najaf.

August 11

Offensive operations pause as the Iraqi interim government and al-Sadr begin peace negotiations.

August 12

Negotiations break down, and U.S. forces recommence attacks. Three maneuver battalions conduct offensive operations: the 2-7 Cavalry in southwest Najaf, the 1-5 Cavalry into the cemetery, and 1/4 on al-Sadr's house and a maternity hospital. Task Force Commando raids the Salah mosque in Kufa.

August 13

Offensive operations pause a second time for negotiations. Al-Sadr is reported to be wounded.

August 14 to 19

U.S. combat operations resume.

August 20

Offensive operations pause a third time for negotiations.

August 21

1/4 raids Kufa Technical College. The 1-5 Cavalry conducts a probing attack west of a parking garage against heavy resistance.

August 22 to 24

Lieutenant Generals Metz and Conway are among those in attendance at a high-level brief for a final attack concept. Combat operations continue.

August 25

Maneuver battalions conduct combat operations inside Ring Road.

August 26

Offensive operations pause a fourth and final time for negotiations between Grand Ayatollah al-Sistani and al-Sadr.

August 27

The cease-fire is announced, and all combat operations are suspended.

Bibliography

Books

Allawi, Ali A. *The Occupation of Iraq: Winning the War, Losing the Peace*. New Haven, CT: Yale University Press, 2007.

Atkinson, Rick. *In the Company of Soldiers: A Chronicle of Combat*. New York: Henry Holt and Company, 2004.

Baer, Robert. *The Devil We Know: Dealing with the New Iranian Superpower*. New York: Crown Publishers, 2008.

Bodansky, Yossef. *The Secret History of the Iraq War*. New York: 10 Regan Books, 2004.

Bremer, L. Paul, III. *My Year in Iraq: The Struggle to Build a Future of Hope*. New York: Simon & Schuster, 2006.

Bruning, John R. *The Devil's Sandbox: With the 2nd Battalion, 162nd Infantry at War in Iraq*. St. Paul, MN: Zenith Press, 2006.

Call, Steve. *Danger Close: Tactical Air Controllers in Afghanistan and Iraq*. College Station: Texas A&M University Press, 2007.

Chehab, Zaki. *Inside the Resistance: Reporting from Iraq's Danger Zone*. New York: Nation Book, 2005.

Cockburn, Patrick. *Muqtada: Muqtada Al-Sadr, the Shia Revival, and the Struggle for Iraq*. New York: Scribner, 2008.

———. *The Occupation: War and Resistance in Iraq*. London: Verso, 2006.

Dobbins, James, Seth Jones, Benjamin Runkle, and Siddharth Mohandas. *Occupying Iraq: A History of the Coalition Provisional Authority*. Santa Monica, CA: Rand, 2009.

Engel, Richard. *War Journal: My Five Years in Iraq*. New York: Simon & Schuster, 2008.

Etherington, Mark. *Revolt on the Tigris: The Al-Sadr Uprising and the Governing of Iraq*. Ithaca, NY: Cornell University Press, 2005.

Filkins, Dexter. *The Forever War*. New York: Alfred A. Knopf, 2008.

Hazleton, Lesley. *After the Prophet*. New York: Doubleday, 2009.

Hoffman, Jon T. *Tip of the Spear: U.S. Army Small-Unit Action in Iraq, 2004–2007*. Washington, DC: GPO, 2009.

Hughes, Christopher. *War on Two Fronts: An Infantry Commander's War in Iraq and the Pentagon*. Philadelphia: Casemate, 2007.

Kozlowski, Francis X. *U.S. Marines in Battle: An Najaf*. U.S. Marine Corps, 2009.

Lacey, Jim. *Take Down: The 3rd Infantry Division's Twenty-One Day Assault on Baghdad*. Annapolis, MD: Naval Institute Press, 2007.

Mahnken, Thomas G., and Thomas A. Keaney. *War in Iraq: Planning and Execution*. New York: Routledge, 2007.

Mansour, Ahmed. *Inside Fallujah: The Unembedded Story*. Northampton, MA: Olive Branch Press, 2009.

Nakash, Yitzhak. *The Shi'is of Iraq*. Princeton, NJ: Princeton University Press, 1994.

Rosen, Nir. *The Triumph of the Martyrs: A Reporter's Journey into Occupied Iraq*. Dulles, VA: Potomac Books, 2008.

Samarae, Wafiq al-. *Eastern Gate Ruins*.

Sanchez, Richard S. *Wiser in Battle: a Soldier's Story*. New York: HarperCollins, 2008.

Shadid, Anthony. *Night Draws Near, Iraq's People in the Shadow of America's War*. New York: Henry Holt and Company, 2005.

West, Bing. *The Strongest Tribe: War, Politics, and the Endgame in Iraq*. New York: Random House, 2008.

Young, Gavin. *Iraq: Land of Two Rivers*. London: Collins, 1980.

Articles

Abdul-Ahad, Ghaith. "I Will Fight Them, Even with My Bare Hands." *The Guardian*, August 9, 2004.

Chaffin, John H., IV. "Tactical Logistics and Operation Pacific Guardian in An Najaf, Iraq—A Company Command Perspective." *Quartermaster Bulletin*, Winter 2004.

Darling, Dan. "Meet Brigadier General Qassem Suleimani, the Commander of Iran's Anti-American Qods Force." *The Weekly Standard*, October 5, 2005.

Fuentes, Gidget. "Lost in the Shuffle." *Marine Corp Times*, May 1, 2006.

Gettleman, Jeffrey. "G.I.'s Padlock Baghdad Paper Accused of Lies." *New York Times*, March 29, 2004.

Gray, Dennis D. "Salvadoran Soldiers Praised for Iraq Role." *Washington Times*, May 3, 2004.

Maass, Peter. "Back-Room Theocrat." *New York Times*, May 11, 2003.

Tahir Amir. "Death Is Big Business in Najaf, but Iraq's Future Depends on Who Controls it." *The Times*, August 28, 2004.

Unpublished Sources

Marine Corps University Archives and Marine Corps History Division

Located at Quantico, Virginia, the Marine Corps University archives and the Marine Corps History Division are rich sources of material for researchers of Marine

Corps history. Their resources include nearly four thousand collections of papers donated by active-duty and former officers and enlisted personnel, documenting every conflict involving Marines. Of particular importance to this book were the oral histories that have been collected by the Marine Corps History Division over the years. The following Marines' oral histories were used in this book:

Apicella, Lt. Col. Eugene N., 30 December 2004
Borneo, 1st Lt. Michael J., 23 October 2004
Butler, Maj. Glen G., 15 June 2005
Cedarleaf, 1st Lt. David N., 19 October 2004
Haslam, Col. Anthony M., 29 December 2004
Johnston, Lt. Col. Gary S., 28 December 2004
Moran, Maj. Coby M., 23 October 2005
Jenkins, Cpl. James T., 31 December 2004
Sellers, 1st Lt. Jeremy T., 29 December 2004

U.S. Army Center for Military History
Badger, Maj. Kevin S., 7 September 2004, 21 September 2007
Beams, Sgt. Joshua W., 6 September 2004
Cosby, Pfc. Thomas F., 6 September 2004
Dunn, 1st Lt. Christopher S., 6 September 2004
Gardner, Capt. Jeffrey, 7 September 2004
Henry, Capt. Antonio, 7 September 2004
Keahtigh, Capt. Darren, 7 September 2004
McFall, Capt. Ben P., 8 September 2004
Miyamasu, Lt. Col. Myles, 3 October 2007
Miyamasu, Lt. Col. Myles, 8 September 2004
Schaffer, 2nd Lt. Douglas J., 6 September 2004
Stauch, 1st Lt. Steven D., 6 September 2004

Operational Leadership Experiences
Beckert, Lt. Col. Chris
Budihas, Maj. Chris
Croft, Maj. Neal
DiSalvo, Col. Joseph
Ehrhart, Maj. Tom
Isom, Lt. Col. Thomas
Karcher, Maj. Tim
Konz, Maj. Matthew
McCoy, Maj. Jeff

McManus, Sgt. Jason
New, Maj. Anthony
Payne, Maj. Matthew
Sarabia, Maj. George H.
Wiltcher, Maj. Barry
Zike, Maj. Peterjess

Personal Interviews
Behm, Maj. Dale, August 2009
Birdzell, 1st Lt. William, May 2010
Butler, Lt. Col. Glen G., April 2010
Campbell, Capt. Jimmy, March 2010
Conley, Maj. Christopher, March 2010
Carrasco, Maj. Sam, May 2010
Demuth, Staff Sgt. Heath J., March 2010
Erwin, Maj. Michael, February–March 2010
Grogan, Maj. Jason, March 2010
Hejlik, Lt. Gen. Dennis J., January 2010
Mayer, Lt. Col. John, August 2009, May 2010
Moorehead, Lt. W. Douglas, May 2010
Moran, Maj. Coby, July–August 2009
Mount, Maj. Stephen H., March 2009
Sotire, Maj. Bruce, July–August 2009, April–May 2010
Throckmorton, 1st Lt. Michael, April 2010
Twaddell, Maj. Edward, February 2010
Zjawin, Capt. Richard, August 2009

Special thanks to Maj. Michael S. Wilbur, USMC, for providing dozens of photographs at short notice and to Lt. Col. John R. Way, USMCR, whose collection of 1st Battalion, 4th Marines, oral history proved to be invaluable.

Internet Resources

Allbritton, Christopher. "Inside the Imam Ali Shrine." www.back-to-iraq.com, August 24, 2004.
Baudaf, Scott. Interviewed by Amy Goodman. *Democracy Now: The War and Peace Report*, August 6, 2004. www.democracynow.org/2004/8/6/as_sadr_calls_off_truce_in
Bereson, Alex. "The Whale Swallows Me Whole." *Salon* (www.salon.com), November 4, 2004.

Fisk, Robert. Interviewed by Amy Goodman. *Democracy Now: The War and Peace Report*, August 6, 2004. http://www.democracynow.org/2004/8/6/as_sadr_calls_off_truce_in

Mufti, Nermeen al-. "Woe Betide Najaf." *Al-Ahram Weekly Online*, August 26–September 1, 2004. http://weekly.ahram.org.eg/2004/705/re11.htm

Robertson, Phillip. "Al-Sadr's Men in Black." *Salon* (www.salon.com), April 17, 2004.

――――. "The Fake Peace." *Salon* (www.salon.com), May 28, 2004.

――――. "Six Days of Fierce Battle." *Salon* (www.salon.com), August 13, 2004.

Sadeq, Kianne. Interviewed by John Vause. CNN.com, August 19, 2004. http://archives.cnn.com/TRANSCRIPTS/0408/19/bn.01.html

Thompson, Dan. "Exploring the Abandoned, Bloody An-Najaf Morgue and Listening to Washington's Take on Iraq." *American, Interrupted: 14 Months in Iraq* (blog), April 30, 2004. http://american-interrupted.blogspot.com/2004_04_01_archive.html

Index